HALFWAY HOUSE

ALTERNATIVE CRIMINOLOGY

General Editor: Jeff Ferrell

Halfway House

*Prisoner Reentry and the
Shadow of Carceral Care*

Liam Martin

NEW YORK UNIVERSITY PRESS
New York

NEW YORK UNIVERSITY PRESS
New York
www.nyupress.org

References to Internet websites (URLs) were accurate at the time of writing. Neither the author nor New York University Press is responsible for URLs that may have expired or changed since the manuscript was prepared.

Library of Congress Cataloging-in-Publication Data
Names: Martin, Liam, author.
Title: Halfway house : prisoner reentry and the shadow of carceral care / Liam Martin.
Description: New York : New York University Press, [2021] | Series: Alternative criminology | Includes bibliographical references and index.
Identifiers: LCCN 2021003110 | ISBN 9781479800681 (hardback ; alk. paper) | ISBN 9781479800698 (paperback ; alk. paper) | ISBN 9781479800704 (ebook) | ISBN 9781479800711 (ebook other)
Subjects: LCSH: Prisoners—Deinstitutionalization—United States—Case studies. | Halfway houses—United States—Case studies. | Criminals—Rehabilitation—United States—Case studies. | Alternatives to imprisonment—United States—Case studies.
Classification: LCC HV9304 .M25 2021 | DDC 365/.34—dc23
LC record available at https://lccn.loc.gov/2021003110

New York University Press books are printed on acid-free paper, and their binding materials are chosen for strength and durability. We strive to use environmentally responsible suppliers and materials to the greatest extent possible in publishing our books.

Manufactured in the United States of America

10 9 8 7 6 5 4 3 2 1

Also available as an ebook

To mum and dad, Pip and Pat, who taught me about words and books

To my love, Aurora, and our babies born as I wrote the words to come

To Joe, for sharing laughs and sadness too, and for looking out for me

This book is for you

CONTENTS

1

Carceral Care

I can hear Joe Badillo's cane clunking on wooden floorboards in the halfway house hallway, one leg dragging with foot scuffing the ground, while he sings the chorus of a hit song by Maroon 5: "I got the moves like Jagger, I got the moves like Jagger, I got the moooooooves like Jagger."

As Joe enters the kitchen, I look over my shoulder from the counter where I eat breakfast. "Morning, kiddo," he says.

"Morning, Joe. Starting the day with a tune, eh?"

"Got to—I woke up today."

* * *

Joe Badillo says he chose to live at Bridge House.[1] To sketch his account of the decision: Joe had been arrested using a stolen credit card while homeless and physically dependent on a cocktail of heroin and prescription opiates. After six months locked up at the county jail waiting for the case to progress, he said the judge offered a deal: a nine-month sentence that with time already served and credit for good behavior could have him out in sixty days. But Joe took instead a year on probation, a risky move carrying the condition that he would be incarcerated another year for any violations.

"A lot of people were like, 'You're crazy. You couldn't do sixty days and get out?'" He recalled.

"I was like, 'Yeah I could do sixty days. But get out to what? Get out to where?'"

Joe said he took probation because it came with the promise of a bed at Bridge House. Like many residents, he talked about getting a place at the program as a kind of lucky break. Joe was on a wait list for public housing and expected to be denied based on his criminal record, then be given the chance to appeal, so faced a long wait ahead.[2] He would struggle to afford rent in the private market even in the unlikely event a landlord was willing to overlook his past. The threat of homelessness was not an abstract fear but a recent experience that he was desperate to avoid repeating. In the absence of alternative housing options, Bridge House filled the gap and provided a carceral complement to the social safety net.

The sentencing judge happened to be a board member at Bridge House. She used the halfway house not as "back-end" support for reintegration but as a "front-end" enhancement to probation.[3] She would have likely viewed the placement as meeting both penal and welfare goals: intensifying the level of supervision attached to Joe's community sentence and, at the same time, providing him with housing. The halfway house was an intermediate sanction between probation and prison that came with a social support component.

In the literature on community corrections, Joe would be described as "halfway-in," his sentence a form of diversion and a final chance to avoid imprisonment.[4] But on the ground it looked messier: he was reentering the community from incarceration as a pretrial detainee and, more generally, had experienced repeated spells of incarceration and reentry spanning more than two decades. At some level, being sentenced to a halfway house was less a form of diversion than an extension of this long-term cycle of confinement, transitioning Joe from one carceral setting (jail) to another (halfway house). At Bridge House, he lived with parolees who are sometimes described as being "halfway-out"[5]—people entering the program as a condition of early release from prison. Often these groups are held separately at specialist facilities; but at Bridge House, the halfway-ins lived together with the halfway-outs, and some men seemed located in-between.

There was a small number of residents who chose to live at Bridge House outside any requirement of the criminal justice system, arranging to stay through friends or personal referrals or remaining after completing a community sentence and being allowed to leave. They found social supports at a carceral institution they could not access elsewhere. And the welfare function of the house was even institutionalized through a contract to reserve one bed for people leaving a local homeless shelter. These men were not being sanctioned for violations of the law but were simply poor and had nowhere else to go, so entered the halfway house as part of a search for housing.

I lived at Bridge House as an ethnographer for nine months spread across three spells of fieldwork between 2012 and 2014 (around June through August each year). Joe Badillo moved in from jail right around the time I first arrived. The project was built around our collaboration, not only while we lived together at the house but during the periods between and after we both left the program—including a return to the field with a draft of the manuscript in 2019. Joe is the main character in the story I tell in these pages. The book follows the ups and downs of his unfolding experience, a sociological biography combining thick description of lived experience with an account of linkages to the broader social forces shaping prisoner reentry in the era of mass incarceration.

This book is also the story of a halfway house. Bridge House was an all-male institution in a two-story former family home in a residential neighborhood (see figure 1.1). Some background: The program evolved out of a national organization with historical connections to the Catholic worker house movement.[6] It had split from the group and had no explicit religious content or instruction, yet the basic model had some unusual features rooted in this tradition. Bridge House invited students from a local university to live alongside residents while working as interns—an opening for my own entry to the site—and recruited groups of volunteers to bring food and "break bread" with the men around the dinner table each weeknight. The program placed no time limit on resident stays. Details were worked out informally and varied depending on the person, but effectively, men were allowed to remain as long as they followed program rules. Occasionally, a resident would stay for years.

Bridge House is probably not a typical American halfway house. The capacity of twelve residents makes it much smaller than the "residential reentry centers" contracted by the federal government, for example, which have an average capacity of sixty-one (around five times the scale).[7] These facilities are commonly called "halfway houses," but most are not really houses at all: they look more like motels or small apartment complexes in semi-industrial areas than family-style homes on residential streets. Quantitative differences in scale imply qualitative differences in social relations. Regulations were often flexible and negotiated based on individual circumstance at Bridge House, but at larger and more impersonal facilities, they are more likely to be applied uniformly through bureaucratic process. The policy of open time frames is very different from the finite schedules ranging from days to months employed at most programs.[8]

Figure 1.1. The porch and main entrance to Bridge House

Yet Bridge House embodies tensions at the heart of the very idea of a halfway house. Staff and volunteers see the program as a charitable service and an alternative to the punitive treatment the men receive elsewhere in criminal justice—the director talks about "embracing" residents. But the halfway house is also part of the same system: receiving funding from the department of corrections, holding interviews with potential residents inside state prison and the county jail, and certified to take probationers and parolees who are forced to live at the program. Even as it seeks to build a welcoming community, it is inextricably linked to the more punitive sources of penal power to which it as an imagined alternative.

Without the threat of prison as a backup sanction, some residents would simply walk away.

* * *

Before the project began, I prepared to move into Bridge House by reading Foucault's *Discipline and Punish*.[9] I had never seen a halfway house up close but, through this theoretical lens, came to imagine the program as an extension of the prison deeper into community life—an alternative to prison that itself is halfway like a prison. I was almost disappointed arriving at Bridge House. It did not look like a prison at all: there was no razor wire or perimeter fencing, no surveillance cameras, no staff in uniform or guarded entries and exits—just a former family home with a fresh paint job and what seemed like a relaxed, informal atmosphere. It had wireless internet and presented as a pretty good place to live.

If I had been better versed in Foucault, I might have realized that the house not looking like a prison was kind of the point. The program was a good example of what Foucault meant by the transport of the penitentiary technique from the prison to the social body,[10] giving carceral texture to the most taken-for-granted architecture: a house. Like prison, it administered punishment by confinement, only this was exercised not through walls and wire but nightly curfews and mandatory meals and meetings. These simple program requirements constructed a circle within which the men could move, the edges set by the distance they could travel between leaving in the morning and returning for dinner. The prison-like rules were barely noticeable to an outsider at first: the drug tests relatively rare, the rule against sex on the premises complained about from time to time but for the most part just accepted by the men as part of the deal. The program incarcerated while blending in with other homes on a residential street.

I frame my halfway house ethnography around the concept of *carceral care*. This uses Foucault's image of "the carceral,"[11] linguistically associated with physical barriers and the prison, to locate the halfway house as among the many ways the human body can be contained beyond walls.[12] Scholars use this metaphor to articulate the often-hidden practices of control and confinement found in diverse social settings: public schools[13] and ghetto neighborhoods,[14] immigrant detention centers[15] and housing projects,[16] drug treatment programs[17] and heavily policed urban spaces.[18] In community corrections, the term has been especially important in drawing attention to how seemingly humane reforms can extend the carceral net and become mechanisms of "net-widening" in disguise.[19] This includes the carceral devolution involved in recent expansions of reentry programming[20]—which have shifted rehabilitation and treatment services once delivered inside to community settings outside and, in the process, introduced new forms of social control to Black and Latino neighborhoods already subject to violent hyperpolicing and unprecedented levels of imprisonment.

In this book, I want to use but also modify Foucault's imagery of the carceral, because in his analysis of the diverse forms of confinement employed at institutions that may seem on the surface benevolent, the other side of the story is sometimes lost—they *can* be crucial sites of care and support. And while Foucault drew on the concept of the carceral to highlight the interconnections between punishment and broader projects to alleviate poverty and regulate the poor, ultimately, the term is better suited to diagnosing coercion than to shedding light on the delivery of material assistance. Joe Badillo says the halfway house saved his life and he will be forever grateful for the support he received there. And by framing this book to center the provision of care at the program, juxtaposed with the exercise of carceral control, I want to examine the contradictions of combining these while imposing criminal punishment.

One reason the welfare function of Bridge House was so important to people like Joe is that more conventional forms of social service delivery in the United States have been drastically curtailed. For several decades, governments have purged welfare rolls and slashed public housing programs while spending record amounts on police and prisons.[21] In this context, even very punitive sites of criminal justice are playing a lead role in providing public aid to a growing pool of destitute people falling through the gaps of an evaporating social safety net. On the front lines of mass incarceration, police officers not only assert control but act as intermediaries connecting the poor with temporary housing and social services,[22] while at the back end, prisons and jails operate as central hubs for the provision of health care, drug treatment, shelter, sustenance, education, and other supports.[23] In the field of prisoner reentry, high-security surveillance and postrelease criminal supervision are routinely blended with welfarist support for reintegration.[24] And at Bridge House, men find parole and probation opening access to a halfway house even as public housing and other sources of affordable shelter have collapsed.[25]

The term "carceral care" is intended to spotlight the institutional tensions of a halfway house meeting essential social needs while adopting an uneasy combination of roles—care and control, reform and repression, punishment and social welfare—placing them at the center of the analysis developed in this book. As the story unfolds, I will turn to examining how the contradictions are experienced and negotiated at a micro-level by the men who live at Bridge House. But I want to start with the bigger picture, locating the program historically in relation to penal-welfarism and the shifting politics of the halfway house.

* * *

In 1964, then–attorney general Robert Kennedy published an article in the journal *Crime and Delinquency* promoting an innovative development in criminal justice: the halfway house. At a historical moment when many experts believed the prison was a failed institution destined to be replaced by more humane alternatives,[26] and support for ideas approaching prison abolition were part of mainstream public discourse,[27] Kennedy was among the many reformers investing their hopes for change in the burgeoning field of community corrections. He had sponsored a federal pilot project opening what were officially termed "prerelease guidance centers" and called for new legislation that would allow for extending these programs from juveniles to adults. Reflecting on the initiative, Kennedy described how he "hit on the idea of the halfway houses" in discussion with the head of federal prisons Jim Bennett:

"We wanted more than just a shelter," he wrote. "We wanted to develop a center where in addition to the basic needs of food and a room the released inmate would be helped to obtain a job, where he would be given the support and guidance to enable him to live with his emotional problems, and where he might make the transition from institutional to community life less abruptly, less like slamming into a brick wall. We wanted a center which would be his sponsor in the 'free world,' introducing him to community life gradually and withdrawing when the process was completed."[28]

The ideal of reintegration, so central to the prevailing ethos of criminal justice at the time, was expressed in the "halfway" house concept itself—residents would be on their way to the community, even halfway there are already. These houses would be an antidote to the isolation and exclusion of large closed institutions, engines of inclusion transitioning residents into the social world beyond. And the penal elements of the halfway house, hinted at by Kennedy's quotation marks around the term "free world," would be secondary to the welfare function of providing support and guidance. The support would be delivered in the service of helping men—the subject was typically gendered—transition from institutional to community life.

This was an era when the policy framework of penal-welfarism attracted the support, or at least the compliance, of all key groups involved in criminal justice policy making.[29] Some claimed that the ideal of "reintegration" was producing a third revolution in the long history of creating a humane correctional system: "Revenge to Restraint" in the early nineteenth century, "Restraint to Reformation" from the late nineteenth to the early twentieth, "Reformation to Reintegration" in the middle of the twentieth.[30] The virtues of reintegration and community alternatives were being celebrated not only by politicians and correctional administrators but radical activists and prison abolitionists.

More broadly, the halfway house movement of the 1960s emerged at a moment of welfare-state expansion and civil-rights liberalization in the United States.[31] The number of people on federal welfare rolls doubled during the decade.[32] With broad-based social movements challenging racial caste, President Lyndon Johnson and the Democratic-controlled government passed historic legislation—including the Civil Rights Act of 1964, the Voting Rights Act of 1965, and the Fair Housing Act of 1968. And in a soon-to-be-closed "progressive moment" in criminal justice policy,[33] the federal government passed laws expanding access to bail, establishing legal counsel for poor defendants, and creating civil commitments as an alternative to incarceration in cases of drug addiction.

In 1965, the Prisoner Rehabilitation Act created legal support for halfway houses by amending the federal penal code to "extend the limits of the place of confinement" where a prison sentence could be served.[34] The act redefined a place of confinement as "any available, suitable, and appropriate institution or facility"—naming "residential treatment centers" as possible alternatives to prison. This broad and permissive language meant prisoners could now be moved into halfway houses at any point during their sentence—even directly from court.[35] And the act included further amendments allowing prisoners to seek work and education outside during their sentence, and to leave on furloughs of up to thirty days for any "compelling reason consistent with the public interest," including to attend funerals or visit dying relatives, to obtain medical services, or to contact potential employers.

The Prisoner Rehabilitation Act embodied core contradictions in the decarceration movement taking hold during these years. The legislation granted the authority for a broad shift from prison to community alternatives, but did this by extending the boundaries of acceptable penal confinement, positioning the halfway house less as a substitute for prison than as a different form of incarceration. The act allowed for the development of residential institutions of a largely unspecified character but, in the language of the penal code of the federal government at least, ensured that these would be themselves sites of confinement. It involved elements of both decarceration and carceral expansion.

Stan Cohen presented the rise of the halfway house as a paradigm case of destructuring rhetoric being used to justify new structures of community social control.[36] In a text that became a classic of criminology—*Visions of Social Control*—he argued that well-meaning reformers intent on replacing prisons mostly succeeded in extending their reach deeper into the social fabric beyond the walls. Cohen pointed out that prison populations remained largely untouched despite the frenzied growth in supposed alternatives, and beginning in the 1970s, the US prison system began an unprecedented period of expansion. Halfway houses and other innovations in community corrections formed a carceral net that complemented rather than replaced the existing institutions of penal power—less a solution than a subtle form of "net-widening."[37]

Bridge House opened in Massachusetts in 1988. The principles of penal-welfarism may have been more influential in the state than anywhere else in the country. At a time when the punitive turn was already taking hold around America, the state closed down almost its entire network of youth justice institutions[38] and relied on indeterminate sentencing to sharply reduce the number of adults in prison.[39] Some prisoners served completely indeterminate sentences (one day to life), and more broadly, a prisoner sentenced to nine to twelve years could be released in as early as three years. This flexible sentencing framework was typically used to shift prisoners into the community as early as possible. The state developed a network of halfway houses—adopting the federal government's terminology and labeling them "pre-release centers"—where people within eighteen months of parole eligibility could serve their prison sentence.[40] A furlough program allowed prisoners to leave up to fourteen days a year to see family or attend job interviews in the lead-up to release.[41]

In the same year that Bridge House opened, the governor of Massachusetts, Michael Dukakis, ran for president of the United States. He confronted a very different political climate than Kennedy had twenty years before. In the wake of civil-rights-era gains for Black Americans, the Republican Party had made an artform of using racially coded law-and-order slogans to attract the support of white voters losing power through the dismantling of racial caste.[42] Dukakis's support for community corrections made him an easy target. His opponent, George H. W. Bush, aired television ads charging Dukakis with complicity in the brutal rape of a white Maryland woman by a Black Massachusetts convict named William Horton—who ran away from a furlough to commit the infamous crime. The ad played repeatedly on network news stations, and Dukakis was vilified as soft on crime—eventually losing the election in a landslide.[43] The Massachusetts legislature repealed the furlough program two years later, part of a punitive turn ushering in dramatic increases in the state prison population.

The rise of racialized mass incarceration in Massachusetts involved a collapse of support for penal-welfarism as the principle of incapacitation usurped the ideal of reintegration at the center of penal policy—with any early release increasingly viewed as a risk to public safety.[44] The use of community alternatives shrank as prison numbers grew. Indeterminate sentencing was replaced by mandatory minimums, which removed the discretion to place prisoners in the community and enforced long prison terms.[45] The state opened Souza-Baranowski Correctional Center—a supermax prison—while closing several minimum-security and pre-release facilities, including Park Drive Pre-Release, Charlotte House, Hodder House, and the Massachusetts Boot Camp.[46] Between 1990 and 2001, the department of corrections increased the number of maximum-security prison beds by 134 percent but cut the number of pre-release beds it contracted by 84 percent.[47] The proportion of men released from prison to parole supervision almost halved—from 65 percent to 34 percent[48]—as prisoners increasingly maxed out sentences inside rather than in the community.

Bridge House confronted a hostile political climate as the web of programs building a bridge from prison to civilian life was dismantled. The program is a registered nonprofit partly funded through "earmarks" inserted into the Massachusetts state budget each year as amendments.[49]

On one occasion, the governor vetoed this funding, and on another, a veto was overturned by the state legislature. It was the mobilization of religious support and private donations that allowed Bridge House to remain in operation. The house was originally purchased with a loan from the Arch Diocese, and the Board of Trustees negotiated for some of the debt to be forgiven. By 2001, the mortgage on the property had been cleared. Around $100,000 was raised when charitable foundations agreed to match the donations of churches and individuals in a campaign allowing them to "adopt" rooms at the program. The money was used for a refurbishment that included adding new bedrooms, bathrooms, and office space.

The political climate had shifted by the time I arrived at Bridge House in 2012, and my research took place in a context of resurgent challenges to mass incarceration and growing movement activism targeting systemic police violence against Black Americans. Policy makers from across the political spectrum were now promoting reentry reform as a pragmatic way to address mounting criticism of the criminal justice system and a fiscal crisis in corrections produced by decades of record prison growth. The Second Chance Act had allocated $165 million of federal funding for reentry programs—during a period of welfare retrenchment and fiscal austerity[50]—and included specific measures for expanding the role of halfway houses in the federal prison system.[51] Some reformers presented a reintegration narrative harking back to the older principles of penal-welfarism, stressing social inclusion and the role of reentry programs in meeting the needs of ex-prisoners in the community.[52]

Programs like Bridge House remain rare despite recent reforms: sporadic estimates in the literature suggest somewhere between 0.5 percent[53] and 1 percent[54] of people released from prison nationwide transition through a halfway house. But it is difficult to know—the breakdown in public funding for the institution during the prison boom has been coupled with a neglect of even rudimentary data gathering. Halfway houses around the country are overwhelmingly run by private providers, and in the absence of a concerted effort to collect centralized statistics, there is a lack of basic information about scale and characteristics. There are no reliable counts of the number of halfway houses in the United States or the population inside them.[55]

Still, the survival of Bridge House long after the end of the Dukakis era points to the uneven impact of the punitive turn and the ongoing influence of the philosophies and institutions of penal-welfarism.[56] The practices of carceral care that I found at the program are rooted in this style of criminal justice, with its blending of punishment and the provision of social welfare—a policy framework dominant in the middle of the twentieth century that is once again being reasserted in mainstream debates. This book examines how the structural tensions of the halfway house are lived and experienced at a particular time and place. And in the context of a national push for decarceration and alternatives to imprisonment, it provides an opportunity to rethink the pitfalls and possibilities of using the halfway house to challenge the worst excesses of mass incarceration.

Liminality in the Halfway House Reintegration Ritual

I have described Bridge House as being in Greater Boston, and to protect the anonymity of the participants and program, I will be no more specific with the location. I name the neighborhood with the pseudonym Clearview Crossing. Clearview hosts a cluster of houses and programs governing addiction and prisoner reentry and shares commonalities with the kinds of neighborhoods where halfway houses are often found in the United States, such as high levels of poverty and unemployment and a reputation for drugs and street crime.[57] The area was hard hit by the collapse of manufacturing and broad shift to university research and high-technology medicine that has transformed the political economy of the region,[58] and in the immediate surroundings of Bridge House, there is both a derelict factory district and an expanding university investing in construction and urban renewal. In a geographical pattern that has been repeated across New England[59]—where old mill and factory cities have often become magnets for Latin American immigrants—deindustrialization in Clearview was coupled with the arrival of significant numbers of Puerto Rican residents to a neighborhood that was once almost exclusively white.

I spend an afternoon walking the old factory district in Clearview. A little more than half a mile from Bridge House, I find a cluster of abandoned buildings and empty lots, which I learn later are the remnants of one the world's largest textile loom manufacturers—a company employing around twenty-eight hundred people at its 1950s peak. I take photos of the red-brick buildings with long rows of smashed windows and plywood (see figure 1.2). I walk for hours jotting notes and taking pictures in what feels like an archaeology of deindustrialization. The paint peels from a boarded shoe company with a portrait above the entrance of a man in a suit and bowler hat having his boots fitted. The concrete smokestacks of an old foundry are overgrown with vegetation and crumbling at one edge.

The architects of the mid-twentieth-century halfway house movement probably imagined men being reintegrated through the kind of industrial labor once carried out in these factories. But capital flight and neoliberal restructuring have been sweeping away the working-class labor markets of Clearview Crossing for decades. At Bridge House, residents searched for a place in the postindustrial economy while carrying criminal records that further amplified exclusion by marking them as suspect whenever they applied for already-scarce jobs.[60] The confinements of a carceral institution were coupled with economic confinement to the social margins.

None of this will be especially surprising to those who are familiar with the literature on reentry and community corrections. US prisons have become satellites to the most racially and economically marginalized neighborhoods in the country[61]—and halfway houses and reentry programs are overwhelmingly located in these same disadvantaged communities.[62] Reentry is typically a transition into poverty.[63] People leaving prison carry criminal convictions that come with wide-ranging invisible punishments,[64] exclusionary sanctions that leave the marked person being denied access to core institutions of social and political life.[65] The position of former prisoners has been described as a kind of "internal exile," a modern-day version of banishment that expels the individual not to an overseas colony but to perpetual marginality at home.[66]

As I accompanied Bridge House residents on the daily rounds, I found that they also experienced important moments of social inclusion tied in part to regionally specific features of the criminal justice system and welfare state. In the years leading up to the fieldwork, Massachusetts had broadly expanded access to free health insurance[67] and made enrollment part of prison pre-release planning.[68] The ability of the

Figure 1.2. The old factory district near Bridge House

men to access health care in a burgeoning high-tech medical sector was crucial given their many complex health needs and the systemic lack of access faced by former prisoners in other parts of the country.[69] Residents could also vote, receive public benefits and food stamps, and apply for public housing—all of which are denied based on criminal records in some jurisdictions.[70] The absence of blanket bans from these institutional arenas created partial openings and precarious opportunities for reintegration, even as powerful mechanisms of exclusion remained firmly in place.

Residence at Bridge House was itself a tenuous foothold in the social mainstream. The program provided a bed in a well-maintained family-style home and wireless internet which opened access to the digital circuits of the knowledge economy. It employed a lawyer part-time to help residents with their many legal problems. There was usually a college student living in the house as a program intern, and every weeknight evening, typically affluent volunteers visited with home-cooked meals to share with the men around a boardroom table donated by a local university. Everyone held hands for a prayer around the table.

Inclusion to the Bridge House community depended on the men meeting idealized and highly normative standards of middle-class respectability.[71] Most important of all was a prohibition on drugs and alcohol. The program adopted a hard-line abstinence model informed by Narcotics and Alcoholics Anonymous, expecting residents to "get clean" and attend three twelve-step meetings each week. Anyone who failed a Breathalyzer or drug test was evicted. The threat of removal gained power in part from the welfare function of the program—for men with few alternative housing options, eviction could be a crushing withdrawal of social support. Most residents were also on parole or probation and faced a rapid escalation of consequences if removed, potentially the most draconian of exclusions: imprisonment.

In this book, I trace the complex dynamics of inclusion-exclusion experienced by Bridge House residents by locating the men in a state of *liminality*.[72] Anthropologists use this concept to describe the middle point in rites of passage used to mark transitions between social locations—rituals ranging from weddings to birthdays and high school graduations—an uncertain in-between period when a person has been unmoored but not yet established somewhere else.[73] And the halfway house as an institution is inherently liminal: the name already implies being in transition toward some new state or position (but not there yet). In postindustrial Clearview Crossing, it was unclear whether the social structure beyond the house was open enough to complete the reintegration ritual.[74] Residents inhabited a liminal position in legal and social space, not in prison but living with former prisoners in a program with prison-like features, marked by criminal records and monitored by parole and probation.

I use the concept of liminality to capture the ambiguities of Bridge House residence, with its contradictory combination of exclusionary and inclusionary social forces. It does not deny that residents are subject to often-extreme exclusions as criminal records interact with and reinforce other markers of race and class disadvantage. But it locates the men in a reintegration ritual in which these exclusionary pressures are coupled with others that push toward inclusion. They live in a social world where lines are blurred and the system seems to operate not by a logic of in or out but different moments of in *and* out that can come in quite quick succession. To borrow Jock Young's metaphor, they are caught in a bulimia nervosa of the social system, at one moment absorbed and accepted, at another rejected and expelled.[75]

Ethnography within the Carceral

Joe Badillo travels around two miles from Bridge House to the noontime meeting of Narcotics Anonymous at a Lutheran church downtown—one of the three he needs to attend this week. I find him afterward among a crowd gathered in the parking lot chatting and smoking cigarettes. Joe says he phoned probation this morning to learn he was summoned to a drug test. He lets me join him on the half-mile walk to community corrections, where he will be asked, as he puts it, to "take a piss."

Just another day really. And Joe's walk between these interconnected sites—the halfway house to the probation office via a mandatory twelve-step meeting—points to the pervasive role of carceral surveillance in structuring his daily rounds. Still, Joe seems very much at home walking these city streets meeting the expectations of various social control institutions. Because he is at home: Joe was born and raised in Clearview Crossing and friendly faces interrupt repeatedly—one man asks how long he has been out, another says how good he looks. I tell him it feels like an episode of *Cheers*.

Joe makes the trip with the help of a cane. And he is physically vulnerable: when we cross the road, traffic slows and stops, and later, he almost falls when an ankle buckles. Joe stops to rest on a sloped window ledge outside the Chamber of Commerce—breathing heavy in the summer heat. I take his red backpack and sling it over my shoulders. Then I ask about the problem behind the cane.

Joe says he entered jail with back pain that turned out to be a cyst on his spine from heroin. He says the jail staff ignored all complaints, even after his legs went numb and he could no longer walk, because they believed it was a hustle for medication. He says he grew feverish and passed out, got rushed to the hospital in an ambulance, and remained in a coma for a month. He says surgery wrecked his spine and he was told he would never walk again. He says that it is still hard to use the toilet and that last time the drug test took two hours. We stop at a service station to buy a bottle of Powerade.

At the probation office, Joe chats with three men wearing crisp basketball gear and silver jewelry. Of course he does. He uses the toilet without drama and the drug test seems mundane and bureaucratic. But the liquid consumed continues to take effect on the bus ride home, and by the time we get off at the bottom of the hill to Bridge House, it is a toilet emergency. I suggest keeping lookout while Joe ducks behind the corner store. He scoffs at the idea: the last thing he needs is a sex offense.

One hand on my shoulder and another on a wobbly cane, Joe sweats and struggles slowly uphill. Things are getting dire, but there is no rushing. Again I suggest a discreet spot that might work. Again he dismisses my naivety. We come across an office chair with a worn orange back and shiny steel wheels discarded by the footpath. Joe slumps in with a humph.

I pump my legs and push him up the hill—our loud laughter filling humid summer air.

* * *

I had only been at Bridge House five days. Joe was fresh from jail. Organic moments of friendship like these were crucial to the long-term collaboration that became the foundation of the project. I worked in the tradition of urban ethnography. This meant violating the canons of the big-sample positivist research dominating the discipline of criminology in the United States[76] and, rather than remaining detached or scientifically neutral, working to build personal relationships among a group on the social margins.[77] I was not trying to correlate statistical variables to predict "recidivism" or "desistance" but, rather, wanted to leverage the power of small samples to create a holistic account combining textured description of events and experiences with a larger analysis of social and historical context.[78]

When I met Joe, he needed all the help he could get—up to and including someone to carry his backpack and push him uphill in an old office chair as he struggled to meet the demands of community corrections. I needed help too: I was an outsider who just moved into an American halfway house around 9,120 miles from my home in New Zealand. I was desperate to find someone prepared to take me under their wing and show me the ropes. It felt from early on like an opportunity to establish a relationship based on trust and mutual support.

Not that I want to draw some false equivalence between our situations. I was an academic who came to Bridge House by choice while based at a wealthy private university in Boston—and could leave any time. Joe was grappling with the rolling aftereffects of a health crisis that almost paralyzed him and, years later, was scrambling to establish a viable existence while in abject poverty and subject to the intensive criminalization of his lifeworld. Some people might say that the arrival of an ethnographic researcher extended the surveillance he already experienced at the hands of the carceral state. I not only offered to carry his bag and push him up a hill, but I recorded the trip in fieldnotes and, later, wrote about it in a book. On that particular day, as Joe traveled from the halfway house to the probation office, I was there watching and recording his movements between these more closed spaces. The blurring of boundaries between research and carceral surveillance is ubiquitous in criminology of all methods, in which much of the "data" is produced by social control institutions engaged in mass supervision— from prison censuses to criminal records. But the human consequences feel far more immediate in ethnography.

The formal process of negotiating access to Bridge House was relatively straightforward: the program director granted permission on the day we met for the first time and I pitched the idea for research. It may appear strange that he would allow an academic to live at a halfway house, but at Bridge House, having people from a university living on-site was central to the program mission. The model was developed in Tennessee by a group of student prison-reform advocates led by a university chaplain who lived with the former prisoners, and in Massachusetts, the house partnered with a university that paid stipends to interns who stayed rent-free while working (there was usually one intern in the house at any time). In this context, I was not given any formal role in the program but simply became part of its "relationship bank"—as the director once put it—fostering resident connections to the social mainstream.

My entry to the site was only the beginning of a far more complex process of negotiating access with Joe Badillo and other residents. My approach was to present openly as a researcher, participate as fully as possible in everyday life, and develop trust slowly by letting the men see up close what I was all about. I did not set out to select a random sample or systematically recruit every resident but, rather, immersed myself in the scene and let relationships evolve as organically as possible. There were men who took me on tours of the neighborhood and introduced me to their families. Others I did not have much to do with. I concentrated my energy on building connections with those who seemed interested in getting to know an ethnographer, negotiating the involvement of key participants and the boundaries of access over many years.

Ethnography is a deeply fraught practice with colonial roots. The genealogy of the method can be traced through the travel diaries of adventurers who embarked on perilous journeys and emerged to tell tales of the "savage" which helped construct the ideals of "civilization" their audiences took for granted.[79] Ethnography was part of the broader colonial project of documenting and recording indigenous cultures that were viewed as primitive and likely to die out through contact with the West.[80] Later, urban ethnographers shifted attention from remote villages in the colonies to the inner-city at home—producing accounts mostly for upper-middle-class readers like them.[81] Some have been criticized for creating modern-day versions of the "jungle-book trope," which circulate stereotypes not of colonized "savages" but of the urban poor in racially segregated neighborhoods.[82]

Before beginning my halfway house ethnography, I read the work of scholars who called for decolonizing social science research,[83] especially the work of white researchers entering the ghettoes and barrios that are the internal colonies of the United States.[84] This work drew my attention to the exploitation that is commonly part of research on marginalized people[85]—for example, the researcher getting grants and promotions for their work, while the researched receive little or nothing in return for their (often considerable) contributions of time and energy. I focused my planning on the nature of the relationships I would try to establish with the men living at the program and, for ideas, turned to gang scholars who engaged gang members less as subjects than as coresearchers themselves involved in fieldwork and analyzing data.[86] I set out to research collaboratively.

During my first three-month spell of fieldwork at Bridge House in 2012, I established a formal collaboration with Joe Badillo, who worked as an interviewer doing life histories with a network of former prisoners in Clearview Crossing (mostly living outside the halfway house). We did half the interviews each, and as part of the training, Joe also recorded my life history. In small but meaningful ways, the arrangement introduced elements of empowerment to the researcher-researched relationship and allowed for a tangible spread of project benefits: I paid Joe for the work, he learned some basics about qualitative research, and gained a credential for his resume. We engaged in joint problem solving and grew closer because of it, sitting on the porch late at night smoking cigarettes and talking about interview technique and emerging themes.

At first, I viewed Bridge House mainly as a base in the community for examining broader issues of reentry and the lasting effects of imprisonment—hence the recruitment of interviewees from outside the program.[87] But the early connection I formed living and working with Joe created opportunities to organize the project more around his own personal trajectory through time. And as Joe became more central to the project, so did Bridge House: for reasons that will become clearer as the story unfolds, he was still a resident when I returned to the program for further three-month blocks of fieldwork in 2013 and 2014. Data collection increasingly centered on Joe's experience and the halfway house as the immediate institutional setting.

In this book, I rely heavily on extensive fieldnotes compiled during these periods. My general routine was to record jottings during the day—using pen and paper or the notepad on my phone—and write these into complete fieldnotes in the evening. When making detailed recordings of important events, I tried to write the notes immediately afterward for accuracy and could spend a day or more rendering episodes of a few hours. Throughout the project, I continued to record open-ended interviews in natural settings, like the city common downtown, and other times Joe or other participants let me record audio of everyday interactions. I transcribed these recordings verbatim and often combined the dialogue with fieldnote descriptions of the people and setting.

I am committed to the idea that people like Joe Badillo—those most directly impacted by the US prison boom—should have a more central voice in public debates over mass incarceration. This idea informed fundamental decisions over the style of representation adopted in this book. For example, one reason I focus on Joe and a small number of connected participants, each introduced with first and last names,[88] is that this allows for showing them as more fully human beings than would be possible if trying to represent the experience of a larger sample. I develop sustained characters by turning fieldnotes into ethnographic vignettes that show these participants speaking and making decisions in varied situations. And with the people involved introduced in social context, I open space in the book for them to speak at length, not setting off this speech with italics or a change in font size but integrating their words as a core part of the text through long passages of extended dialogue.

Power dynamics at the heart of ethnographic representation shaped the whole process of making the words of participants central to the book. For one, this involved extensive editing and selecting from the transcripts of hours upon hours of conversations recorded over the years of fieldwork.[89] To try to maintain the vividness and force of participants' speech as words on the page, I cut phrases and paragraphs and whole sections, removed redundancies and clutch words, and occasionally changed the order to help with flow and coherence. I never added or substituted my own words, except to insert pseudonyms, and focused on maintaining as much as possible the original meaning and message. But the work of selecting and editing meant that I always had the final say over how the words of participants were conveyed and, ultimately, what words were included at all.[90]

My attempts to push the envelope in collaboration came with their own problems—rooted in the structural inequalities that make this kind of ethnography an inherently fraught exercise. As I grew increasingly wary of my control over how the research would be represented, I engaged Joe Badillo as an analyst through a process of shared reading and writing together. I will develop this more fully in chapter 8 but, for now, will simply note that it was tumultuous and took a heavy toll on Joe at a time when he was already stretched and vulnerable. The problems ran deeper than limits to literacy: the basic social conditions in which he lived were severely disruptive to the practices involved in producing not only this book but writing more broadly. And the contrast between our respective social conditions—Joe's and mine—is symptomatic of the broader forces enabling some people to have a voice in public debate while others are excluded.

I have come to see many of the issues raised by the research less as problems to be solved than as unavoidable dilemmas.[91] As an example, I am splitting the book royalties between Joe and another key character, Tim Williams, as part of a commitment to sharing the project benefits and finding mutually beneficial ways to engage participants in ethnographic research.[92] But might this be interpreted as purchasing their stories and involvement? I never talked about royalties with Joe and Tim, or even had a book contract, until long after we developed close relationships and the fieldwork was effectively finished. And yet it is impossible to separate my role as a potential resource from their participation, when from the outset, I was looking for ways to be helpful to them as they were being helpful to me (by giving rides in my car, for example). I viewed providing support as a necessary part of doing ethical research with people experiencing chronic social marginalization—a project I would clearly benefit from in a range of ways—but because of their marginality, this support also introduced a subtle element of coercion to participate.

A key strength of ethnography is that the involvement of participants can be talked through over time in the context of long-term relationships: I lived with these men at Bridge House, and by sharing a roof, we developed sustained personal connections. And in 2019, I traveled to Clearview Crossing with a draft of this book. I was living in New Zealand working an academic job in my hometown of Wellington and returned to the United States, where Joe hosted me at his house for two weeks. I used this time to show him the manuscript while also approaching other participants to talk about the book and to offer to show them the draft—providing people the chance to raise concerns or clarify details before publication. All were anonymized in the text and named with pseudonyms. Yet this consultation was still an important safeguard against information that people viewed as damaging or stigmatizing being attached to them despite the changing of names.

Joe had more pressing issues pulling on his energy and attention during my visit anyway. But that will have to wait, for we are getting too far ahead in the story. There is a lot more to be told about the time between that day I pushed him up the hill to Bridge House in a discarded office chair—befriending and supporting as well as observing and recording—and more than seven years later, when I returned with a draft of this book. It is a story that opens a window on the tensions and contradictions of the halfway house as an institution. Perhaps it is fitting, then, that my whole ethnographic approach was brimming with dilemmas of its own.

2

A Blessing in Disguise

A connecting thread running through this book is the story of Joe Badillo's residence at Bridge House. The structure is loosely chronological—tracing the time from entry to the program to exit from it—with the broader themes developed out of this unfolding experience. But the first step is looking backward and taking a longer view of Joe's biography and the many years he spent shuttling in and out of prison and jail. Locating his experience during the fieldwork within this larger cycle of confinement raises important questions about the role of the halfway house as an alternative—issues that will be returned to throughout the book. It also provides an opening to examine how this history of incarceration intersected with the health crisis that left him desperately in need of housing and other support from the program. Part of this will involve presenting Joe's own narrative of the tumultuous period leading up to his arrival at Bridge House. But let's start with the official record of his imprisonment.

* * *

I smoke cigarettes on the Bridge House back porch with Joe and talk about his criminal record. He holds a printed copy of the six-page document in his hands. We laugh that his ethnicity is listed as "Black" at the top of page 1—Joe has light skin and identifies as part Puerto Rican. He talks about the irony that during all the years of hustling, he was oblivious to this ever-growing record, but it has now become a problem as he tries to make positive change. Joe is especially concerned about his application for public housing and says he has been on a wait list for around three years. He believes that when the application reaches the top of the list, he will be denied based on his criminal record but be given the chance to appeal. So he waits.

Joe lets me make a copy of his criminal record. It is the first time I have ever properly looked at one, and I struggle to make sense of the technical jargon and acronyms presented without explanation or commentary. I learn that the label "CMTD" being attached to a case disposition indicates that a prison or jail sentence was imposed, and later, I separate the CMTD cases from all the others to create a history of Joe's incarceration (see table 2.1).

TABLE 2.1. A Cycle of Confinement: Joe Badillo's Prison and Jail Sentences

Year	Charge(s)	Sentence length
1988	Disorderly Person	Not listed
	Distribute/Dispense Class B	5 years
1993	Attempt to Commit Crime, Possession Burglarious Tools, Disorderly Person	90 days each charge[a]
	Compulsory Insurance Violation, Attaching Wrong MV Plates	Not listed
	Escape	90 days
1994	Possession to Distribute Class B	2½ years
1997	Violation of Probation (VOP)	1 year
1998	Operating After Suspended License	10 days
1999	Possession Class B Controlled Substance, Use Without Authority, Operating After Suspended License	6 months, 6 months, 10 days
	Conspiracy to Violate Controlled Substances Act, Distribute/Dispense Class B	2–4 years each charge
2004	Larceny More, Operating After Suspended License, Resisting Arrest	3 months, 60 days, 30 days
2008	Possession to Distribute Class B	18 months

a Sentences with the same disposition date are shown on the same line.

Joe experienced incarceration not as a single long stretch behind bars followed by a discrete process of reentry to society, but as a cycle of confinement spanning two decades of recurring movements in and out, in and out. Within this cycle, the "reentries" were less transitions from prison to freedom than preludes to further spells of incarceration. The record suggested he was sentenced to prison or jail on twelve separate occasions. Sometimes multiple sentences were imposed together at the same time—as in 1993, 1999, and 2004—and as far as Joe could remember, these were served concurrently in groups.[1] On the other hand, what might seem like meaningful periods on the outside really involved other incarcerations missing from the record. For example, the record did not show the many times Joe was detained waiting for cases to progress because he could not afford cash bail.[2] These incarcerations could be lengthy and were especially important between his release in 2009 and arrival at Bridge House in 2012—including the around six months he said he was locked up on a charge of "Larceny Over" before receiving the probation sentence that came with a halfway house placement. The record also missed incarcerations outside Massachusetts, and Joe said he served time in Florida in 2006.

A criminal record is a decontextualized account of individual criminality. One reason records are such a potent source of stigma[3] is that they filter politically and ethically complex human experiences through the seemingly neutral legal categories of the carceral state and, in the process, focus attention on personal failures rather than the problems with the categories themselves or the racist and discriminatory way they are often policed and enforced. One way to shift perspective is to locate Joe's cycle of confinement within the broader history of the rise of racialized mass incarceration through this period.[4] All his sentences longer than a year involved drug offences as the most serious charge. And the war on drugs was under way: as Joe became a teenager in the 1980s, law enforcement in Black and Latino neighborhoods around the country was being militarized and violently escalated.[5] The Massachusetts legislature introduced mandatory minimums among the harshest in the United States, replacing judicial discretion with fixed prison terms of up to fifteen years depending on the weight and type of drug.[6] These macro changes in penal policy forged a prison-community pipeline in places like Clearview Crossing: a 1997 study of concentrated incarceration in Massachusetts found that Hispanics were eighty-one times more likely than whites to receive a prison sentence for a drug offense.[7] In this context, Joe's experience might be considered representative of the hypercriminalization of young men growing up poor and Puerto Rican under a racially targeted war on drugs.[8]

But Joe was not a typical member of the community: he was unusually criminally active, and his drug use and dealing were associated with serious violence. He said he was often armed with a gun and told me stories about "pistol whipping" people over debts, attacking strangers in the street while high on crack cocaine, and undertaking brutal robberies of drug dealers. This locates him among the small percentage of persistent offenders who criminologists have long identified as responsible for most violent crime.[9] The extreme behavior of men like Joe often gets used to justify treating all young men of color as if they are armed thugs. But given the pervasive stereotypes, it is worth stating directly: experiencing hypercriminalization may be a normal part of growing up in some minority neighborhoods, but engaging in the kind of serious criminality described by Joe is not.[10] And he might have spent much longer imprisoned. As he once put it, "I was doing some shit out there that should have got me buried under the prison and well deserved."

Looking back on Joe's past, the picture that emerges is of a mutually reinforcing cycle of individual violence and state violence imposed through imprisonment.[11] When Joe was seventeen years old, he was sent to state prison for five years on a drug-distribution charge. He said the sentence was largely indeterminate, and with good behavior, he could have been out on parole in six months—but he ended up serving most of the term. Joe described prison as incredibly violent and like "going from the streets into a criminal university." Not long after being released, he faced two fresh sets of charges for violent offenses in the same year (1991): first armed robbery, then armed robbery and assault and battery with a dangerous weapon. Both cases were dismissed. Then Joe successfully challenged a charge for firearm possession without a permit in 1993—he told me he simply tossed the gun and, when police found it, claimed the weapon could have belonged to anyone. He was locked up again the same year on different charges anyway. And on and on.

Tracing this cycle as a linear chronology starts to make it seem inevitable, and the endless complexity of the whole backstory gets lost in the presentation. Real life is always messy and unpredictable—it might have gone differently. And we could fill a book properly unpacking this history: dealing with the steep problems of accurately reconstructing what even happened and when, tracing the linkages to a broader context, and teasing out the nuanced interplay between structural oppression and individual responsibility.

In this book, the bigger question is how we might understand Bridge House in relation to this cycle of confinement. Joe was sentenced to the program as an alternative to imprisonment. Was it a meaningful alternative? Should we think about Joe's entry to the halfway house as a genuine break from this long history of incarceration in prison and jail? Or should we view his experience at the program as an extension of the more obvious confinements he had so often experienced behind walls and razor wire? Is Bridge House better understood as a substitute for or addition to imprisonment? These questions center on the particulars of Joe Badillo and Bridge House, but how we think about them has much-broader implications—they raise issues at the heart of how we imagine decarceration and alternatives to mass incarceration.

* * *

Joe's understanding of his own experience at Bridge House is central to the analysis in this book, and as the next step, I want to focus on his narrative of how he ended up at the program. The account hinges on his contracting an epidural abscess—a collection of pus and germs between the outer covering of the spinal cord and the spine—a life-threatening condition that kills around 14 percent of all people diagnosed with it.[12] I want to let Joe tell the story in his own words, drawing on this personal and textured view of social suffering to open a window on the institutional response when he was at his most vulnerable.[13] It points to the contradictory role of the criminal justice system as a source of abuse and neglect as well as respite and support.

The story begins at Richmond County Jail. Joe was intimately familiar with Richmond and was usually sentenced to incarceration at the jail rather than in the state prison system.[14] This is partly because of an unusual feature of criminal justice in Massachusetts, where sentences of up to two and a half years can be served at the county level, while in most other states, jails are typically reserved for pretrial detainees or those convicted of misdemeanors.[15] The harsh conditions at the facility were symptomatic of conditions prevailing more broadly through the years of the US prison boom.[16] A damning investigation by the federal Department of Justice, for example, found that the Richmond jail was "significantly overcrowded," designed for around eight hundred people but consistently holding around fourteen hundred, and was especially critical of severe shortages in mental health services. And Joe could narrate the long-term decline in conditions through stories of his own experiences there over many years—from deteriorating food quality to the growing use of extended cell lockdowns.

Joe said he left Richmond County Jail in 2009 with $5,000 saved from time in work-release and immediately started "hustling," his dealing intertwined with his own growing dependence on the consumption of heroin and crack cocaine. He described being at a "trap house" buying crack when he was asked to join a group of men confronting a rival dealer selling within their territory. A fight ensued and the rival was stabbed. He said he was arrested along with the other men and taken to the Richmond jail the same night. It was there that the first symptoms of the abscess appeared.

"I start getting back pain the second day," Joe says. "I'm saying to the nurse, 'I'm getting this back pain. It's killing me.' I don't know what it is—might be a pulled muscle or whatever. When you come into the jail, you get a physical, and right away, I'm saying, 'I'm dope sick. I need to go to the infirmary. I need to detox.' When you're in the detox part of the jail, you're in the facility where all the doctors and nurses are, so you have access to nurses all day long. They bring you medication three times a day. I remember telling her every time I seen her, 'It's getting worse. It's getting worse.'

"First day, 'Let's see how it goes. It might just be a sprained muscle.' Second day, I'm like, 'Yo, this ain't getting any better.' She's like, 'Yeah, whatever'—just totally blew me off, talking about I want pain medication because I'm an addict. That goes on for a few days, then gets to the point where I can barely walk. They still wouldn't give me nothing. They wouldn't let me see a doctor or nothing. Then it comes to where I'm done detoxing, and they send me to general population.

I ask, "In the infirmary, is every man and his dog in there detoxing and telling every story in the world to try to get something?"

"No. Because when you're detoxing, you know you're not getting anything special. You could tell them that your arms falling off, and you're not getting anything. And if that was the case anyways, as your medical right, they're supposed to follow through with any complaints as a precaution. If I said I was sick ten times prior to that and was lying, on the eleventh time you don't know if I'm lying or not. You have to give me medical attention. It's my right as a human being. It's my right. They were denying my right to medical attention. I don't care if you have a history of lying about whatever. That don't give them a right to—you don't know."

"How long were you in the infirmary for?"

"Five days, I believe. Yeah, five days. And check this out. I get locked up in June. It's like this weather now but hotter. If you can imagine, you're in this unit, maybe one, two, three, four, five, six, seven, maybe eight beds. No bunk beds—five beds against this wall, three or four against this wall. It's a little room. And they got a shower and a toilet, that's it. No TV.

"My back is killing me, so I start taking showers all day long. I'm talking about, I'm in there twenty-four hours a day showering, letting this hot water get on my back. That gets to the point where it's steaming up the whole room. So they are telling me, 'You can't shower. You're showering all day.' I'm like, 'Yo, it's the only way I'm getting relief for my back, man. You guys don't wanna do nothing for me.' You know what they did? They end up bringing me to a room where there was no shower. I'm just by myself. I ended up staying in there for like two days.

"That's when I moved to general population. When they moved me, I was telling them, 'I can't walk over there.' They wanted me to pack all my linen, uniform, underwear, socks, blankets in a bag. By the time you're done putting everything in this like sack, a plastic bag, I'm like, 'I can't carry that over there.' So they have another inmate carry my bag over. But I'm walking hunched over, man. I can't move. And I'm telling them, 'Listen, my back is—I can't move, man.'

"A two-minute walk took me a half hour. I get over there, get inside my room. I just wanna lay down at this point. I get inside the room, and I'm on the top bunk. So I go to the CO and say, 'Yo, I can't get up there.' They're like, 'You got a medical slip for a bottom bunk?' I say, 'No, but my back is killing me, man.' They are like, 'You got no slip. You get on the top bunk.' So I had to climb up there, man. As painful as it was, I got up on the top bunk and just stayed up there for the whole day. We locked in for twenty-one hours a day anyway, but I stayed in any time I was allowed to go out.

"My roommate was like, 'What's wrong with you, man?' I was like, 'Man, my back is fuckin' killing me. I can't fuckin' . . .' So after the second day, he was like, 'Here, you can take the bottom bunk.' But I still wasn't going out. I lost my appetite. I was all fucked up. That went on for like a week. I was filling out doctor's slips this whole time."

"Were you getting any indication from them they were paying any attention at all?"

"When I left [the infirmary], they put me on Tylenol. When I got to general population, you have to go to med line to get your medication. I told my roommate, 'Can you let them know I can't make it? I can't walk, man.' I lost sensation in my legs. If you touch my legs, I literally couldn't feel nothing. Couldn't even use them. Couldn't walk. Yeah, couldn't walk. He would go get his meds, and I was like, 'Tell them I can't move. I need to see a doctor or something. Bring my meds over here, or let them bring my meds.' He would go over there and give them the message and then come back and just—'Tell him get up and walk over. Tell him it's procedure. He must get up and move.'

"There was a lieutenant who worked there that I knew from doing time. He ended up grabbing me a few Motrin 800s, which he wasn't supposed to do. He said, 'I'll talk to the medical staff and see if they can start bringing your meds over.' I said, 'Listen, you need to do more than that. You need to tell them I need a doctor.' After that, the next day or something, that's when the CO brung me over there on his own, which he wasn't supposed to do. The CO went to get a wheelchair and said, 'Fuck these people, man. I'll bring you up there myself.' Put me in a wheelchair, took me out to the infirmary, and said, 'Listen, this dude is fuckin' sick, real sick. You need to see him now.' That's out of protocol. They're not supposed to do that. The only people that are classified to put you in a wheelchair is the medical staff. CO ain't supposed to do none of that. That's going way out of their line. They'll get fired for that. But he knew there was something seriously wrong with me."

"Did you know the guy?"

"Just from doing time. He's a CO that's been there forever, and I've been going there forever."

"Do you remember his name?"

"Yeah, Hawthorne. I'll never forget it. He probably saved my life. He and another CO bring me to the infirmary. They rush in and say I'm being seen and I'm being seen now. I go into the nurse practitioner's office. They had to pick me up out of the wheelchair, put me on the examiner's table. She removed my shirt and asked me some questions. I told her, 'I can't feel my legs.' She says, 'Oh, you're all right. You probably have back spasms.'

"I'm like, 'Bitch, I can't fucking move my legs!' They had to calm me down because I'm ready to spaz out. I'm like, 'How the fuck you gonna tell me everything's fucking all right, and I can't fucking move my fucking legs? These people had to bring me up here in a fucking wheelchair. They had to carry me and put me on this table that I'm on. And you're fucking telling me I'm all right?' She's like, 'Calm down, calm down. We'll keep you up here in the infirmary under observation, just to make you satisfied.'

"At this point I'm breaking out in a fever. They put me back in the infirmary, the detox place. I get right in bed. Fucking can't move. I ain't eating. I'm burning up a fever. Next thing you know I'm pissing myself and shitting myself, and they are leaving me in my shit. They are not cleaning me up. They are not nothing. They left me like that for like twelve hours. Then they got a doctor in there. The doctor was like, 'You've got to rush this kid to a hospital ASAP.'"

"At that point, it's like code red?"

"Code red brother. Code red. I get to the hospital. I'm in the examining room, got these doctors asking me all these questions. I'm telling him, 'I'm thirsty.' The first thing I'm saying, 'I'm thirsty. I'm dehydrated.' Because I had a fever. I had an infection. The cyst got infected and was spreading in my bones. I'm telling them I can't feel my legs, I'm having back pain. They put me in a CAT scan, you know, the big machine that your body goes in the thing—a CAT scan or an MRI. And that's the last thing I remember. Next thing I remember, I woke up like a month later in a different hospital.

"That's when they told me, 'You're paralyzed.' The doctor explained that I was a paraplegic. I couldn't move my arms at the beginning of the month, then I started getting that feeling back, so instead of a quad I was a paraplegic. They said, 'Yeah, you're paralyzed. You'll never walk again.'"

"At first you couldn't move your arms even?"

"They told me no, that I was a quadriplegic, meaning my arms and legs were affected during the surgery. But this movement [rotating his forearms] came back surprisingly right away."

"Do you remember your response to that news?"

"When they told me I was paralyzed, I didn't really comprehend. It wasn't until maybe later on that I—hold on—because I was so medicated I didn't understand. I think like a couple of weeks later. Like, they would never—they would come and all be talking, but they were not talking to me. I would be right there, but they would talk like I wasn't there. They would be discussing my case like one doctor to another. They were like,

'Diagnosis is showing he's not gonna walk.' I was like, 'Hold on. Wait a minute.'

"That's when it finally kicked in. I look to my legs, tried to move them, and they wouldn't move. I was like, 'Oh my God.' Yeah, it was fucked up, man. Definitely something I never want to experience ever again. It was definitely fuckin' ssshhh—it definitely was a nightmare. Yeah.

"You know what though? From the doctor saying I would never walk again, eight months later, my toes start moving, man. I started moving my toes. Every day they used to take a pen and rub it on my foot, to see if I get any reaction. None, none. Eight months, man. Then one day my toes—I called the doctor: 'Yooooooo!' Because I wanted to know, maybe it was nerves just acting on their own, man. They was like, 'Can you stop it?' And I stopped it. 'Now wiggle it again.' And I wiggled them. They were like, 'Yeah, they getting feeling back. Absolutely.'

"I didn't get out of bed for eight months. I stayed in a hospital for two months, and then I went to a nursing home. Because they can't keep you in a hospital. You have to go to a nursing home. I went to a nursing home to learn how to live in a wheelchair, how to be self-supportive in a wheelchair. But let me tell you, when I went to the nursing home, I didn't get out of bed for—from the day I had the surgery, it took me eight months to sit upright. So eight months later, I got up on my bed. I learned how to do exercises, build up my body strength, my upper-body strength. Then a couple, a week later, I got in a wheelchair. Altogether, I did eleven months and something in the hospital and nursing home. So almost a year after surgery."

"After eleven months you got out?"

"Yeah, but it's more like I was forced out. My insurance said I'm capable of leaving the nursing home. They said, 'We ain't paying for him to go there no more.' Because, every month my physical therapist would have to give the report about my progress. And basically, I can dress myself at this point. I can get up out of the wheelchair to get to a walker. So basically—"

"Could you go to the toilet?"

"I could do that by myself."

"Showering?"

"I don't know about showering. No, because you know what, the whole time I was there, I was never allowed to shower by myself. I always had to have a CRN shower me. What they do is that I would transport from my wheelchair to this other chair that's built for the shower, that they rolled into the shower and washed me. But I can get dressed on my own."

"So what happened with the insurance?"

"My insurance says, 'He's capable of taking care of himself. We're not paying for him to stay there no longer.'"

"Do you remember how you felt about that at the time?"

"The thing is, Liam, where am I going? This is what they said: 'You're not getting kicked out right away but within the next month.' So I said, 'What's my options?' I mean, I already filed for [public] housing. I was getting Social Security, but you don't collect it while you're in there. You get like $600 a month. I knew I was going to have an income when I got out but it wasn't—"

"How much?"

"$700 a month, $700 or $800 a month. So I went to my caseworker and said, 'What's my options here, man? I'm still waiting for housing. I'm on the handicap list. I'm handicapped. I'm in a wheelchair. I'm going to need somebody to bathe me. I need all this.' And honestly, I wasn't ready to leave, but that was my options? They said, 'Well, you can go to a shelter in Boston. You ever heard of Pine Street Inn?' They want me to go to Pine Street Inn. I know Pine Street, and that's a bunch of alcoholics. I'm in a wheelchair. That's the last place I want to be, man. So I was like, 'Let me make some phone calls, man.' It was a rush decision, but that was my only option. I moved in with my friend Eddie Jones. He was active though."

"How do you know Eddie?"

"I know Eddie for over twenty years. I grew up hanging around Eddie, getting high with Eddie. He's a mechanic. He used to own a garage and then started getting high and lost his garage. He's been around forever. He's a dinosaur."

"So Eddie says he'll put you up at his place?"

"Yeah, but he's active."

"He's a heroin addict?"

"Crack."

"What's the apartment like?"

"He got it through SMIT [a nonprofit social service provider]. He went through the shelter. They gave me a year of free rent there."

"How many bedrooms?"

"Two. Well, one, but the living room made into a bedroom. So I'm still in the wheelchair. I can get up the stairs. He lives on the second floor. I need help getting out. I need help getting down. Showering by myself though."

"How would you get up and down?"

"Because he had railings on the thing, so I was lucky."

"What would you do with the wheelchair?"

"He would bring it up and down for me. Yeah, it was a pain, man. And the girl who I was running with, she was still active, she would come and visit. Eddie's got people in and out. He's getting high. I started getting high. Then I got to the point I was spending my SSI on that shit. Or selling my medication, all my Percs [Percocet] and shit. I found myself back on Main Street in a wheelchair."

"When you were in the hospital before you moved in with Eddie, how were you imagining life after that?"

"I figured I would be in housing, that housing was going to get me a place. I would be away from all the bullshit. A normal life. But when they came and told me my insurance ran out, they ain't paying no more and I was leaving, that just, ppfffttt. My thinking started going into survival mode. 'I'm going to get out. I'm going to pick up a package, start selling and shit.'"

"You are thinking that even before you got out of the hospital?"

"Pretty much. Knowing that I was gonna move in with Eddie."

"What do you mean by 'survival mode'?"

"Come on, man, I'm getting kicked out with nowhere to go. What else am I gonna do? My dreams or perfect scenario was, I get my housing, I go get SSI, I pay $200 a month to get my own place. I get into the gym, get back on my feet. That all changed when I was like, 'Oh, you ain't got nowhere to go.' All right, what else am I supposed to do? I got nowhere to go, man. Nowhere. In a wheelchair with nowhere to go. So fuck it, man. I said, 'Fuck it, I'll go back to hustling, get a place.'

"When they tell me I gotta go, my insurance stopped paying, that set me back so far mentally. I was so depressed, man. I was like, 'What the fuck am I gonna do, man?' It's just so much stress, so much—I just wanted to give up at that point, like, 'What the fuck, man? What am I gonna do?' Yeah, man, it fucked me up. I truly believe if I would've stayed there, got my housing, I would've been fine. I wouldn't have had to go through this struggle that I went through of fuckin' catching another habit, out there runnin' in a wheelchair, going back to jail."

"How long from when you left the hospital last time to when you got locked up again? How long is that?"

"A year maybe."

"Are you living with Eddie the whole time?"

"Nah. I live with Eddie for a couple of months. You know, I'm chasing the hustle. At first it's like, I pick up a package, stay at Eddie's house, try to sell. But he wants to get high, I want to get high, and just sitting right there ain't happening. So I go to what I know best—Main Street, where it's constantly people looking for shit. The best way I can hustle is on Main Street. And the more I'm on Main Street, the less I'm going back to Eddie's. So it just gets to the point where I'm not living at Eddie's no more. I'm just living in crack houses now.

"So you're literarily selling on the streets in a wheelchair?"

"Yep. Selling in the wheelchair, fighting in the wheelchair, smoking in the wheelchair. Fuckin' miserable. I hit my rock bottom. Not only was I homeless, but I was a homeless, wheelchair-bound addict. A successful hustler is being in numerous places as fast as you can be. Basically that was taken away from me. When you're selling drugs, especially a successful drug dealer has got a phone, and you're getting phone calls: 'Hey, I need five over here.' 'But I can't go over there. You've got to come to me.' Nine out of ten times somebody who's smoking crack or buying crack, they don't want to leave their house. So it definitely affected me that way. Getting around, avoiding police.

"Thank God I had that reputation where, 'Hey, he might be in a wheelchair, but it's still Joe Badillo. Don't try to rob him. Don't try to fuck with him.' Because there were times where I was having bags of crack, bags of dope in a wheelchair, where anybody else would've been robbed, kicked over. Know what I mean? I still had that: 'Don't fuck with him.'

"It got to the point where I was beating people in my wheelchair. 'Let me see your money,' shhwwwt. Because my hustle got bad, yo. My hustle got to the point where I couldn't really hustle, man. That's when I came up with another hustle. If you get a blank check, you go to Stop and Shop, you write on the check the amount—$100 cash and $100 for groceries. You write a check for $200 to Stop and Shop, you don't have to show them no ID or nothing. Bam. They give you $100 cash back. That was my hustle for a while. I must've done a hundred checks. Stolen credit cards. Go to Walmart, they wouldn't ask you for ID. Actually that's how I ended up getting arrested. They had me on camera buying a laptop for $500. They got me maybe two months later. The cops were looking for me. They said they had a warrant. It was for larceny. They said they had me on camera. That's when I went back to the house of correction."

"Did you bail out that time?"

"I could've bailed out. I was still getting my SSI checks. I got arrested with my EBT card and told my mother to call the place up, act like you're me—I gave her all the information, my password—and she got a new card sent to her. She would take the money off my card and put it on my books. That was my plan. My bail was like $1,000, so that would've taken like two checks. I was planning on doing that, then bailing out. But the first thirty days my mind started changing. I do want to go back out there, man. I really don't.

"And you know what? I go to L block [a unit at the jail], and I go right back into survival mode. Running the block. I opened a store. I'm gambling, selling drugs. But this time I'm not doing them. Every time I went to jail, I always got high. This time I was like, 'No, I'm not doing shit.'

"My mind-set started changing, like, 'If I bail out, where am I gonna go? I got this handicap. How am I gonna survive out there?' I said, 'No, I don't wanna do that.' I didn't want to get sentenced, because the block I was in, I was running the block, I was getting one-third of all the drugs in there. I had the store. But if I got sentenced, I would've had to go to another block. So I told my lawyer, 'Keep on getting it continued, continued, continued.' I did that for six months, then I told her, 'Listen, I want to go to a program.'

"I had six months in, and the judge said, 'I'll sentence you to nine months. Do three more months, and with good time, in probably forty-five or sixty days, you go home free. No paper, no probation.' I said, 'Hell no, I won't last. I want to go to a program.' So the deal was I had to take a year probation with a year suspended. I said, 'Put a year over my head. I don't care if I've got to piss in a cup for a year. I'll risk having that suspended sentence if I fuck up. I'm willing to take that. This time I'm giving myself a chance.' That's what I did. I gave myself a chance. I gave myself a opportunity.

"This is how God works, man. I went in front of Janet Pryor. She's a board member of Bridge House. And my attorney was a public defender, but in the public defender's office, there's a caseworker that works just to get people into programs. My attorney is a caseworker strictly for that—getting people into programs. Her name is Jenny. She happened to work for Bridge House before that. She was like, 'Listen, I'm going to pull some strings, get you into Bridge House. Just don't fuckin' disappoint me.' PPPffffttttt. Damn. Without having an interview or anything, I get right in there."

"It seems like you came to that decision, determined to do something different, quite quickly when you went in. Do you remember a day where you're sitting there like, 'Okay, I'm done'? Or is it more gradual?"

"I hate to even bring this up again, but there goes again: God works in mysterious ways. For the longest time, I wanted to be out of that lifestyle, but God's honest truth is, if I didn't have this disability, I would still be out there right now running up and down. If I didn't have this disability, to be honest with you, I would probably still be out there trying to hustle. For the longest time, I wanted to not be out there, and that's why I say God works in mysterious ways, man. Yeah, if it wasn't for this disability, I would still be out there. Absolutely."

"What you mean for the longest time you wanted to—"

"There was many days, many, many days, where I would be saying, 'I don't want to live like this no more. God, please help me. I'm tired, tired of going in and out of jail, tired of . . .' But I just didn't know how to stop. That's why I say that this whole thing, this whole disability, is a blessing in disguise. And if I don't recognize it like that, then I'm going to miss out on a big fucking blessing. It truly did save my life. It almost took my life, but then again, it gave me my life back."

* * *

Joe Badillo narrated his experience of illness at Richmond County Jail through stories of neglect. He says that when he first complained of back pain and losing the ability to walk, the nurse brushed him off, dismissing him as an addict seeking medication. And when he took long showers to cope with the pain, steaming up the infirmary, they simply moved him to a room without a shower. He said that despite being barely able to walk, he was transferred to general population and given the top bunk in a shared cell, where he lost the feeling in his legs and became unable to leave. After several days, Joe said he convinced a guard to take him to the infirmary in a wheelchair—where he was "pissing" and "shitting" himself: "they left me like that for like twelve hours."

Joe's anger at the jail was palpable. He had filed a lawsuit against the County Sheriff's Office, which ran the facility, and three specific medical staff. He gave me a copy of the civil action complaint, which presented the following timeline: he arrived at the institution on June 1, was prescribed Ibuprofen on June 4, was disciplined for excessive showers on June 5, was moved to general population on June 7, and on June 10 returned to the infirmary, where he was diagnosed with a "back strain." He was not seen by a doctor for the first time until the evening of June 11. The doctor recorded him "laying in bed, unable to stand," with "belly distended, tense, diffusely render" and appearing "yellow, dehydrated, with sunken eyes, chapped lips." At that point, Joe was rushed to the hospital, diagnosed with an epidural abscess, and underwent emergency surgery.

One result of the seeming indifference of jail medical staff was costly delays to surgery that increased the risks of an already dangerous intervention. The procedures used to remove epidural abscesses are known as "laminectomies" because they involve cutting out the portion of the vertebral bone called the lamina—the roof of the spinal canal—to drain pus and decompress the spinal cord.[17] The key to success is acting early, and on the flipside, "late diagnosis or inadequate treatment may leave the patient with long term severe or disabling incapacity."[18] For Joe, the result was a "nightmare" of emerging from surgery to find he could not move his arms or legs.

From one perspective, Joe's treatment at Richmond County Jail might be viewed as a case study of the inhuman punishment inflicted on ill and vulnerable prisoners more systemically around the United States.[19] In California, federal courts held that the entire state prison system was violating the constitutional rights of prisoners by holding them in facilities that could not provide adequate medical treatment, and in 2005, the prison health-care apparatus was put under a court-appointed receiver.[20] At one point, Joe himself framed his experience in terms of a denial of basic rights, arguing that jail staff had refused to provide medical attention that was his "right as a human being."

But the picture of the jail that emerges from Joe's narrative is ultimately more contradictory. After describing his harrowing postsurgery experience as a "homeless, wheelchair-bound addict," he said that he was arrested and brought back to the very same jail—which this time appears in his account as a form of housing and respite from the brutal conditions outside.[21] Joe said he was originally detained because he could not afford the $1,000 price for his release, but after figuring out how to collect Social Security and gathering the money for bail, he decided not to pay and even worked with his public defender to try to slow the progress of his criminal case. Joe said he leveraged his social standing inside to access resources, "opening a store" selling goods and taking a cut of the profits from drug dealing in his unit.

Joe presented the jail as a resource in the struggle for survival. Yet his narrative centered not on the goods or services provided by the institution but instead on the bleak prospects that awaited beyond the walls. As he put it, "I got this handicap. How am I gonna survive out there?" Joe's most recent experience "out there" was one of homelessness and poverty-level income from Social Security that he estimated first at $600 a month, then revised to $700 or $800 a month. He had historically supplemented the inadequate provisions of the welfare state with hustling in the underground economy but described his physical condition making the old strategies untenable. And while there are moments in Joe's narrative suggesting opportunities—like the single line mentioning that he was given "a year free rent" to stay at his friend's apartment—he nonetheless came to view jail as a more desirable location than what was available outside.

Joe's evaluation of Bridge House also needs to be understood in the context of this grim assessment of the alternatives. He described the opportunity to get a bed at the house appearing as almost a divine intervention: "this is how God works, man." As Joe surveyed his options and searched for a program placement, he found two key people who had existing relationships with Bridge House: the sentencing judge was a board member, and his public defender was a former employee. The public defender "pulled strings" and got him accepted without an interview as part of plea-deal probation sentence.

Among the most striking features of Joe's narrative is a sense of agency that extends even to the destruction of his body. The epidural ab-

sce
alsc
mak⸱ownsend stands at the Rotary Club podium in a white shirt and
was ⸱ tie, brown hair cut short and beard neatly trimmed, an Ameri-
In th⸱ ⸱ hanging loosely from a pole a short step from his left shoulder.
again⸱ are important moments in generating support for a program that
myst⸱ ⸱n private donations to cover baseline operating costs. It helps that

Th⸱oks like an insider—there are lots of white men in suits among the
ple v⸱nce—and can tell the gathering that before having children he was
cha⸱ ⸱member of Rotary. He thanks the audience for a recent donation,
of p⸱ ⸱ames his short talk around the role of Bridge House in respond-
of v⸱ ⸱he "opiate epidemic."

a "⸱ want to share a brief story about an experiment called 'rat park,'"
oth⸱ ⸱ys. "Years ago, there was an experiment where they had rats in
tan⸱ ⸱ and gave them the opportunity to drink either heroin-tainted
re⸱ ⸱r regular water. They found these isolated rats would choose the
na⸱ ⸱laced water and drink it to the point where they would die. So
ir⸱ ⸱ound that it was an experiment that showed the level of addiction
r⸱ ⸱iat it could do to people.

⸱n⸱ars later, there was a psychiatrist who decided to twist the experi-
⸱ient and set up something called 'rat park.' It was a rat's dream: it was
⸱not just one cage; it was multiple cages. There were wood chips, there
⸱vere cans to hide in, there was more than one rat around, and they could
⸱m around and engage with one another. It was a happy place for a rat.
fo⸱ And by the way, don't mention to any of my residents that I'm com-
a⸱ ⸱g them to rats, because that doesn't go over very well with former
⸱ers," Pat says to a ripple of laughter.

⸱ut what they found was, when they introduced the water to the
s⸱ts ⸱t rat park, that the rats at rat park would choose the regular water
th⸱er the heroi⸱ induced water. Why is that? What they found is that
⸱ ⸱community the rat goes into has a major effect on the health and
⸱ ⸱-being and the level of addiction of the rats involved. So the rats at
⸱ne happy park did not become addicts; the rats who were isolated did.
⸱⸱⸱The same parallel can be drawn for people in our community. A lot
⸱f us have gone to hospitals. People have had wisdom teeth out. People
⸱end up having oxycodone and other painkillers to deal with the surgery
and so forth—and why is it millions of us come out of the hospital in the

United States, we don't end up having an addiction to those painkillers, after we have to use them for pain and that kind of thing, when other people do have those addiction issues?

"And the reason is that in a lot of circumstances—not all; by all means, this is not a total solution—but in a lot of circumstances those of us who have surgery come home to a loving community. We come home to a family that embraces us. We come home to connections in the community and have groups and associations that we belong to that give our lives meaning. But for other people, those who have belonged to abusive families, those who have had struggles their whole lives, they don't have that to come home to—and we create a whole new generation of addiction.

"At Bridge House, we are no longer the cage. The rats are free; they come into Bridge of their own free will. And the question we are left with at the end of the day is, What kind of rat park do we want to create? And at Bridge, what we try to do is create a welcoming, loving environment. We have a saying, which could be considered a little corny, 'Bridge is family.' And that's what we try to create. We try to re-create a family environment in our home.

"And just to show you we are living at an unprecedented time with this opiate epidemic: two of our former residents just recently died in the last month from overdoses. What we have is a crisis. But I do think that the response has to be a welcoming environment, creating community, creating a solid foundation like we have in our families, where we have a combination of opportunities for people to do well in the community and we have expectations for their behavior, and they are not using drugs and alcohol while they are recovering and entering into recovery.

"I would invite you all to come and see Bridge House anytime. It looks great. Especially now we have put in the landscaping you guys afforded. I can't tell you, as someone who's been involved in the front lines in the struggle, with people who are really trying to get their lives back together, how deep our appreciation is for the work you guys do. So let me just say one more time, thank you, God bless you, we appreciate the support."

* * *

Pat Townsend presented Bridge House as a "welcoming, loving environment" that, like the rat park built by laboratory researchers, alleviated the social causes of addiction. The laboratory "park" he referenced was designed to be spacious (about two hundred times the size of a standard cage), scenic (a forest painted on the plywood walls), comfortable (with empty tins and wood scraps around), and sociable (with sixteen to twenty rats in residence at once).[3] Rats housed in these settings rarely used problematically the morphine they were offered (unlike those in cages).[4] And at Bridge House, Pat set about constructing the program as a family-style home without the kind of heavy-handed security measures—like secure perimeter fencing and guarded entries and exits—common at many US halfway houses.[5] He even invited the Rotary audience to visit themselves and see how nice the house looked with landscaping paid for with their help.

Pat drew on the rat park experiments as an analogy to present a clear separation between Bridge House and the broader prison system. "We are no longer the cage," he said. "The rats are free; they come into Bridge of their own free will." This language belied core tensions of an institution that imposed criminal punishment on the same residents it aimed to support. Is it fair to say these men chose the program freely when most entered as part of parole or probation conditions? Can they really be described as "free" while living under overlapping systems of halfway house and probation/parole regulation? And while the rats in the laboratory park were not being threatened with return to the cage, at Bridge House, it was the desire to avoid prison (either by diversion or early release) that brought many residents to the program in the first place and often prevented them from leaving.

In evoking the rat park experiments, the larger point Pat was making was that addiction is a symptom of social failure and therefore requires a collective social response.[6] And his approving references to the research point to his relatively progressive views within a broader landscape of US criminal justice more often relying on punitive discourses of drug use as an issue of individual pathology. In reentry programs located at the fuzzy edge between drug treatment and criminal justice,[7] practitioners tend to reduce drug problems rooted in large-scale structural inequalities to the individual level,[8] with addiction approached as either a moral failing deserving punishment or a disease requiring medical intervention.[9] In contrast, Pat presented addiction as a social problem and, in the process, positioned Bridge House as part of a broader set of solutions centered on building healthy and supportive environments.

Pat faced hard choices implementing these ideals at a halfway house in Clearview Crossing, with the issues of many residents intimately connected to the drug crisis unfolding openly in the city streets around the program. His allusion to two former residents dying in a month points to life-threatening consequences within the Bridge House social milieu. In my first year of fieldwork in 2012, more people died of opiate overdoses in Massachusetts than died in car accidents,[10] and the annual number of deaths had jumped 130 percent by the time Pat was addressing the Rotary Club three years later.[11] A report by the Massachusetts Department of Public Health found that people released from state prison during this period were fifty-six times more likely to die from an opiate overdose than were members of the general public.[12]

This was the context in which the progressive elements of the Bridge House program were uneasily blended with a more hard-lined abstinence model, drawing on the twelve steps of Narcotics and Alcoholics Anonymous, in which any resident failing a Breathalyzer or drug test was removed from the house. As Pat said in his closing remarks, all communities place expectations on behavior, and at Bridge House, this meant most of all "not using drugs and alcohol." In the background of this brief statement hung the challenges of policing substance use and punishing transgressions—which relied on practices that threatened to disrupt his vision of the house as a site of care and support.

There were compromises being made as Pat juggled the tensions and trade-offs of halfway house governance. For even as he often criticized the punitiveness of other sites of drug treatment and criminal justice, in some ways, Bridge House mimicked the harsher edge of this wider system with a policy that residents "get clean" or face expulsion from community life. At the core of the program were the same black-and-white notions of prohibition that drive the war on drugs more broadly. And the contradictions were hard to miss: the halfway house expelled people who used drugs from the social supports that its own model presented as necessary to prevent drug use. Residents punished in this way could also be subjected to escalating sanctions in the punitive system to which Bridge House was intended as an alternative.

When Pat spoke at Rotary, he glossed over these contradictions by focusing squarely on the role of the program in supporting (rather than punishing) residents. And he spoke from a position partly removed from the messy ground-level work of implementing his vision of the halfway house. He lived around thirty minutes away in a different town, with his wife and children, commuting several days a week to an office at the site. He no longer attended the evening meal or had much to do with residents day-to-day. Pat's role centered instead on raising the funds to keep the place running and recruiting and supervising volunteers, leveraging his cultural capital and social networks in religious and charitable organizations to attract the resources that made Bridge House a relatively comfortable place to live.

The hands-on work with residents was devolved to the operations manager, Kevin Smith.

* * *

I sit with Kevin at a gray picnic table in the grease-stained Bridge House driveway. He is smoking Newport cigarettes, as usual, and wears a familiar outfit of polo shirt, jean shorts, and sneakers. Kevin has around fifteen years "clean time" and is a staunch advocate of the twelve steps of Narcotics Anonymous. He shares a similar background and social location with the other men at Bridge House, an ex-convict and former resident whom you might mistake for a current resident. At the same time, Kevin is the most identifiable site of carceral control at the program: managing the drug testing, for example, and handling any evictions. And when I ask him about his division of roles with Pat, he quickly transitions to talking about basic differences in their views on how best to help residents.

"Like Pat, I love 'im to death, but like he basically got aloootta compassion. And there's a fine line between enabling and helpin' someone. I mean, you can't always just run around, 'yeah okay, yeah okay, yeah okay.' Because these guys, some of them will run amok and walk all over you. So I think he [Pat] likes that I kinda guide 'em and toughin' 'em up into seein' like—his level of compassion and helpin' can sometimes also really be enabling. If you understand what I'm sayin'.

"I mean, that's like you, Lump," Kevin says, turning the conversation toward me and shortening my nickname, "Lumpy" (more on that later).

"To be for real, like basically if you worked here, you'd probably be more like, 'Yeah, okay, you don't gotta be at supper. You don't have to do your [twelve-step] meetings.' I'm not sayin' that in a negative note, because you don't understand that some people who come from the background we come from, that isn't always helpin' them. You needa sometimes be firm and let 'em know—no, no, no, no, no, no, wait a second."

"Is that ever hard, this thing of being firm?" I ask. "Like giving urines [drug tests], for example?"

"It depends on the situation. Because I had people that I've known for years come through here. Friends and everything come through. And it's not fair for me to give them special privileges and be harder on the other guys. I try to keep it real with everybody. I had a friend come through here that I had to end up discharging. And every time that I had somebody come through here that I've known for years, I let them know right up front, 'We can be friends, but I also need to do my job. Just because me and you are friends, that doesn't mean you're gonna be able to break curfew. That doesn't mean you're gonna be able to not do a chore. No special privileges.'"

* * *

Kevin was a long-term member of the community with an organic social network overlapping with the residents he was employed to supervise. This meant the personal stakes in performing the role were high: he said he once had to "discharge" a friend from the program. And in our conversation, Kevin drew on this insider status to present Pat Townsend as well-meaning but ultimately out of touch with residents. He argued that his shared experience with the men—his knowledge of "the background *we* come from"—provided a more realistic vantage point on what was needed to support them. He said that Pat showed too much "compassion" and, without his guidance, would probably just let residents "run amok."

Notice the word Kevin used to describe the problems of showing compassion: "enabling." The term is used in the twelve steps to charge the friends and family of drug users with fueling the addiction of their loved ones by being overly permissive or forgiving. The language of recovery is flexible—a core theme of chapter 5—and, for Kevin, was often a tool for emphasizing the personal responsibility of residents and justifying the more disciplinary aspects of his role.[13] He routinely weaved the concepts and idioms of Narcotics Anonymous into everyday conversation and, in this case, used to the idea of "enabling" to suggest that being too lenient around program rules might cultivate addiction among the men.[14]

Kevin grouped me with Pat as a naïve college type who needed toughening up. To be fair, Kevin was right to question my experiential credentials. I had never seen up close the effects of dependency on drugs like heroin and crack cocaine before starting my ethnography. And as I became more acquainted with this world while living at Bridge House, I grew increasingly sympathetic to the appeal of enforced abstinence. I came to see residents' support for drug testing and evictions as rooted in their personal experience with chaotic cycles of drug-related harm. They did not want to live with men who were shooting heroin or smoking crack cocaine. Neither did I.

I also believe there was a healthy dose of naïvety in Pat and Kevin expecting the men to meet standards of abstinence that few people maintain in a society awash with drugs of different kinds.[15] And here the two men were aligned: inclusion to the Bridge House community was based on the binary division between "clean" and "dirty" that is so central to the twelve steps.[16] Only the "clean" were allowed to stay—with urine testing used to remove the "dirty." Whereas many Bridge House rules were flexible and open to negotiation depending on the circumstances, when it came to this principle, the usually relaxed approach disappeared. Any resident failing a drug test was evicted. And this required intrusive day-to-day monitoring and control to regulate the substances the men put in their bodies—most importantly, using informal surveillance to identify suspects and drug testing them.

In practice, Pat devolved to Kevin these more punitive elements of Bridge House operations. And it was Kevin who confronted most directly the tensions of halfway house governance, when as a routine part of the daily rounds, he was called on to balance program goals of care and control in concrete situations dealing with specific individuals. This was the location from which he argued that showing compassion could easily do more harm than good. He said it may be tempting to bend the rules and let things slide, but leniency on even basic program rules was a slippery slope toward "enabling," when people from backgrounds like his own needed firm boundaries. This was not a matter of punitiveness for the sake of punishment.

For Kevin, the exercise of control was itself a form of care: tough love.

* * *

Kevin pulls into the Bridge House driveway, exits the car, and almost immediately confronts Aidan Meaney, one of a group of men gathered on the porch.

"You hang out at the Allerton?" he asks accusingly.

"Who?"

"You."

"What are you talking about?" says Aidan, growing frustrated at the accusation.

"You weren't at the Allerton last night?"

"Absolutely not. Fuck that. We gotta get the cup real quick? I wasn't at no fuckin' Allerton."

What Aidan calls "the cup" is a euphemism for the plastic container in which he now needs to urinate for a drug test. Both the use of slang and automatic assumption that he will be tested points to the normalization of this carceral practice. The trigger for the test is Aidan being seen—though the facts are disputed—on the stairs to an old hotel, the Allerton, which has been converted into a boarding house. Simply being near the Allerton invites suspicion.

The stakes of the drug test are high within the linked systems of criminal punishment framing Aidan's experience at Bridge House. I am about to drive him downtown for a court appearance, where he will face charges for a string of burglary offenses committed while physically dependent on heroin. His two children are with relatives, and his wife is in a drug-treatment program. His best shot at avoiding prison and regaining custody of his kids is building "clean time" and establishing a track record of drug abstinence at the program.

Aidan passes the test. But he is angry about being accused and, on the drive to the courthouse, rehearses the conflict with Kevin.

"He said, 'Aidan, I know what I seen.' I said, 'Well, you need glasses.' He said, 'You had the green shirt on. You're drinking a Monster [energy drink].' I said, 'It sounds the fuck like me, but I did not go up those muthafuckin' stairs at the Allerton.'"

"Even if you did, you can go anywhere," says Toa Mackie, another resident who joins us for the drive.

"Yeah!" Aidan agrees, before continuing to describe the exchange: "He [Kevin] goes, 'I was just worried. I didn't want you to put yourself in a situation you couldn't handle.' I said, 'Listen, dude, I walk the fuckin' beat four nights a week, looking at hookers going to [twelve-step] meetings. I got a pocket full of money half the time. If I'm getting high, I ain't coming back. I would never do that to the house. If I'm going out to shoot dope, I'm going on a fuckin'—I'm going out to shoot dope, you know what I mean?'

"You hear me tell him to send the cup? Send the cup! I'm in a tie and shirt going to court. I ain't fuckin' dirty. I said, 'Send that shit.' But don't be fuckin' calling me out in front of everybody."

"He ain't supposed to put your business out there like that to the public," says Toa.

"What's the matter with your uncle?" Aidan says from the passenger seat, jokingly referring to Kevin as my relative.

"Quick-cupping me at 8:30 in the morning. I'm fuckin' heated right now. I swore on my kids that I wasn't going up the stairs to the Allerton. He's like, 'I know what I saw. I saw you going up the stairs.' I said, 'No the fuck I wasn't.' He said, 'I was going to come and see you last night.' Yeah, well you would have found me at St. Peter's [an NA meeting], where I said I was gonna be."

The car goes quiet for around fifteen seconds.

"'I know what the fuck I saw,'" Aidan says quietly, quoting Kevin. "Fuck you, dude. Lem [shortening Liam], I'm fuckin' pissed. I just don't wanna be on his fuckin' radar. Hey, pissed right in that cup. Tested it, looked at it, folded it in a paper towel, and threw it right in the trash. I said, 'Am I free to go now? CO, am I free to go now?'"

* * *

Aidan used the label "CO"—prison slang for "correctional officer"—as an insult implying that Kevin had crossed over from convict to guard. Kevin was very sensitive to this kind of language presenting him as an agent of social control in a prison-like hierarchy. For example, he said it was inappropriate for residents to use the words "rat" or "snitch" to describe people coming forward with information about rule violations from other residents—arguing that the words were evidence of a "jail mentality" with no place in a program. Without Kevin around, Aidan was free to call him what he liked.

Kevin was an encyclopedia of local crime news. He trawled the newspaper daily for stories about the misdeeds of people he knew—especially residents—and spent much of his time chatting about the latest comings and goings with others in the recovery scene. There were rumors that he sometimes drove the neighborhood looking for residents gone astray. Whether or not the rumors were true, they point to a general feeling among the men that they were under surveillance inside and outside the house. Perhaps it was during one of these drives that Kevin believed he had seen Aidan.

It was not only the establishment that was suspicious but the general location, Main Street, the central roadway through Clearview Crossing. Aidan sometimes called Main Street the "dirty boulevard"—a reference to a reputation for hard drugs that twisted the clean-dirty binary of the twelve steps to color the entire geographical location. Kevin seemed to share the evaluation. Aidan being seen walking this dirty street evoked suspicion that he might personally be dirty and triggered a drug test.

Aidan passed the test but experienced the whole process as insulting anyway. There was indignity in being forced to urinate in a cup. And while the act of using the toilet was done privately, Kevin made the accusation very publicly in front of a group of residents gathered on the porch. Drug tests at Bridge House almost always had this embarrassing public dimension, declaring the person had been up to no good. Being tested was itself a kind of punishment.

* * *

Joe Badillo had been at Bridge House around three weeks when he got drug tested for the first time. I did not record in my fieldnotes the cause for suspicion or whether a reason was even given. But I did record that Joe seemed very philosophical about the whole thing. As was standard procedure, Kevin had him wait in the lounge until he was able to use the toilet, security against any effort to acquire "clean" urine or otherwise cheat the test. Joe asked me to bring a plastic bottle filled with warm water to help move the process along.

Joe's abstinence was being doubly monitored by Bridge House and probation. Sitting on the living-room couch waiting patiently for the piss to come, he told me how probationers were called for drug tests in groups according to color. Joe had been assigned the color brown. Each morning, he was required to call probation to hear by automated message whether the browns needed to travel to the office and provide drug tests that day. He said they had the same system during his last community sentence, that time parole, and he would purchase drug-masking drinks for $60—but the money was often wasted when he did not get called. He believed more recent tests were able to beat the drinks and detect drugs anyway.

Joe told me these stories, in the middle of being drug tested, to make the point that he did not have to worry about all that anymore. The stress of dodging drug tests was in the past so long as he stayed "clean." And that was the plan: Joe was forced to attend three twelve-step meetings a week as part of the program requirements of Bridge House but was going to meetings every day, sometimes more than one. After many years of runaway drug dependency, he was embracing the message that total abstinence was the key to self-transformation. On this point, the rules enforced by Bridge House and community corrections aligned with his personal goals for development and positive change.

Joe's philosophical attitude to being drug tested was also rooted in the utter normality of the practice. Unlike Aidan Meaney, who had never been to state prison and spent less than a year total spread across short stints in jail, Joe had been inside much of the past two decades—and was usually under community supervision in the times between. Being drug tested was part of life. In the past, it came with the stress of trying to beat the system and evade prison guards or parole and probation officers. But at Bridge House, Joe seemed to view the drug test as a welcome reminder that things would be okay so long as he did the right thing.

The test came back negative, and Joe was free to leave.

* * *

Speculation is growing about the whereabouts of the Bridge House resident Zak Lopez. Kevin is asking among the men if Zak came home last night. Apparently, a former resident saw him on the other side of town early this morning—who knows how Kevin got the sighting or knew to ask.

Zak chose a bad day to go missing. The volunteers dropped the food for dinner early and left without eating. The men are gathered and eager to get on with things. We start around 5:30 p.m., half an hour before the scheduled time, and would usually have the weekly house meeting immediately afterward—but Kevin says we cannot begin until 7:00 p.m. unless Zak returns. Bill Morris is protesting that he needs to get back to work at a local gym.

Zak shows up and goes into the office with Kevin. The suspicion that he broke curfew will undoubtedly trigger a drug test, but first, he needs to attend the house meeting with the other men. Zak slumps in the chair with arms folded tightly, hat pulled over a bandana and low to his eyes, looking exhausted and ready to cry. Kevin adds "program" to the agenda. He stands by the door while the other men sit—as he always does at the house meeting—delivering a long spiel about respecting the curfew.

Zak has only lived at Bridge House three days. Awkwardly, there is a tradition that new residents are asked a question by each of the men at their first house meeting.

Jim Caine opens in a typically grumpy and confrontational fashion: "You came here all loud and gung-ho on Friday, but something's different today. What's up?"

Zak grunts a one-word response: "Family."

The other questions receive similarly brief answers.

Kevin goes last, still standing in the doorway: "How much clean time you got?" he asks accusingly.

Zak mutters something about thirty days.

After the meeting, Kevin tells Zak to wait in the lounge until he can provide a urine sample. But Zak will not stay in one place: he goes upstairs, outside, into the kitchen. Then he jumps on a BMX bicycle and rides out the driveway. It seems that the matter is settled: he has refused to complete the drug test and has left on his own accord. As Kevin puts it, "He discharged himself."

But Zak returns on his bike. There is music playing from a phone in the front pocket of his hooded sweatshirt. He is nonchalant about the disappearance, announcing that he went to the corner store to buy cigarettes, but when he got there, somebody gave him one so he did not buy a packet.

Kevin seems insulted by the very idea he would accept the story. Believing Zak may have just purchased "clean" urine, he demands to watch him use the toilet. Zak argues back, and Kevin compromises, proposing that he watch Zak drop his underwear and then leave, providing a measure of privacy while he uses the toilet. But he is adamant about making sure Zak is not hiding something in his pants.

"I feel like I'm in jail right now," Zak protests. "It's like an invasion. You want me to strip down and stare at my dick?"

A group of residents are gathered on the porch smoking cigarettes and listening while the conflict unfolds in the kitchen on the other side of the wall. When Zak questions the legality of being forced to strip, Ross Whitaker looks up from his phone and laughs skeptically to the group. Zak comes outside and appeals directly to the men for sympathy.

"Come on, man, we all been to jail," Joe Badillo says dismissively.

Kevin now says he is simply going to discharge Zak—not coming home last night was grounds enough, let alone refusing a drug test. Zak says several times that he has nowhere else to go. They continue to argue as Zak begins packing his possessions in a bag. Kevin comes into my bedroom, which is next door, and starts circularly justifying the logic of the discharge: that Zak did not come home last night and should not have disappeared from the drug test.

"I ain't gonna call probation," says Kevin. "If they call me, I'll tell 'em, but I ain't gonna call. I don't wanna get him in trouble."

It is after 9:00 p.m. when Zak finally leaves. A group of residents are still gathered on the porch. Kevin is loudly justifying his actions, but no one seems very interested. He asks what I would have done.

"I don't think I could do your job," I say.

"You got too much compassion," says Joe Badillo, rising from his chair and heading inside. "You probably just say, 'Don't do it again.'"

"I got compassion for the dude," says Kevin, "but I'm juggling all these things. I got compassion. I'm feeling aggravated. Like, he's tryna play mind games. Now I gotta go home with that."

I am the only one left listening as Kevin continues to justify the discharge. One resident calls him "the treadmill" for a tendency to repeat the same points in conversation. But tonight Kevin is especially circular, rehashing again and again the reasons for handling the situation the way he did: that Zak did not come home last night, that he should not have run away from the drug test, that Kevin wanted to work with him, that he has only been a resident three days.

Kevin becomes a very visible agent of social control in these moments. Much of the time he passes as one of the men, but when he is drug testing and evicting, his position of authority is laid bare and becomes open to criticism. So he stands on the porch trying to validate his actions publicly. Kevin's ability to maintain order relies on fostering a measure of goodwill among these men. He is outnumbered and there are no guards or security personnel at his disposal. When someone like Zak refuses a drug test, the only thing preventing mutiny is other residents taking his side. And that is exactly what they did. The idea of Zak avoiding a drug test after breaking curfew was treated as laughable. Zak knew the rules and chose to break them. Few residents showed signs of sympathy as he left at 9:00 p.m. on Monday night with nowhere else to go.

Kevin juggles feelings of compassion and aggravation as he tries to support and control Zak at the same time. He says he will "go home" with these emotions, suggesting they will linger for the evening as he broods over his decision-making. He is clearly frustrated at Zak and, ultimately, sends him on his way. But he also decides not to call Zak's probation officer, providing some protection from further sanction, breaking the chain of carceral power rather than reinforcing it. Tomorrow, he will be back to work as a member of the group that he is also charged with controlling.

* * *

Tim Williams sits at the head of the large table that hosts the Bridge House evening meal. It is around 10:00 p.m. in the dimly lit room, and the wooden chairs are upside down with arm rests on tabletop—except for the one where Tim sits making cigarettes. He wears a black do-rag and plain black T-shirt with sleeves that hang almost to the elbow. As always, he has a phone stuck to his left ear—I estimate in fieldnotes that he talks to his wife around three hours a day.

Tobacco spills from an open bag and scatters around the Top-O-Matic cigarette machine, a plastic black box with a silver lever and an imprint of the American flag on the side. Tim sprinkles enough tobacco for one cigarette into a thin groove that runs along the edge. Then he reaches into a red-and-white carton stamped with the image of a smoking cowboy, pulling out an empty paper cylinder with a filter and sliding it over a round metal tube protruding from the end the machine. He winds the lever in a semicircle, pushing the tobacco along the groove and into the empty mold. A cigarette is ready to be smoked.

Tim is rolling cigarettes for just about every resident at Bridge House. A thick callous with blister fluid underneath forms on the inside knuckle where his thumb rubs the machine lever. He nicknames the blister after his biggest customer, Steve Reynolds, who he says once smoked two hundred cigarettes in a weekend. He usually drinks two cans of Rip It, an energy drink purchased for ninety-nine cents at the same store as the tobacco, on the nights when he rolls. The empty cans sit discarded among the debris. Next to the rolling machine is Tim's laptop, a Dell Inspiron Mini bought secondhand from a friend of Joe Badillo's, and between phone conversations, music booms out through the headphones attached. A current favorite is the song "Hustle Hard" by Ace Hood.

The cigarette hustle has solid economic foundations. At the nearest corner store to Bridge House, a packet of twenty cigarettes sells for between $8.15 and $10.15 depending on the brand, but Tim can purchase enough loose tobacco to roll a packet much more cheaply (the exact cost is never quite clear). He asks if I want to sign up to the scheme shortly after we first meet. The deal is as follows: I will pay for the bags of tobacco, which he says cost $20, and in exchange receive ten packets of twenty cigarettes. The cigarettes arrive in batches as they are rolled. Tim makes a point of theatrically playing up how many there are—"hoooo weee, look at that bag"—quickly mixing handfuls of cigarettes with others already stored in ziplock bags. The only time I count, what he said was seven packets was less than five. I go with Tim to buy the tobacco at a small market down the road. He pushes the door open and raises both arms in the air, shouting, "I'm here, baby!" Tim barrages the man at the counter with a stream of words and haggles on the price of everything, leaving with two bags of tobacco, three boxes of filter tubes, and a lighter for $25. So much for the bags costing $20.

Kevin asks if I am buying cigarettes from Tim. The question stems from an unstable compromise: he has allowed Tim to continue the operation only so long as cigarettes are not sold directly for cash. It is not the first time Kevin has confronted a black market for the product at

Bridge House. During my first spell of fieldwork, Matt Carmine was selling packets for between $3 and $4 and sometimes "singles" for spare change. But when Matt expanded and started selling to residents at the rooming house next door, Kevin closed the operation down, saying it was too much like a "jail hustle."

Tim's operation seems a lot like a jail hustle too. In fact, it is very similar to a hustle Tim had in prison: he is on parole and says when he was in state prison, he paid guards to smuggle in chewing tobacco, which he broke down into smaller quantities and sold to other prisoners. The system of gift giving and bartering that evolves under Kevin's ban on cash only makes the whole thing seem more prison-like. I watch Tim pay with cigarettes for a haircut from another resident. More commonly, as in our arrangement, the customer purchases the bag of tobacco, and perhaps some supplies, and Tim receives some of the product in return for his work. This allows Tim not only to smoke for free but to accumulate surplus cigarettes. Sometimes these are sold when Kevin is not around—for example, when Tim takes a weekend pass and leaves the city.

The flourishing black market for cigarettes at Bridge House pointed to ambiguities in the very idea of drug abstinence. Many residents at the program consumed the drug nicotine with impunity twenty times a day or more. Kevin himself was a heavy smoker. Never mind that the drug is highly addictive and carries serious long-term health consequences. No one argued that smoking cigarettes should be considered "relapse" or jeopardize a person's "clean time." To the contrary, cigarette smoking was about the only social activity the men undertook as a group.

Bridge House sidestepped the thorny issue of exactly which chemical substances counted as "drugs" by simply policing whatever showed up "dirty" in urine samples. Billy James was evicted for using an anabolic steroid. There was tension when one resident accused another, who worked at a local gym, of selling Billy the steroids. But no one seemed to object to the eviction. One could imagine a debate over why using a steroid should be considered more harmful than smoking cigarettes. But this was precluded by the drug test—it proved that Billy was no longer "clean" and so would have to leave. On the other side, there were powerful pharmaceutical drugs that did not produce failed tests and were tolerated. Jake Christie arranged colorful pills by days and times on a bed-stand tray in his bedroom. He squirmed and fidgeted, jaw chomping up and down with mouth closed and no food inside, and often ran his tongue along the top lip of a toothless mouth. Jake said the medication was messing him up. But it did not affect his drug tests or ability to present as "clean."

Kevin's problem with the cigarette hustle was not the drug nicotine, which was clearly permitted, but the black market that emerged for the product. He said it was too much like the underground economy of the prison: most US penal institutions ban smoking and possession of tobacco, and in the shadow of these controls, prisoners build elaborate trade networks in the substance.[17] At Bridge House, the regulatory context was not a blanket ban but heavy taxation driving up prices in the formal economy, creating financial incentives to search for alternatives. Tim Williams got a rolling machine and went to work.

I believe Kevin would have liked to shut the whole thing down. He said as much a few times. But not surprisingly, the arrangement was popular among the men, smokers with little money, as Tim provided cigarettes at a fraction of the usual cost. Kevin would have paid a heavy price in goodwill for a crackdown. The trade lay just outside the borders of what he could control without jeopardizing the basic level of support among residents he relied on to do his job. So he compromised and everyone smoked cheap cigarettes.

* * *

Among the most important ways that Bridge House expressed an ethic of care toward residents was by adopting a general attitude that they should be allowed to stay as long as needed. Pat Townsend criticized the standardized schedules used at most other halfway houses as a "factory model" that creates "false beginnings and ends in people's lives that don't make sense." And he described the Bridge House policy of open time frames as crucial to the mission of fostering "supportive community." He talked about this idea again and again: when we recorded a conversation about the program, he used the word "community" thirty-four times in a little more than an hour. And for Pat, creating supportive community meant being generous with the core resource provided by the program: a bed in a house. In his words, the goal was to "embrace a person for as long as you can and support them along their journey."

There were clear trade-offs involved. Bridge House was already a small program. The capacity of twelve was spread across eight bedrooms—half of them "doubles" with two beds and the others "singles" with one bed. And when residents stayed beyond the placements mandated by parole or probation (sometimes even for years at a time) or when bedrooms were held open during periods of emergency absence (like hospital visits), scarce space became even scarcer. The approach was grounded in recognition of the dire social conditions that many residents would face if forced to leave prematurely. But at the same time, it excluded other potential residents who may have also been in desperate need of transitional housing. Among the most distinctive features of the Bridge House program was an unorthodox approach to this fundamental trade-off: the decision to provide sustained support to a small number of people for long periods, rather than offering more limited support to a larger group moved through on shorter stays.

Pat Townsend's language of "supportive community" can easily obscure a more complex situation facing long-term residents. Consider the case of Jim Caine, an elderly resident who had lived at Bridge House for years beyond any community sentence or criminal justice mandate. From what I could gather, Jim had tried leaving the program several times but quickly spiraled out of control drinking vodka all day and growing volatile and violent. At Bridge House, you would often find him on the porch, smoking back-to-back filterless cigarettes and telling improbable stories—like the one about robbing a bank with a skunk. Jim once told me he had served a combined sixty years in prison. Whatever the real count, in old age he was clearly short on options for finding housing and social support outside the halfway house.

Jim responded to his long-term residence at a carceral institution by refusing to follow basic program rules. Most notably, he did not seem to attend any twelve-step meetings at all—despite the Bridge House policy mandating three every week. If asked, Jim sometimes said he went to meetings in a different town. But he did not have a car, and frankly, the story was not believable in the slightest. Some residents called him a "dry drunk," a colloquialism of the twelve steps that refers to a person who is abstinent but fails to engage in the associated self-improvement work—that is, they are alcoholics who quit drinking, so are "dry," but still behave like "drunks." Jim was a hard man to live with and could be openly hostile to those around him.

It is hard to imagine that many other halfway houses would allow this kind of blatant disregard for core program policy. But at Bridge House, Jim's rule violations were overlooked based on a broader consideration of his needs, the assertion of control superseded by a commitment to the provision of care. It seemed reasonable to assume that any removal would place both Jim and the people around him at immediate risk of harm—so he was not removed. Provided he was not actively drinking, Jim could stay until he made the decision to leave.

Day-to-day, Kevin Smith was left managing a rebellious old man who undermined his authority at every turn. These two men had spent far too long in each other's company through little choice of their own, and I learned of their bitter conflict in my first days of fieldwork at Bridge House. Jim Caine was a great early connection in the project. No doubt he could be volatile and even shouted at me a couple of times. But he also took me on tours of Clearview Crossing and told great stories over cigarettes on the porch. And as I got to the know both Jim and Kevin—and grew familiar with their mutual animosity—I came to believe Kevin was actively trying to make life so unpleasant for Jim that he might choose to leave Bridge House voluntarily.

I had been at the program little more than a week when Kevin suggested I should move into Jim's basement bedroom. Raising the proposal seemed from the outset like part of cynical plan to torment Jim. Having a room of his own provided Jim precious independent territory in an environment over which he otherwise had little control. The surroundings may have been bleak—the room was located at one end of a dark and dingy halfway house basement with a concrete floor—but this also had the advantage of increasing Jim's privacy by discouraging other people from going down there. Kevin knew very well what it meant for Jim to have that room—and used this as leverage. I was placed at the center of their conflict.

Kevin eventually raised the proposal around the dinner table—on a night when volunteers had dropped food for the evening meal without staying to eat—in a transparent attempt to provoke Jim.

"Ain't no one fucking coming downstairs with me!" Jim snapped back angrily.

It started a fierce argument with another resident, Jensen Tyler, who chimed in to support the plan. The two were seated diagonally next to each other—Jim at one end of the table as always, Jensen at the nearest end of the horizontal edge—and it threatened to erupt into a fistfight but died down after about fifteen seconds. Jim finished eating and quickly left the table. The moment he walked out the door, Kevin and a group of residents started ridiculing him and laughing loudly, saying that if anyone went down to the basement, they would get killed, that there must be every disease imaginable down there, that you would have to check every drink you made for poison.

Kevin tried to drag me into the conversation as I cleared plates and cups from the table: "You shoulda heard him flip on Liam yesterday—I think he shit his pants," said Kevin, referring to an incident the day before when Jim berated me after I tried to help him load garbage into the dump outside.

I did my best to appear nonchalant, muttering something about "Jim being Jim" and the guys being too ruthless, before escaping to do dishes in the next room. Another resident, Peter Tennant, was already starting despite it being my assigned chore. I said thanks for helping while the sounds of the men mocking Jim and laughing boisterously filled the room. Peter paused from the dishes, turned his head slightly, and said quietly under his breath, "No problem. You got my back, I got yours." I imagined Jim brooding in his bedroom and wanting to have a drink.

* * *

Jim Caine was just the kind of person Pat Townsend had in mind when he talked about "embracing" residents over the long term. But Kevin openly wanted Jim out, and despite lacking the authority to enact this directly, he could certainly make life miserable in other ways. That night around the dinner table was the last time I recorded in fieldnotes Kevin talking about the plan to move me into Jim's bedroom, and to the best I can recall, he simply let it go. But their conflict was never far from the surface. And Jim's experience of the program was always framed by a fundamental lack of power over key features of his daily rounds and physical environment—which, again, was being imposed outside any formal criminal punishment.

Still, the Bridge House program and especially the open-time-frames policy was a crucial intervention for Jim. The housing was part of it, but more broadly, I also watched many people in that house put aside his general hostility and relate to him with kindness and goodwill. The situation may have been more complicated than being "embraced" in a "supportive community," but this general philosophy did at least partially translate into practice. Residents often listened and showed interest when Jim told the same old stories smoking cigarettes on the porch. Pat Townsend would bring his family dog to the house, and Jim would take the dog for walks and let it nap in his bedroom. Jim rarely said a word to the volunteers at the dinner table in the evening, and yet he got a lot of affection from the visitors, who seemed to treat his grumpiness as endearing.

Against this backdrop, maybe it was unfair to build my account of Jim's long-term residence around the conflict over Kevin's proposal to move me into his bedroom. And there is another possible interpretation of that situation altogether: perhaps it was a legitimate plan from Kevin to juggle scarce program space. I do not believe that to be the case. Jim's basement bedroom had only one bed and had never been shared, and given his temperament, the idea of me or anyone else going in there was hard to take seriously. And yet the conflict did highlight institutional pressures around the allocation of halfway house space—and the ethical tensions of me living at the program at all.

* * *

Kevin leaves a message on my answering machine as I prepare for a final spell of fieldwork:

"Lumpy, what's goin' on?" He says. "You that lazy you can't even pick up the phone? All you gotta do is move ya arm. Anyways ah gimme a call so we can set up a date when you plan on comin' [to stay at Bridge House]. All right, I'll talk to ya take care, Lump."

* * *

The already limited space at Bridge House was further strained by efforts to recruit college students to live there while working as interns—and ultimately my own filling a bed—which like the policy of open time frames, was justified through appeals to the supportive community ideal. Pat traced the origins of the program through the Catholic worker house movement. He argued that student interns continued this longer tradition of applying the general principle of showing hospitality toward the poor to the work of prisoner reintegration. In practical terms, there was not a huge amount for interns do, because Bridge House did not really run formal programming, counseling sessions, or even twelve-step meetings. But Pat nonetheless described students living in the house—even if only doing relatively peripheral work—as an important contribution to the program mission.

This was the context in which I was allowed a bed at the program. My presence in the house was always ethically fraught, given the high demand on these spaces, but at the same time was quite consistent with what Bridge House was all about. I was not an intern but was allowed to stay on similar grounds, and without having a formal position within the institution, my ethnographic goals of immersing myself in the daily rounds and building personal relationships with a small number of people over time fed into the program mission of fostering supportive community.

When I first approached Pat Townsend about the research, he seemed happy to have found someone like me willing to stay at the program. But it was ultimately Kevin Smith who was left figuring out exactly what I was doing there. I introduced myself to him as a researcher from the beginning. And with increasing levels of completeness as our relationship developed, I told him about everything from the process of writing fieldnotes to the details of specific grants and the ins and outs of doing a doctorate and writing a book. We recorded an interview about his role at Bridge House and views on the program. And yet I still do not think Kevin ever *really* understood what I was doing. Ethnography lay well outside his usual frame of reference, and anyway, I met other men at Bridge House who also claimed to be writing books. Book writing was not an activity that seemed to be taken very seriously.

The college types Kevin was used to seeing at Bridge House had clearly defined roles as "interns." Take James Keene. James lived at Bridge House for a gap year while working on medical-school applications and earned the nickname "Doogie," after the child doctor in the TV sitcom *Doogie Howser MD*. He did not have a huge amount to do with residents day-to-day and was mainly involved in desktop work, like writing letters to solicit donations or helping publicize the program over social media. James worked in the office and spent much of the rest of the time in his bedroom.

I was not an intern. I generally resisted however I could when Kevin tried to get me to do work in the office. I was concerned about being aligned with halfway house staff, not only for how this might shape how I was perceived by residents but also because of the effect that too close an alliance with carceral power would have on my efforts to form meaningfully collaborative relationships with the residents subject to this power. I avoided the office at the program as much as possible. Unlike the interns, I was included in the rotation of assigned chores with other residents, and more broadly, I dedicated much of my time to smoking cigarettes on the porch among the men. But if I was not an intern or a resident, what was my role at Bridge House?

Kevin parodied my unusual presence by nicknaming me "Lumpy." It was a caricature of what he apparently believed I was doing: lumping around. To my university peers, I was hard at work doing ethnography, and more personally, I often felt overwhelmed by the scramble to get it all done. But one man's work is another man's lumping. To Kevin, I seemed to spend a lot of time hanging out smoking cigarettes. And the nickname was only the tip of the iceberg. Kevin relentlessly hassled my work ethic and took every chance to publicly declare my laziness.

Kevin calling me "Lumpy" was most obviously an insult—even the sound of the word was offensive. But there was also affection in that nickname. Nor was I the only one berated: "busting balls" was a common style of social interaction among the men, a way of doing community through humor that was both cruel and caring at the same time. At Bridge House, the many verbal barrages I received on the porch and around the dinner table—which could be hard to deal with at times— were socially integrating and at some level expressions of acceptance. And as the Lumpy nickname caught on, it was an important way I was included, flaws and all, within a program framed by an ethos of long-term membership in a supportive community.

Whatever Kevin's motivations during the conflict over Jim's bedroom in my first days at the house, ultimately, he invited me back year after year. And his support was crucial to the project, given his sway over the allocation of program space. It was Kevin who usually interviewed potential residents and in large part decided who was accepted—hosting visits from state prisoners preparing for release, for example, or entering Richmond County Jail to interview inside. In theory, these applications were wide open: the only people excluded outright were those with sex offenses or arson on their criminal records. But it seemed like Kevin used his personal experience to make quite-selective qualitative judgments about who would be allowed entry—and sometimes even left beds empty at Bridge House. As he once said, "I look for people that are gonna probably make my job a lot easier."

And when it came to Kevin's support for my staying, I sometimes wonder if he ultimately just viewed me as easier to have around than the resident who may otherwise have been in my bed.

* * *

Beyond the recruitment of interns, the Bridge House program mission of fostering supportive community was enacted as a regular part of the daily rounds through the ritual of "breaking bread" at 6:00 p.m. each weeknight. The general idea was that volunteers, many of them college students or members of area churches, would bring food and share a meal with the men. The participants were seated around a wooden boardroom table donated by a local university—Pat Townsend said it was the only original piece of furniture remaining from when the house opened in 1988—ringed by twelve wooden chairs with cushioned backs and arm rests. I was told the twelve chairs symbolized the disciples at the last supper, but when I asked Pat, he laughed at the suggestion. On evenings when more than twelve people were present, a foldout table was set up to accommodate the extras, placed in the opening between the dining area and a lounge that shared the same light-brown, finished wooden floors.

The Bridge House evening meal not only provided material support to residents by meeting a basic need for sustenance day-to-day—which many could not take for granted outside the house—but operated as a social practice that contributed to the community ideals of the program. It was intended as a reintegration ritual cultivating relationships between the men and people outside the house that might create bridges to the social mainstream. At least in theory, the evening meal always began the same way. Each person held hands with those on either side of them—forming a circle around the table—and after a resident said a prayer, participants took turns sharing their names in a clockwise fashion. These were liminal encounters blurring social boundaries and bringing together people who would usually never have much to do with one another. And they were often fraught.

* * *

The cooks arrive in a Mercedes-Benz SUV with college stickers on the back window. All three are students: Maddie has painted fingernails, Mario sports neatly trimmed facial hair, and Mike wears a long-sleeved Patriots Super Bowl T-shirt. The meal is burritos, one large bowl of ground beef and another of rice and beans, sour cream and grated cheese, a small container of store-bought guacamole.

The participants link hands while resident Michael Richards says the prayer: "Thank you, heavenly father, for this opportunity you have given us. Thank you for the food. Thank you for the volunteers who have brought it in. In Jesus's name, I pray. Amen."

Jim Caine is annoyed when eating begins, and the men—myself included—serve themselves before the volunteers.

"I see you got yours," he says to me gruffly. "Same as these guys. Look at 'em. *They* all eating." He turns to Maddie: "Don't let the food get down there before you get yours—there wont be nothin' left."

She smiles but does not reply.

The cooks do not eat much anyway. Mario and Mike have small burritos, Maddie a single scoop of the rice and beans. I assume that they will eat a proper dinner later. They are bunched at one end of the table: Maddie at the head and Mike and Mario next to each other at the nearest end of the horizontal edge. A resident tries to engage Mario in a conversation about the NFL, but it goes nowhere. Mostly the cooks just chat among themselves about a hectic schedule of upcoming exams and assignments.

* * *

The volunteer cooks drop food for the men but do not stay for dinner. It is Friday night, and some residents are eager to leave on weekend passes. We start well before the scheduled 6:00 p.m. start time and skip the predinner prayer and introductions—as far as I remember, the prayer was always skipped when there were no volunteers. Kevin Smith announces that these cooks do not usually bring much food, so go easy on the portions. The meatloaf is bland and dry, the French bread stale, and the potatoes unpeeled and cooked whole in tinfoil. Like most of the men, I smother it all in BBQ sauce.

Tony Gonzalez got out of jail this morning and is the most talkative at the table. As he trades notes about the past with Steve Adams, who sits to his left, they identity several shared acquaintances. When Steve asks Tony about a man going by the nickname "Boone," it turns out that Tony himself is Boone, only older and with less hair, and the two men had hung out together in their younger days. Small world.

Michael Richards has the assigned dish night and sits silently at one end of the table without eating, leaving his paper napkin and knife and fork on the plate. Around five minutes after the meal begins, Michael starts cleaning up, telling Tony as he clears the table about plans to go out tonight with his girlfriend. After around ten minutes, Tony is the only resident left, finishing the last of the meatloaf while Michael cleans around him.

Tony tells Michael it is the first food he has eaten all day.

* * *

Anna Arcuri shelters from the rain under the open trunk door of her Jeep Grand Cherokee. Steve Adams and Matt Carmine grab the food, and she greets both men by name. In the kitchen, she slides a large silver tray covered in tinfoil into the oven and says it is a "funky meal" but "super delicious": Spicy Italian sausage, peppers, potatoes, and onions. Garlic-bread sticks. A large bowl of colorful salad decorated with assorted nuts and cheeses. Ambrosia with a choice of cookies-and-cream or coffee ice cream for dessert.

Anna wears a floral top with sleeves rolled to just above the elbow, bangles on both arms, dangling jeweled earrings, and heeled shoes with a buckle across the toes. It is all action in the kitchen in the lead-up to the evening meal, people coming and going constantly, plenty of talking and laughing. Simon Kenny sits on the stool next to mine with an elbow on the counter and yarns away about his job at a scrapyard and the family turmoil of having a six-week-old baby and a wife in drug treatment.

Anna alternates between working busily and listening intently—at one point stopping completely to stand with hands on hips, a tea towel hanging from one.

I ask Anna about her volunteering at Bridge House. She says she has been coming for seventeen years. Jim enters the kitchen with a mug and pours a cup of coffee from the machine.

"Jim has been with me a long time—right, Jim?"

"Best woman in the world," he says, with a rare show of affection. "Alotta people come through here, but she's the only one who cooks with this," he says, tapping a finger on the heart in his chest. "She cooks with love, not like what some of 'em bring—makes me sick," he says, spitting the word "sick."

"Yeah, well, they're trying," Anna says as Jim exits.

"But I do—I come here with a grateful heart," she says to me. "I love being here. I love being with these guys. I love hearing things, and I don't pry or ask what they did or where they've been or how come. If they tell me it's okay, I'm not here to say, 'Ooohhh my God.' It's not like that, you know. I lived a different life. And that's not to say I don't know: my brother's a drug addict, forty-five years dependent, and he's been clean for about six. So it's a loooooong road. I have a heart for it. I understand that part of it, to a degree. But I never was involved in it or lived it or did it. I'm just a country bumpkin. But for Jim to say that about me, that's the biggest compliment. It's just—I want people to know that no matter what they did, I want them to know people care. People still care. You're still a good person. And I don't even think that, but I feel it. There's a difference."

Joe Badillo enters the kitchen while Anna fries eggs on the stovetop.

"What do we have here!? Breakfast?"

"We are gonna have sausage, peppers, potatoes, onions, with an egg on top, if you want it."

"Can you make one fried hard?"

"Yep."

"I don't like the yoke."

"Really?"

"Nope, not at all."

Joe exits after this simple exchange. And in the flow of Anna finishing the meal among the hustle and bustle and cooking around fifteen fried eggs—timed to be eaten hot—she remembers his usual seat at the dinner table and serves the one fried hard to his empty plate.

* * *

Anna Acuri clearly cared a great deal about the ritual of breaking bread at Bridge House. And her hard work was especially important to Joe Badillo: the kind of healthy food Anna served was tangible support for his physical well-being and ongoing struggle to overcome the rolling aftereffects of the spinal abscess and surgery to remove it. Perhaps even more important than the food itself was the social dimension of Anna being concerned enough to tailor the cooking of eggs and remember his preferred seat at the dinner table. The years leading up to Joe's arrival at the program had been stamped by chronic marginalization, culminating in brutal neglect during a health crisis at Richmond County Jail. At its best, the Bridge House evening meal enabled him to form new relationships of support and experience meaningful moments of social connection.

Not that all the evenings meals were like the monthly contribution of Anna Acuri. The quality of the food varied widely—probably more typical than her elaborate multicourse affair was the dry meat loaf and stale French bread dropped by the volunteers who did not stay to eat. And the very fact that the program relied on volunteers to provide food every weeknight is a concrete manifestation of the ongoing struggle of the halfway house to generate the revenue required to meet the fundamental needs of residents.

Anna was also exceptional in the quality of the relationships she was able to establish with the men. More common was the rather awkward encounter involving Maddie, Mike, and Mario, in which the dinner table talk devolved into separate conversations. The social distance between residents and volunteers—with the basic division of criminal status intersecting with a series of other markers of privilege and disadvantage clustering on either side—often seemed to materialize physically in divided seating around the large table (volunteers together at the kitchen end, residents together at the living-room end). When residents were seated at a separate foldout table, this was usually the liveliest site of conversation.

Anna said she wanted the men at Bridge House to know that, no matter what they may have done in the past, "people still care." And she spent long hours working a gendered second shift to ensure her contribution to the evening meal was a meaningful expression of this sentiment.[18] She was employed full-time as an office manager at Harris Dental, and she told me she prepared the food described earlier over several days: cutting and freezing the sausages and most of the vegetables on Sunday, adding the potatoes and partly cooking everything on Tuesday, and after leaving the dental office on Wednesday, finishing the meal in the Bridge House kitchen. Anna said she also cooked elaborate dinners for her husband, an industrial mechanic, and father, who lived with them. Once a month, she extended the household labor she already juggled with paid work to support not only the men in her own family but the men at Bridge House.

Anna carried out this care work as part of a ritual framed by coercion. The evening meal may have been an important element of the social support provided by the halfway house, but at the same time, the men were given no choice over whether or not to attend. Being at the evening meal was a compulsory requirement, and because of the precarious criminal status of residents on parole and probation, this seemingly basic rule was backed by the ever-present possibility of rapidly escalating punishment. The evening meal also subtly contributed to the experience of spatial confinement by requiring residents to be physically present each weeknight. In other words, the same ritual through which care was provided was also less obviously an exercise in carceral control.

Perhaps this was one reason most residents seemed to treat the evening meal as little more than a formality—it was usually ten or fifteen minutes from the prayer to when they started leaving. The standard line among the men was that they were thankful for the generous volunteers cooking and bringing food, but ultimately, most ate quickly without saying much. Not once do I remember dinner opening out to a longer, more substantial conversation around the table. People who took their time eating usually had residents cleaning up around them, eager to get on with the evening.

This did not prevent volunteers like Anna Acuri—and there were others who performed the work similarly—from trying to make breaking bread a more substantial encounter and genuine contribution to the lives of residents. And that made all the difference to Joe Badillo's experience at the program.

* * *

When Joe completed his probation sentence and was free to leave Bridge House, he decided to keep living there anyway. It was a vote of confidence that complicates any analysis that might treat the halfway house as simply a site of carceral control and extension of the prison into the community. Joe not only chose to stay but talked about the program in glowing terms. He told me more than once that it saved his life.

Still, I met other men during the project who said *prison* saved their lives. Their stories were less endorsements of prison than implicit critiques of the collapse in alternative sources of support. After decades of policy makers systematically dismantling the social safety net while dedicating unprecedented levels of public funding to criminal justice,[19] these men experienced prison as a refuge providing access to services they could not find elsewhere: a place to eat regular meals, sleep indoors, and receive medical care.[20] The prison provided crucial support even when delivered as part of penal confinement and sometimes brutal state punishment.

A key difference: I do not believe these men would have chosen to stay in prison if given the chance to leave, whereas Joe did make that choice at Bridge House. But even this is unclear. Joe himself talked about deliberately prolonging his stay at Richmond County Jail the last time he was locked up (see chapter 2)—choosing not to pay bail and working with his lawyer to try to delay his criminal case so he could remain a pretrial detainee. In a desperate situation after a chaotic period of homelessness and drug dependency, still physically recuperating from spinal surgery, he found the jail meeting basic human needs. Joe tried to extend his own incarceration.

Now Joe had finished probation and was extending his stay at the halfway house. Relying on poverty-level Social Security income left the alternatives severely limited and made getting public housing—in which rent would be subsidized and priced at one-third his income—the lynchpin of his exit strategy. But he remained on the public housing wait list when probation ended, so he stayed at Bridge House, a kind of confinement not by criminal justice fiat but by poverty and blocked opportunities. The confinement was partial, and there were other options despite the structural exclusions. Joe had friends and family in the neighborhood and, in a pinch, could have moved in with one of them. He could have searched for a different program or a homeless shelter or even returned to the street, as he had done so many times before. And he decided to stay at Bridge House, in part, because it was a pretty nice place to live. There was wireless internet. He had his own room with a TV and a fairly comfortable bed. He was well liked among residents, and when the volunteers brought food to share in the evening, he often held court around the dinner table.

Beyond Joe's own account of the virtues of Bridge House, I observed ethnographically the important role of the program supporting him throughout this period. Stable housing provided a foundation for sustained engagement with the health-care system, and more generally, he was eating healthier food and sleeping on a regular schedule. Joe had grown physically stronger and was walking without needing a cane—remarkable progress given the initial postsurgery prognosis that he may never walk again. And however valid the academic critiques of twelve-step recovery,[21] there were clear benefits to Joe "getting clean" and breaking a long cycle of dependency on various combinations of crack, cocaine, heroin, and pharmaceutical opiates. His commitment to abstinence provided a clarity of mind without the influence of powerful chemical substances day-to-day, allowing him to reflect on the trauma of the past, plan for the future, and think rationally about the overwhelming obstacles he confronted. I found Joe calm and level-headed in the face of what often seemed like a constant stream of personal crises.

These are the tensions of carceral care—because Joe's residence at Bridge House beyond the end of probation was also symptomatic of the invisible punishments[22] so many former prisoners face long after "doing their time." He had completed the criminal sentence imposed in court but lived in a halfway house, a liminal location in the shadows of the carceral state.[23] The institution received some public funding but operated at arm's length from the state agencies of criminal justice, and Joe would not have shown up in conventional measures of the reach of mass incarceration, like counts of correctional populations or the number of people under community supervision. He may have been officially unshackled from any criminal sanction, but he was still subjected to the intense carceralization of his lifeworld, from drug testing and curfews to subtle spatial confinement.

Even as Joe became a long-term resident at Bridge House, I rarely heard him describe it as "home." He used a more impersonal term instead: "the house." For example, if we were out in Clearview Crossing and talked about returning, he would say something like "let's head back to the house," rather than "let's head home." At some level, the program was providing Joe with more than simply housing—physical shelter and a place to eat meals and sleep at night—but with a set of relationships and social supports that some people might associate with a "home." And yet, consciously or unconsciously, Joe rarely used that word in the conversations of everyday life.

* * *

I ask Joe what it means for Bridge House to be a halfway house.

"Exactly what it means—you're halfway home," he replies. "A halfway house originated from prison, where you go from maximum to medium to minimum to pre-release to halfway house. This is more like a three-quarter house—meaning you're that close to just moving on to your own house or back into your family's house or whatever."

"Does it ever feel prison-like in that way?" I ask.

Joe pauses to think, then continues. "Anytime you're not in *your* home, it's gonna feel like some kinda institution. Even here. You can't have sleepovers. You got rules in place. Anytime there's rules involved, of course a convict's gonna think about prison. Even though it's far from a prison, it's still got a prison mentality as far as you gotta follow rules, when there's another person telling you what you have to do. And Bridge House does that: you have to be home at ten, you can't stay out late, you can't have people staying over. There's rules involved. And anytime I feel that there's rules involved, there's a part of me is, 'How can I get over? How can I manipulate the rules to work for me, instead of against me?' So yeah, I think you could label it as a prison environment."

I take over and share some of my own impressions of Bridge House: "I had never seen a halfway house before I came here, and I thought of a halfway house as like halfway out of prison. Then when I got here, it's very relaxed. It doesn't feel like there's too many rules and stuff. But even acknowledging that, I am still—in what ways does it feel like a prison is something I want to ask the guys—"

Joe interrupts: "When you're home, like when you go back to Boston, is there a list where somebody's telling you you gotta do dishes?"

I shake my head.

"So anytime there's somebody in authority figure, telling you you have to do something, your instincts kick in, and it's—like I said, with Kevin being, even though he's not like a police, you view him as a police, because he's the one in charge of the rules. You can view Pat as the warden that make sure the prison runs right, make sure it's funded. Then you got Kevin, who's in charge of discipline and makin' sure everybody abides by the rules.

"As lenient and flexible as these rules are, there's still rules in place. In summertime, for example, let's say my family wanted to go to the beach for the week, I wouldn't be able to go because I have to be home for suppers. Yeah, that's a big one—I have to be home every day. So I have to set my schedule not according to me but according to the house. That make sense? If I got plans, I gotta make sure my plans don't interfere with the house. Whereas if I was home, I make my own plans. I'll be home when I get home. That's hard.

"A gigolo like myself, I can't have a woman spend a night over here. If I do, I gotta keep my door open like a teenager. So that's hard. It's hard knowing that, you know. That makes you feel like you're not home. That's when the reality kicks in, and you understand you're not home yet. Whenever you gotta have a visitor, you gotta have your door open.

"It's not home, man. As much as it feels like home, as much as it's saving people's lives, it's still not home. Home is home, man, where you can let the dishes pile up and not have to worry about discipline. Home is when you can come home when you wanna come home, and if you wanna bring a girl home. That's home. I can't bring nobody here to spend the night.

"There's rules I got to follow, just like in prison there's rules you got to follow. I don't want to make it sound like it's a prison. But it is what it is—and it's not home. They make you feel like you're home, and they welcome you like it's your home. But it's not home."

4

Bridge Is Family

Tim Williams got married at Bridge House. He lost contact with Tanisha during a long stretch in state prison, but after release, he reached out to her on Facebook. Tim said that Tanisha showed no interest in reconnecting at first—"she was like, 'Fuck you, you ain't changed, ya piece a shit'"—but he was persistent about seeing twelve-year-old Denise and sixteen-year-old Terrell, who he called his daughter and son (I learned the relationships were complicated). He said Kevin Smith helped "advocate" to Tanisha about his personal development. They started talking on the phone every day, and after completing forty-five days at the program, he was able to take weekend passes. Tim would catch the train almost one hundred miles and stay with the family in their old home in the town of Colchester. In other words, his reentry from prison was also a slow process of family reunification—consecrated with a halfway house wedding.

"It was great, bro!" he said, describing the event. "Everybody was there. They showed up, they gave—I don't care about the gifts, but at least they came and enjoyed the moment with me. Takin' pictures. Cake smeared all on my face. I got on a tuxedo. Broke-ass nigga with a tuxedo! I had the piss-test cup and Breathalyzer 'cause everybody was so happy I thought somebody was high in that muthafucka! That's how happy we was!

"I went out shopping for myself: tuxedo, tie, shoes. I enjoyed it, and it was fun. Pat was there, Mary [his wife] was there, couple of the other [volunteer] cooks was there, Tullys was there, I was like, 'What? For me? Oh, heeelllll no.' I ain't think that many people liked me. For real, man, it was fun. Like, everybody showed up on time. Everybody was smilin'. Helpin' the wife. Doin' everything. I'm like, 'What?' You know, 'cause that's, that's like, that's like, know I'm sayin'?

"Not to be disrespectful, but that's not no type a wedding that normal people go to. After the [normal] wedding, it's poppin' bottles and—know I'm sayin? Yeah, we popped a bottle, nigga, a bottle a muthafuckin

Pepsi! That was about the only bottle we popped! This is recovery. If I was out there using and said I wanted a wedding, they woulda brung a thirty pack a beer and said, 'Fuck everything else. I ain't got no money for that.' But I had alotta people at the wedding. And it was all the people from Ray of Hope, YWCA, Counselling and Assessment [where he attended therapy and sometimes chaired twelve-step meetings]. Know what I'm sayin'?

"Kevin and Pat and them was my supporters. You know, they was helping me out with everything. Even the other organizations that I work with, they was helping me out. Like, I was grateful for a $400 cake for free as a wedding present. I was grateful to get ten homemade pizzas for free. My boy Chris took time outta his day to cook ten pizzas for a whole day, for my wedding.

"I was grateful to have a couple of women in the organization, like Mary and them, take me to get little things—even the little things count. I was grateful they came over with two bags a salad and told me, 'Get right.' I was grateful one of the residents, Tony, was there to cook the chicken. It was teamwork. Meg made the cake, and she decorated. Yo, it turned out beautiful, bro. I got rides to go and get the food and all that. I even had James helpin' me, the other intern that was at the house, I had him helpin'. I had other people give me rides to go to Dollar Tree gettin' the gifts for people. I spent, no lie, I spent like $1,000 alone on the wedding. And I was only makin $300 a month. How you do that? Know what I'm sayin'?

"I had people lookin' out for me, givin' me money here and there if I need it. And alotta people knew I was getting married, so they were like, 'If you need something, let me know.' All right, I will. This ain't easy man, and I was doin' it all on my own. I had to set up for the bridesmaid, I had to call my brother, have my brother come all the way from Vermont. I put up on Facebook, and everybody was hitting me up. I went out and got the invitations, I was writin' 'em. It was a big process, man.

"Thanks to Bridge, we were able to have it there, man. I don't know where I would be at if I didn't have Bridge. I wouldn't be married right now. 'Cause I couldn't afford no ballroom for fifty people—that's like $1,000 alone. Know I'm sayin'? And bringin' the food and the tables. Dudes goin' out buyin' ice, dude goin' out and buyin' fruit salad, dude goin' out and buyin' flowers, dude goin' out and buyin' this. Even the guys in the house was serving, cleaning up, settin' up. Where else they do that?"

* * *

Tim talked excitedly about the outpouring of community support for his wedding to Tanisha. Friends in recovery provided food—Mary brought the wedding cake and Chris homemade pizzas—while a Bridge House resident, Tony, cooked the chicken and other residents helped set up, serve, and clean. Tim talked about the help of specific staff and volunteers: director Pat, operations manager Kevin, intern James, and the husband and wife he called "the Tullys," longtime volunteer cooks. Unnamed supporters gave rides or paid for ice and flowers. With typical good humor, he expressed surprise at this mobilization of support: "I ain't think that many people liked me."

There was a saying at Bridge House: "Bridge is family." This expressed the program vision of modeling family life for residents, for example, through the ritual of sitting around the table and sharing a meal in the evening. In practice, it was often used ironically, say, by one resident cajoling another to help them with the dishes—"Come on, man, you know Bridge is family"—and I heard Pat Townsend preface it in public settings by acknowledging that the saying was "a bit corny." But at Tim's wedding, the Bridge House community really did act a bit like a family.

It would usually be family members performing the collective labor of planning, financing, and executing a wedding. But Tim was a halfway house resident on parole a long way from home, and in the absence of substantial support from blood relations, members of the carceral community filled the gap. Despite his living in conditions of poverty and social exclusion, this support opened access to some of the most important symbols of a "perfect day" presented as necessary by popular culture and a powerful wedding industry: he wore a tuxedo, for example, and had a wedding cake he valued at $400. He said the halfway house itself provided a free alternative venue to a "ballroom."

At the same time that the wedding helped firm up Tim's family relationships on the outside, it absorbed these relationships within the carceral apparatus that was already so dominant in his lifeworld. His children watched him exchange vows and rings with Tanisha in the halfway house lounge and, in the process, established the institution as a central site in their shared memories and family history. Bridge House made the wedding possible but also located the ceremony at the fuzzy edge between freedom and captivity. A ritual ostensibly undertaken as part of a project of personal change and escape from the criminal justice system also entrenched Tim's place within it.

It may have been that Tanisha only agreed to marry Tim because he was a resident at Bridge House. Consider that the wives and girlfriends of prisoners sometimes view their relationships as benefiting from the institutions that contain and control their partners, and come to appreciate the role of prison regimes in shaping men's behavior and suppressing dangerous or difficult conduct.[1] Perhaps Bridge House provided a similar source of security. Tim said that Tanisha rejected his initial advances after his release and only became more open to their relationship over time. And he was experiencing an unusual degree of stability during this period: for the most part not drinking alcohol or using drugs, at home at night, eating healthier food. Tim said they talked on the phone every day, suggesting a reliable and predictable avenue of communication in their relationship. Kevin Smith even advocated about Tim's personal development to Tanisha.

Tim was able to attract support for the wedding in part because it was a very popular symbol of successful reintegration among people in the community. Tim was following a highly normative and gendered script for parole success,[2] forming not just a family but a quite conventional nuclear family of husband and wife with two children. The outpouring of support emerged in part from the appeal of this kind of domestic arrangement, with the ideal of the nuclear family central to the whole Bridge House program model: perhaps Tim would even share meals around the table with his wife and children after leaving the program.

Bridge House is hardly alone in emphasizing the importance of family relationships to successful prisoner reentry. Desistance researchers present marriage as a crucial "turning point" in the life course, in which social bonding and strong ties to family are a source of informal social control, facilitating the movement away from crime.[3] And on the ground in criminal justice systems, having (or not having) a stable home is treated as an important factor predicting the likelihood of recidivism, with the family life of prisoners routinely considered in decision-making about whether they will be released on parole.[4]

For the time being at least, Tim was not part of a nuclear family sharing a household. He lived instead in a halfway house, while Tanisha lived almost one hundred miles away and was prohibited by program rules from staying overnight with him. The same institution that allowed them to be wedded in marriage was central in keeping them physically separated. But there was an exception: after forty-five days at Bridge House, Tim was able to take weekend passes from after dinner on Friday until Sunday evening and, almost every weekend, caught the train to Colchester and spent this time with his family.

I offered to drive Tim on one of these visits. He took the opportunity to deliver gifts to the family. We collected an enormous old television he was given by a friend from the Clearview Crossing recovery scene—it was almost too heavy to move, and we could not close the trunk of the car after loading it inside, driving the neighborhood with the television hanging dangerously loose. Back at Bridge House, we decided against driving like that to Colchester and traded it for the smaller television that Tim had in his bedroom at the program. Tim was also able to rustle together a set of wooden drawers for Denise, and for Tanisha, a crockpot and some plates and cups.

And with the car loaded, we were off to Colchester.

* * *

It is a sunny day and beautiful drive, and as we approach the state border, the freeway is lined with open-faced rock formations and tall trees waving in the wind. After exiting to Colchester, we drive past a country club with rolling hills and perfectly mowed lawn and a driving range with rows of shiny SUVs in the parking lot. Tim calls it "the rich white area." But Tanisha's street also looks kind of suburban—even slightly rural—with forested mountain tops decorating the horizon. She lives in a thin, cream-colored house with three stories, one in a row of eight.

It was the market forces of the drug trade that first brought Tim here. With oversupply collapsing the price of crack cocaine in New York, where he was dealing, Tim said he could sell the product for three times the price in Colchester, and he made the trip so often that he eventually settled for good. The move took place as part of broader regional migrations of African Americans leaving deindustrialized northern cities—like New York and Boston—for smaller towns and suburbs where the cost of housing was more affordable.[5] By the time of our visit, around 5 percent of the population of once almost entirely white Colchester was Black.

Tim introduces his son and daughter in a dark lounge with a large TV. Denise watches Nickelodeon, while Terrell dozes on the couch under a blanket with only his head showing, still wearing a do-rag. We walk down a short hall to the kitchen, where Tanisha washes dishes in the sink of a cluttered room, the top of cupboards covered with pots and bowls, a collection of miniature Smurfs on the microwave. She says hello without turning around.

Outside, we struggle to get the wooden drawers from the backseat of the car. We are worried about breaking something while squeezing it out the passenger door, so we stop for a cigarette. Denise plays on a handrail by some concrete steps outside the house. Tim goes to give her a rough hug.

"Eew, don't touch me with your cigarette mouth," she says.

They play fight, and she pushes him away.

"Yo, did you shower this morning?" she asks. "Okay, then lift your arm and let me smell."

Tim lifts his arm, and she tickles his armpit, running inside.

"I knew she was gonna do that," Tim says with a grin.

We carry the drawers upstairs, then the television, and make space in Denise's bedroom for the new furniture.

"I told you to do this yesterday. I'm about to slap you!" he says to his daughter. Then again, "I wanna see this room clean all the time, or I'll fuckin' punch you."

It is the familiar style of mock confrontation I have seen Tim use so often among the convicts at Bridge House—not that Denise seems to mind:

"You won't punch me!" she says defiantly.

* * *

Tim is expecting a visit from his brother, Dee. While we smoke a cigarette by the car waiting for him to arrive, it appears that Terrell wakes up, because shouting erupts inside—going mostly from mother to son.

As time passes and the shouting continues, I start thinking of the house as a hostile place I shouldn't really be.

"Shut the fuck up!" Tanisha screams, the words bellowing out onto the street. "Shut the fuck up!"

Dee shows up and stumbles from the car in a white tank top and low-hanging skinny jeans. He has lots of tattoos—up and down both arms, a teardrop under his left eye, a Chinese symbol on his neck—and starts talking about all the girls at a drunken "cookout" the night before.

"You tell him about your other baby mothers out here?" he asks Tim.

"It ain't nothin' criminal," replies Tim, shooting a glance at Denise, as if to say, "Don't say that with her around."

Dee talks about Black people taking over Colchester: "The whole Bronx is out here now," he says. "They be doin' there thing out here."

Denise watches from the step, playing with a white bandage wrapped around her left bicep, where a patch of eczema appears infected. The shouting continues inside the house.

"That right there is why I don't live with women," says Dee.

* * *

We drive to Big Y grocery store. I ask Tanisha if she likes it when Tim visits.

"He's a pain in my ass sometimes, but I love him—seventeen years, Liam," she says.

Tanisha says she likes my name, and there's someone called Liam in the soap opera *The Bold and the Beautiful*. Tim helps her and Denise unload three black rubbish bags of cans and bottles for recycling. Tim and I leave them to do the shopping and drive to Tanisha's mother's apartment, delivering the crockpot he brought from Clearview Crossing. He introduces me as a Boston College "professor" from New Zealand. There is a photo of Tim at Norfolk State Prison on the wall. He is dressed in blue denim from head to toe and wears bright white sneakers. Tim jumps from the chair and waves his arms, telling the story of our trying to carry the enormous television the day before. We leave with the crockpot, which apparently Tanisha's mother did not want.

We collect Tanisha and Denise from Big Y and park the car by the back door for unloading. There is a flurry of activity bringing the shopping inside, and bags pile up on the kitchen floor.

"If you ain't helpin', get the fuck out the kitchen."

I exit for the TV in the lounge. The opening sequence of the movie *Old School* is playing. The scene shows the main character coming home to find his wife in the middle of a swinger's gangbang. I have seen the movie before and found it funny but feel a bit awkward watching with Denise.

Tanisha shouts at Tim as they unload the shopping: "Not there, here, muthafucka! I will knock you out!"

Some of the shouting seems directed at no one in particular: "Oh my fucking God. Muthafuckers, who left the cereal open? This is ridiculous."

Tanisha is definitely upset at the kids: "Lazy-ass teenagers not helping around here. They can eat though."

When Tim eventually leaves the room, Tanisha calls after him: "Yeah, you just walk away like you do best."

Tanisha gets a phone call. Tim says she is being blamed for a cash register not being counted correctly at the McDonald's where she works the graveyard shift as a night manager.

* * *

Dee returns, and we smoke a cigarette out back. He talks more about getting drunk the night before and shows me pictures on his phone. He gives a twenty-dollar note to Tim, who grabs at the other notes in a crumpled pile and ends up getting another five dollars in one-dollar bills. Tim goes inside to talk with Tanisha.

"Don't you dare touch me! I will knock you out!" she shouts.

Tim leaves, with the screen door slamming threateningly behind him.

"I'ma divorce you, muthafucka!"

We drive downtown to buy a Fourth of July outfit for Denise. Dee and Tim know the store owner—all three are from New York. Hip hop booms onto the street, where two men sit on plastic lawn chairs at the entrance. One has a ponytail and a deep scar stretching from the edge of his mouth to his ear. Inside, clothes are arranged in three rows to suggest matching outfits: flat-rim caps along the top, T-shirts and tank tops in the middle, shorts and pants along the bottom. I struggle to keep up with a conversation about fashion trends that feels like a long in-joke that I do not understand. Dee tries on a hat and strikes poses in the mirror, asks Tim to take a photo, then takes a selfie himself. I become conscious of what I am wearing: dirty Nike sneakers with soles worn through, army-camo shorts given to me by a Bridge House resident, a two-year-old white T-shirt. I notice that Tim is also much less put together than Dee is.

Back at the house, Tanisha is cooking chicken, and the conflict begins immediately: "Why the fuck would you come around the front when you could come round the back?"

I want to stay out of the way and so station on the couch in front of the TV—*Old School* is still playing. The conflict escalates, and Denise goes upstairs to her bedroom. Among the barrage of angry words coming from the kitchen comes a line that instantly makes me feel awkward as hell: "You have your little friend here who I don't like and I don't trust!" Tanisha yells.

I decide it is time to get out of the house and exit to stand by the car. Tim follows behind soon after. The shouting is relentless, the words flying out the door and echoing down the street: "We're done! It's over! We're done! You may as well cancel your [train] tickets 'cause I don't want you coming out next week! Don't ever call me again!"

* * *

It is a tough ride back to Bridge House in the car. For much of the drive, we cannot get radio or internet reception and so have no music. We talk it through, but I feel out of my depth and struggle to come up with any sensible advice. Tim keeps bringing the conversation back to Tanisha being too easy on the kids and them being lazy and not helping. I do not really know how to voice that I totally disagree: it seems like the opposite of being too easy on them. I want to say that Tanisha needs rest and time away from that house and those kids—it feels like she is on the verge of nervous breakdown—but know enough to realize that the supports that would make that possible do not exist.

The car goes quiet. Tim leans his head back on the chair and goes to sleep. He was awake most the night and has barely eaten all day.

* * *

Tim hands me the phone with Tanisha on the line, and she apologizes for the weekend. I do not record in fieldnotes the specifics of what she says, but it is enough for me to decide it would be okay to return to the house. This time the visit would be longer: we would drive Denise to the dentist on a Monday morning but arrive on Saturday, spending the weekend with Tim's family.

I suggest we cook dinner on the first night. But we do not arrive until 4:00 p.m. and have errands to run, so settle instead on Domino's Pizza, which becomes the focal point almost immediately after getting out of the car. Tim shouts inside to Denise to find the coupons. Terrell demands bread sticks. Tim gets on the phone to order, and I feel resentful: first, we went from cooking to takeout; now he is ordering without checking how much it will cost. It comes to $32 plus tip for the driver. Tim hands over the phone, and I give my credit card details.

Tim distributes the food on paper plates. The pizza boxes are not opened on the table; instead, each person is served a set number of bread sticks, chicken wings, and pizza slices.

From the other room, Terrell talks loudly on the phone: "I'm up here eatin' Domino's!"

Tim jokes sarcastically that he is telling the world about his dinner. Tanisha says, "Leave him alone"—they do not get to eat Domino's very often.

* * *

Tim says that he brought a $5,000 diamond ring for Tanisha when he was dealing crack cocaine. An addict was at the house trying to sell the ring for $10,000, and Tim negotiated down to half price, an impulse buy paid in cash. We are heading to the mall to visit Kay Jewelers and get one of a cluster of diamonds on the ring replaced. Tim does not want Denise to come but gets overruled by Tanisha, in the process negotiating for one condition: Denise will not ask to be bought anything.

Tanisha and Denise start at Victoria Secret, Tim and I at Footlockers browsing sneakers. At Sears, Tanisha argues with the lady behind the counter about mistakes on a receipt for a previously purchased jewelry chain, saying that she paid $300 but the receipt lists $129 and that the chain is longer than the measurement listed. Tanisha decides to take Denise "back to school shopping." Tim is annoyed, saying that there is still a month before school and that clothing styles will change in the meantime.

The last stop is Dollar Store. I hover while they walk the store buying things from a list, then join them at the counter, where there are bumper stickers for sale with patriotic slogans like "God Bless America" and "Proud to Be an American"—three for a dollar. Some Bridge House residents joke about my being anti-American, based on my being from New Zealand and having critical political views, and I decide that putting these bumper stickers on my car will be a nice counterjoke. As I go to pay, Tim quickly grabs a pen for his cell-phone screen and hands it to the person behind the counter.

"Give me two dollars, and I'll pay you back," he says.

Resentful that Tim is asking for more when I just drove him across the state and bought the family dinner, I ignore him, paying for my bumper stickers but not the cell-phone pen. There is a moment of confusion as he realizes that I did not get the pen that he has already given to the person at the counter. Tanisha steps in and pays, clearly unhappy about it, saying to Tim, "Don't borrow nothin' from him."

Tim tries to put an arm around Tanisha's shoulder on the walk back to the car. She is annoyed and pushes him away. Tim rushes off in front, and as the distance grows with each step, I position myself in between the two, consciously trying not to take sides. The drive home is angry and silent.

* * *

Tim suggests a game of table tennis at the YMCA to escape the conflict bubbling at the house. We trash talk our skills on the way down, only to find they no longer have tables, so instead do a walk around downtown. Two young women swagger along the sidewalk wearing too-short jean shorts.

"You look good," one says to Tim. "What you doin' tonight?"

I start crossing the road and try to pull Tim along with me: "Let's go, man."

He turns to engage them anyway: "Nah, I know her."

They chat on the sidewalk, one girl standing off to the side looking away, while the other tells Tim that it is her birthday and she just got back from out of town.

"I'm lookin to have a good time but don't got no money," she says, noticeably cross-eyed and slurring slightly.

They exchange phone numbers.

"What time should I call you?" the girl asks as she walks away.

"Around nine," he calls back.

"Why did you give her your number? They look like teenagers, man," I say to Tim, shaking my head.

"Nah, they like twenty-two. She was seventeen back then and getting into the clubs."

Tim starts talking in circles, telling a story about the girl and then claiming it was not his "real number" but one to an old phone. I know he still uses both numbers.

* * *

We stand around the back of Tanisha's house smoking cigarettes. The sun is going down, bringing evening coolness to a humid day, and the air is alive with the sound of kids playing basketball on a portable hoop held in place with stones. A beaver runs past at the edge of some bushes. A man in a big brown truck talks out the window to the woman watching the troop of children.

"I used to buy weight from him. That's my boy right there," says Tim.

He hopes the man will stop and give him some money before leaving. While we wait, a man in baggy jean shorts and a white T-shirt hurries past and into the house two doors down. Tim says the guy was jealous about his growing operation, and after telling Tim to stop stealing customers, he called the police about Tim's dealing. Tim says that he was "getting everyone" by selling $50 bags of crack cocaine for $40 or even $37—only paying $10 for the half gram of crack they each contained. He says that he drove different cars every day, belonging to various "crack heads," in an effort to throw off the police.

The man in the brown truck pulls out from the parking space, drives a few feet, and stops not far from where we sit. Tim walks over and jumps in the passenger seat, returning after a couple of minutes to reports that he received no money from the man in the truck. Preempting what I have been thinking basically the whole time we have been sitting here—that Tim is destined for a return to prison if he ever moves back to Colchester—he says, "See the temptations I got out here."

Tim says that being on parole is actually kind of helpful. Otherwise, the police might see his ring and chain and suspect that he is dealing again.

"Would you move out here after your parole finishes?" I ask.

"Hell no," Tim replies in an instant.

Denise plays in a patch of dirt by the wall to the kitchen, digging a hole she imagines to be the foundations for a new house. Then the hole becomes a swimming pool: she lines it with a plastic bag, held tight around the side with stones, and fills it with water. I sit in a kitchen chair and ask a few questions as she goes along—trying to reserve judgment in this scene where I am so out of place—as Tim ignores Denise for the screen of his phone, offering no more than a few gruff comments about the silliness of playing in the dirt.

* * *

We take a trip to the lake. The morning is overcast and the weather predicts rain, but we decide to go anyway, getting there around noon. Tim sits on the grassy bank smoking cigarettes, Tanisha wades in ankle-deep water, Denise swims. The air and water are both warm. I teach Denise about skipping stones: how to hold the stone with an index finger wrapped around the edge, the semicircle motion of the arm before releasing, the logic of getting the flat edge to bounce along the water. I gather flat stones and hand her the best ones.

Tanisha retires from the water and sits on the shore with Tim. They take a couple of photos for Facebook. Tanisha's brother comes and smokes a blunt on the shore, the smell of weed wafting out over the lake. We stay around two hours. Tim grabs Tanisha by both hands and lifts her from the towel where she sits. They walk back to the parking lot holding hands. I am a little behind and take a photo for Tim on my phone: the pair walking side by side on the grassy shore by the lake.

* * *

Tim hangs out in the kitchen while Tanisha cleans chicken in the sink for frying. I missed the negotiation, but apparently he started cleaning the chicken but gave up due to poor eyesight—he has glaucoma—and so handed her the work. Hunched over the sink, Tanisha says she can cook but hates cooking. As far as I can tell, Tim has not eaten all day.

Tim and I duck outside for a cigarette. Terrell shows up for the first time since the night before and starts loudly demanding chicken. Tanisha suspects that he has been smoking marijuana, and the conflict rapidly escalates into a physical scuffle. Through the screen door, I see

Tanisha take a couple of big swings at Terrell, who seems unfazed and continues his defiant demands for chicken. The same woman from next door is again watching a troop of kids playing basketball: "I got one like that too," she says to Tim. "Only comes home to shower and eat. One of us is going to jail—that's how that's gonna end."

The conflict spreads to Tim and Tanisha. I exit to the TV room and leave them in the kitchen. I can hear Tim losing his cool and shouting back at Tanisha, charging that she spoils the kids and lets them disrespect him. When the food is ready, and Denise and I join them at the table, the arguing continues unabated. Tanisha stands hunched over the sink with back turned. Tim tries to get her to sit down, but it only makes her angrier. Denise is the first to leave, and as it escalates into threats of divorce on both sides, I hurriedly cram chicken and rice and beans into my mouth before again exiting for the lounge. There is no opening to say thank you: I am hungry, and the food is awesome.

* * *

Tanisha goes to bed. We sit in the lounge, and with Tim and Denise next to each other on the couch, it feels like a nice scene, more affection between them than at any other time on the trip. Tim plays *Big Barn World* on his phone—a game he shares with Tanisha—while I chat with Denise.

Denise asks how many brothers and sisters I have. I say, "One of each," and then return the question. She goes through a list of half brothers and sisters who all seem to be older, and Tim looks up from the phone, rolling his eyes to signal that I am being misled. Then he says that he wants to go upstairs and bring Tanisha down. Almost immediately after he leaves, Denise looks at me and says, "You know he's not my real dad, right?"

* * *

We sit around the kitchen table with Tim and Tanisha playing *Big Barn World*. Tanisha gets a phone call from a man who says Terrell was at his house last night. In the ensuing conversation, I learn that Terrell is part of a program for juvenile offenders that tracks his location remotely, and when he did not come home last night, there was a missing-person report automatically filed with police.

Tim beckons me into the lounge to say that it was Tanisha's ex-boyfriend who called on the phone. He says that is why he encouraged her to answer the call even though we were sitting together and complains that she will not let him talk to women but still talks with other men. Soon Tim and Tanisha are arguing again in the kitchen. I doze on the couch in the lounge, listening to music and zoning out the sound of angry voices.

Terrell barges into the house sounding frantic. It must be around midnight. He says he needs money for gas.

"Excuse me, sir—you got five dollars?" he asks.

In a fog, I shrug my shoulders and say no.

* * *

We are up early the next morning, driving an hour to the dentist's, where Tanisha is appealing a decision by MassHealth to deny Denise braces. There is lots of Spanish spoken among the people gathered in the waiting room. A security guard with a bushy moustache sits in the corner. Tanisha and Denise disappear inside and return to say that the appeal was unsuccessful.

Tanisha is philosophical and thinks that their lawyer did a good job anyway. She says Denise got a score of twenty but needed twenty-eight. Apparently, the orthodontist believes that Denise has a deep impinging overbite but could not be sure it was the overbite causing the pain in her teeth and so argued that there was not enough evidence for why she needs braces. MassHealth agreed to keep the case open another thirty days to give time to gather more information. Whatever the result, they will be allowed to reapply in six months.

* * *

We pick up Tanisha's father, Tony, who wants a ride to Clearview Crossing. Tony is angry at his landlord and talking in circles about the problems from the backseat. No one seems very interested. At Tanisha's, we eat lunch at the kitchen table while Tony smokes cigarettes outside—the two have an ongoing dispute and so are not really talking. Tanisha had left the door unlocked in case Terrell returned but found it locked when we got back, so she speculates that he may have been home. Tim says they found three knives on the table this morning.

Tony shares his landlord problems over an after-lunch cigarette. He wants to move to Clearview Crossing to be closer to his daughter Roseanne, and already handed in thirty days' notice for his house in Colchester, getting Section 8 papers sent from one jurisdiction to the other—only to learn that his new landlord was unexpectedly charging not only a security deposit but first and last months' rent. Tony says he earns $900 a month on disability and cannot afford the $2,100. He is angry that the landlord did not raise the first and last months' rent payments earlier. The plan is to head to Clearview Crossing anyway, then try to negotiate with the landlord and new public-housing authority.

Tony calls Roseanne from the backseat of the car on the drive. He wants to stay with her and asks if she will attend a meeting with the housing authority. Roseanne says that Tony probably should not come to Clearview Crossing and might not even get an appointment this week. After hanging up the phone, Tony considers getting out of the car and turning around but directs his frustration at Roseanne for being reluctant to have him. There is no recognition that the reluctance may be reasonable: I know Roseanne as a single mother with two children under the age of seven, whose husband was murdered around a year earlier and is already hosting Tony's ex-wife and new boyfriend in her two-bedroom apartment.

Back at Bridge House, Tony realizes that he forgot not only his phone charger but his housing voucher, the most important document he needs to meet with the housing authority. I leave him pacing in the driveway smoking a cigarette.

* * *

The belief in marriage as a "turning point" toward desistance is based on a vision of family as a site of stability. It is an ideal rooted in a postwar Golden Age of high employment and secure family structures underpinned by the safety net of the welfare state.[6] It is doubtful how open these arrangements ever were to a Black couple like Tim and Tanisha—the Golden Age was always reserved primarily for white America[7]—but the social supports for a stable family life are even more distant today, in a world of economic precariousness and welfare provisions slashed systematically.[8] Tim's family home is a site of interpersonal conflict and stress—much less stable than the halfway house where he usually lives.

The gendered vision of family life embedded in the Bridge House model appears most clearly in the core ritual of breaking bread: the men sitting down to eat meals around the table in the evening. The volunteers who cooked and brought the food were usually women, imitating a male-headed nuclear family, in which the wife is home during the day with the time and resources to cook and generally keep the place running. The regular schedule of the meals at Bridge House—6:00 p.m. each weeknight—was underpinned by resources and support that were absent from Tim's domestic arrangements in the real world. The simple ritual of breaking bread was based on a highly normative vision of family life that did not resonate with his experience outside.[9]

Much of the conflict in my visits to Tim's household centered on food and its preparation. There was no one bringing dinner for Tanisha and her children—*she* did that work and it was a constant source of stress, even more so when there were visitors and her son was running out of control. There was no male breadwinner working during the day and leaving her the time and economic security to dedicate to child care and home maintenance. It was just Tanisha, living effectively as a solo mother while working night shifts at McDonald's.

Tim was unlikely to ever have stable work again. He was a Black former prisoner living under a de facto system of racial caste.[10] Not that Tim would not talk about the situation in such dire terms: he seemed much more interested in opportunities than obstacles. And his efforts to provide for his family centered on various forms of hustling—for a long time drug dealing, and then, living under intense criminal justice supervision in the community, befriending ethnographic researchers with cars, rolling cigarettes for bartering and selling, getting money from his brother, and gathering used goods like wooden drawers and televisions to deliver as gifts.

No matter how hard Tim hustled—and it required constant hard work[11]—it could not possibly be enough to create the economic foundations for a stable family life. And his return from a long spell in state prison was itself destabilizing for the family.[12] Not only Tanisha also but Denise and Terrell faced having to accommodate Tim and figure out the nature of their new relationships and his role in the family unit. The process had similarities to other situations of family reunification after forced separation—for example, when war veterans return from overseas and disturb established domestic relationships.[13] But one important difference was that Tim returned to the family as a convict who was still supervised by the criminal justice system, back from prison but not fully present, there on the weekends but living in a halfway house on the other side of the state during the week.

Tim negotiated the tricky dynamics of family reunification under severe material hardship. The poverty could easily be missed for all the consumer goods around the house: Denise had an iPhone that was apparently worth $500, and the downstairs basement was strewn with clothes, bicycles, and DVDs. But Tim did not even have a bank account. He went long stretches during these visits without eating and, on one occasion, had his first meal of the day around 4:00 p.m. Domino's Pizza was a special occasion with portions carefully divided so that everyone got a fair share. The family did not own a car and there was no proper public transport. My role in the scene was largely as a driver: I took the family to do grocery shopping, and they recycled cans and bottles to get some money.

Tim charged Tanisha with spoiling Denise, saying that she asked for too much without doing her share of work around the house. And he reprimanded her throughout these visits with angry words—"bring me this," "clean your room," "wash the tub"—without asking questions about how her life was going, about her friends, her basketball team, her teachers, or her favorite subjects at school. It was hard to be around. But Tim's attitude toward Denise also seemed rooted in the poverty under which he negotiated the tricky dynamics of reentering the family. Perhaps he felt frustrated and self-conscious about being unable to support the family. And if the many stresses Tanisha faced could be explained by the kids being spoiled and not helping out, it would mask his own inability to provide for them financially or help with the day-to-day labor of the household.

I spent a lot of these visits feeling like I was being hustled by Tim. He made constant small grabs for resources involving subtle deceptions: the ordering Domino's without asking how much I would pay, the cell-phone pen added to the order at the Dollar Store counter, and many other moments in between. I felt annoyed but also unable to get proper perspective on what was reasonable and what was not. I started saying no to requests, believing that giving too much was more than a financial issue—it might leave me labeled a sucker to be hustled. On the last day of our visit, after driving Denise to the dentist's and returning to the house, Tanisha needed five dollars for a taxi to do grocery shopping. I did not offer to pay or give them a ride.

The need and crisis seemed constant: the son gone missing with knives on the table, the infected eczema and failed effort to get braces for hurting teeth, the family conflict escalating to physical scuffles and threats of divorce, the being stuck between public housing. None of it seemed out of the ordinary—it felt like the days of our visits were a fairly representative slice of life in this Colchester family. I quickly ran out of empathy and simply drove away, taking Tim with me.

Tanisha stayed with the kids.

* * *

"Did I ever tell you I might have a son?" asks Joe Badillo.

Joe tells me the story about this possible child over lunch at the counter in the Bridge House kitchen. He says he had a casual relationship with a woman and, after being sent to jail and then released, bumped into her at a club. On the spur of the moment, she led Joe home and revealed a sleeping baby she said was his son. Now they are exchanging messages on Facebook. He shows me a photo of the teenage boy on his phone, then a photo of himself as a teenager, and there is clear resemblance. Joe says the mother and the other possible father are very short, but the boy is over six feet tall.

By chance, just the night before, Tim Williams had told me that a woman contacted him about a possible child. He presented the mother as crazy and after money, but as he talked in typically elusive circles, he shifted from denying that it was his daughter to effectively confirming it. At one point, he used the phrase "baby's mama," and when I tried to clarify, he switched for the phrase "maybe baby mama." As the conversation went on, it turned out that his grandfather looked after the girl until she was eleven, when apparently the mother claimed that it was not really Tim's daughter and took over the caregiving. When I asked what the daughter thought—she was fifteen years-old—he said that she recently sent a text message starting with the words "hi dad."

Joe and Tim both appeared to have teenage children who they played no role in raising or supporting. They were only vaguely aware whether these children were even their own. So when Bridge House created obstacles to their forging family relationships—preventing overnight visits, for example, or holding them at physical distance from their homes—it conformed with existing situations of absence and dislocation. The practical consequences of their being separated from their children while living at the house was limited by their already being separated.

There are problems with Bridge House presenting itself as a model family while paying little attention to the actual families of the men. But this structure also fit with the roles—or lack thereof—that many of them already played in their families. One reason the program was able to ignore the men's wider networks of family obligations was because the men often already did.

* * *

Joe Badillo's adult daughter spends a few days visiting Clearview Crossing. Layla is in the military and lives in Washington, DC, but has come to drop her son with Joe's ex-wife for child care, so she can participate in the Fourth of July parade and stand guard at the White House during the festivities. Joe has not seen her for years, and the fledgling moment of family reunification comes at a critical juncture. He has only been out of jail around five weeks, still adjusting to Bridge House but dedicated to making positive change in his life and desperate to piece together the broken relationship with his daughter. He meets his eighteen-month-old grandson for the first time.

I do the first life-history interview with Joe on the final day of Layla's visit. He shows up late after farewelling the family and is still processing the encounter. I ask open-ended questions about his relationship with his daughter—and with his own father—and Joe describes learning that his ex-wife was pregnant with Layla while he was incarcerated in state prison at twenty-three years old:

"It was feeling of joy that part of me is gonna be in this world, but then it was fucked up because, you know, I'm in prison," he says.

"I felt good being a—you know, but it was a fucked-up feeling at the same time. Know what I mean? To talk about this, you need to really know my past. My father was in and out of jail all my life. I reflected on that, like, 'Wow, I'm doing the same thing my dad did to me'—something I promised myself I would never do. Here I was repeating the same cycle that he did to my mom.'"

"Reflecting back now, what kind of man could really be happy about that? You can't be too happy, can't be too proud. 'Yeeaah, I'm having a baby.' But you're in prison. Who you gonna tell? The prison guards? Who you gonna tell? The murderer who sleeps next to you? Who you gonna tell? The rapist who sleeps up the hall?

"So it was a double-edged sword. It was—it is what it is, you know mean? I spent the next three years in jail, and I got out. And everything was supposed to be perfect, the Walt Disney movie. And it just didn't happen. I ended up going to jail again a year later."

I take over to ask a question: "So the early part of your daughter's life, you were inside. Do you want to talk a bit about the relationship you had with her at that time?"

"I didn't have a relationship with my daughter."

"Would your daughter's mother bring her up to see you?"

"Well, she did, but then when she got married and had her other child, all visits stopped, all communication stopped. She was living in New York, then they went to New Jersey."

"How old was your daughter the first time you had a relationship with her?"

"Maybe eighteen. I mean, I wasn't there for my daughter for none of her life. I was absent her whole life—not absent where she didn't know who I was. I would see her here and there and try and give her money to make everything better or make her promises and break 'em. I didn't see her graduate from high school. I didn't see her graduate from boot camp from the Marines. I didn't see her get married. I wasn't there for her baby's birth. I missed everything important. Every important thing in my daughter's life that was important to her, I was absent. Absolutely.

"For a long time, I blocked it out. 'Accept me for being a drug addict,' you know, blame it on the drugs. That's how I dealt with it. Always one excuse after another why. But what it all boiled down to was the same excuse: too high to go to anything. If I wasn't there, it was either because I was too high or I wasn't high enough to go. 'Oh, I cant go to your gradu-ation. I need a bag a dope to go.' Or 'I can't make your wedding because I'm too cracked out.' Or 'I can't see you graduate from boot camp because I don't got the money to go down there because I've gotta buy drugs.'

"Now I'm man enough to say what a fuckin' shit bag I was. But, you know, she understands. I don't know if she—yeah, she understands. She understands that I have a disease, and that's not the man that I am when I'm on drugs. For that, I'm grateful."

"You said she came back into your life when he was eighteen. What was happening then that made you reconnect with her?" I ask.

"She was going into the Marines, and this was during the war . . ." Joe pauses to recompose himself, choking up slightly. "It was just real hard knowing that my baby girl was gonna go to the Marines and go to war. What happens if something happens to her? If she goes over to Afghanistan? She don't know me really. She knows the drug dad, but she don't know her dad though.

"She don't have my last name because I wasn't working, and I didn't want child support after me and all the other bullshit that goes with it. She really wanted my last name before she graduated from the Marines. The day before she was supposed to go to boot camp, we were supposed to go to city hall to give her my last name. I promised, 'Yeah, I'll be there tomorrow. We'll go down to city hall and do it.' But I just got high and never went. So, yeah, it's fucked up.

"So she went to boot camp, and I went back to prison. Then I got a letter from her. She was like, 'I'm still proud of you. I love you. I am who I am today because of you.' She sent me pictures of her Marine shit. I promised her, 'I'll do things differently.' The whole time that I was in jail, she would write me, I would write her. We kept in touch. But the day I got out, I forgot all that shit, man, and just went right back running the streets. I went back to the streets, and of course I went back to jail. And that's when this shit happened to me [referring to spinal infection]. And I was in the hospital, and she got in touch with me again through emails and Facebook. I told her that was it, that's enough. Just the same excuse over and over. Ain't nothin' changed, you know. Just the same shit, man.

"So now, I don't tell her I'm gonna do things differently—I'm gonna show her. I already made enough promises, man. I don't even tell her anymore, 'I'm gonna do things differently. This time it's different.' I don't even tell her that. I don't. I don't make no more promises because I don't know if I can keep a promise. The best thing I can do is just show her one day at a time that I'm available. Like I was available when she came up, and I was available when she left. That's huge. I seen her when she came up, I seen her in between, and I seen her when she left. That's huge. That's huge, man. The first time. It's a big breakthrough, man.

"Hopefully it stays on the track that it's going. The only way that me and her relationship is gonna work is if *I* work it. She already doing everything she has to do: she's a daughter. Now it's my job to be a father. No promises, no anything in the world is gonna make our relationship stronger except if I show her I want a relationship. I can say I want a relationship till I'm blue in the face. Unless I show her—like the past couple of days, I've shown her that I want a relationship—that's the only way I'm gonna continue staying in her life. She's tired of my bullshit in the past. And she's told me, 'Dad, you're getting too old. I'm getting too old. You have a grandson now. You wasn't there for me. At least be there for him.' I think about that. I don't promise her, but I promise myself. That's all I can do."

There is an alert on Joe's phone while he talks, so we pause, giving him time to check the message.

"It's her," he says.

"What does she say?" I ask.

Joe reads from his phone: "I sent you a friend request on Facebook—accept it now."

"Just so she can keep track of you and monitor you," I suggest jokingly.

"Let me jump on Facebook to accept her," he says, chuckling. "She said 'now.'"

There is a silent pause while he fiddles on his phone, and then:

"She won't give up, man. Unconditional love. That woman has unconditional love for me, man."

* * *

Joe's family separation went well beyond the around six months he had just spent locked up at the county jail. He said he had not seen Layla for four years and, longer term, had missed every important milestone in her life: her high school graduation, her wedding, the birth of her son. He missed Layla's birth too—Joe was in prison. And he described the guilt of learning about the pregnancy while incarcerated: having experienced firsthand the hardships of a father cycling in and out of prison, the news came with a realization that he was extending the cycle intergenerationally.

But Joe might have missed Layla's birth even if he was not in prison. He said he was absent from her life inside *and* out and, in fact, talked about their most meaningful communication taking place during periods of incarceration. Layla sent him photos, he wrote her letters, and they generally kept in touch. It was after Joe's release that he really became absent: outside prison, he was "running the streets" and breaking the promises he made inside. Joe rarely had a stable address and was sometimes homeless during these periods. At least in prison, Layla could find him when she needed.

Bridge House also provided Joe a stable foundation for building a relationship with his daughter. He was predictably available for the few days of Layla's visit—there when she arrived and when she left and around in between—which he described as a "big breakthrough." Being a resident at the halfway house also helped demonstrate his growth and personal development. Joe said that the time for making promises was long gone—he had broken too many already—and now it was about *showing* his commitments. He brought Layla to Bridge House and introduced some of the residents.

Joe being available during the visit may have been a milestone, but it was only three days and his grandson stayed with his ex-wife, a conventional gendered division of family responsibilities. And the halfway house was a source of separation as well as stability—creating barriers to his relationship with his daughter that were more subtle than the bars and walls of a prison, but barriers nonetheless. Joe could not share a meal with his family on a weeknight or travel to Washington DC to be with them for longer than allowed by the weekend pass. He could not have hosted his daughter and grandson during their stay even if he wanted to.

Joe's narrative of neglecting his daughter was dripping with regret. Like many of the men at Bridge House, he talked about his history of family abandonment with a deep sense of guilt. He had not only abandoned his daughter but, having experienced the same thing as a child, knew what that felt like viscerally. The opening for change was provided by Layla, who remarkably continued to show her father "unconditional love" regardless—providing him hope at this critical crossroads.

Joe drew on their fledgling relationship to articulate a changing vision of what it meant to be a man.[14] Central to the narrative was a story about Layla not having his last name—part of an effort to avoid child-support payments—and him breaking a promise to meet at city hall and legally change her name to his own. The story critiques his failure to meet traditional masculine ideals of heading and providing for a family. But he also located that man in the past: he talked about being "man enough" to recognize that he used to be a "shit bag," made a distinction between "drug dad" and the dad he was now, and said that Layla understood, "I'm not the man I am when I'm on drugs."

At the Monday-night Bridge House meeting held the same day Layla left Clearview Crossing, residents shared an update about their week, and Joe talked about the gratitude he felt meeting his grandson for the first time. He was not the only man to tell a story about family. Matt Carmine talked about going to the movies with his father, and Steve talked about going to the beach with his daughter. Peter Tennant described exchanging Facebook messages with a son he had not seen in almost two years, and Bryan Charles talked about spending the weekend at a Boston College High football training camp with a son he said we might be seeing on television.

Day-to-day, these men were only peripherally involved in the hard work of raising children and caring for dependent blood relations—their family dislocation institutionalized by the confinements of the carceral state. But the men constantly talked about these relationships when articulating their desires for making positive change. They relied on family less as a concrete set of supports and reciprocal obligations pulling on their time than as a set of ideas through which they imagined and narrated the future. Family was a site of aspiration.

* * *

Bridge House at once limited Joe Badillo's ability to cultivate outside relationships and itself became a crucial site of social connection. It was a carceral institution involved in controlling and regulating his movement—the restricted mobility intensified by rolling health problems that made it physically difficult to get around and, more broadly, not having a car or other reliable transport. But it was also a deeply social space that he shared with other men who came to operate a bit like his family: they lived together in the same house, ate food together around the table in the evenings, and generally looked out for each other. There was lots of mutual support, sharing of cigarettes, of clothes and sneakers, of cologne and shampoo. Joe had once built family-like bonds with the men he grew up with and navigated the drug economy alongside. Now it was Bridge House residents playing this role.

Joe was usually at the center of the interaction when the men gathered to smoke cigarettes and talk on the porch. Often this was part of the spatial arrangement, with Joe taking the chair closest to the kitchen door and ending up in the middle of a group: one person on the remaining chair to his left, another leaning on the railing to his right, another standing in the driveway out front. He was an avid user of social media and *always* on his phone—a digital escape from his confinement—so as others talked, he was typically looking down and half distracted. Yet the conversation still seemed to bounce off him: "Right, Joe?" someone would say. "You hear what he said, Joe?"

Joe also seemed increasingly comfortable around the Bridge House dinner table in the evenings. He made an obvious effort with the volunteers: remembering their names and the kinds of things they liked to chat about, asking the Fletchers about their kids, exchanging updates on the latest news from the Boston Red Sox with Mary Taylor, and talking classic cars with Bruce Michaels, who apparently once put $300,000 into a single vehicle. Joe often stayed to talk or share dessert when other residents left for the customary after-dinner cigarette on the porch. And the dinner-table conversations sometimes evolved into broader relationships, like when Bruce invited him to attend a wine-and-cheese party to farewell a church pastor.

This was the context in which Joe talked about Bridge House as a family-like setting:

"I got a good family, but we didn't have the family traits as far as sitting down as a family eating supper. Here [Bridge House] you get that atmosphere where you feel like you're in a family and you belong to a family. Believe it or not, I got a lot out of sitting down talking to the [volunteer] cooks. Really helped me out tremendously, man. Getting involved with—them just being like asking—you know what—just asking if I'm okay or how my day went. That goes a long way, man. People might not realize that, but for Pat [Townsend] to even ask how my day's going, that means a lot to me, because it means they're concerned. And you don't get that a lot.

"I don't remember so many days when my own family asked how my day was going."

* * *

Over time, "Bridge is family" became a rather apt description of the role the program was playing in Joe's life. And yet the language of family can easily obscure that it was also a halfway house and the site of his criminal punishment and penal confinement. And the whole idea of Bridge as a surrogate family has more ominous connotations when this part of the story is brought more clearly to the surface. The program providing a substitute for kin relations in the intimate setting of a former family home was a crucial source of care and support for Joe but, at the same time, involved a profound carceral transformation of his lifeworld and personal relationships.

5

The Recovery Hustle

The residents of Bridge House needed to speak the language of addiction recovery. This began with gaining a place in the program: the screening interviews I watched Kevin Smith carry out with potential residents were very much focused on assessing the person's commitment to living "clean." And once the men were inside, the expectation was that they would attend twelve-step meetings as a regular part of the daily rounds, face-to-face gatherings where they were called on to provide personal testimonials and develop an understanding of how recovery related to their own biography and experience.[1] The twelve-step slogans for everyday life were a staple of casual conversation at the house:[2] the men recited the serenity prayer, talked about living "one day at a time" and accepting "life on life's terms," argued that "this disease does not discriminate" and warned that "if you hang out in a barbershop long enough, you eventually get a haircut." Many of the men adopted recovery as a kind of master frame for explaining what they were doing: "getting clean" and "working the program."

Residents' engagement with recovery was always framed by the coercive model of drug abstinence at the carceral institution in which they lived. Still, the house did not have any structured drug-treatment program of its own, instead leaving the men to attend meetings in the surrounding neighborhood, where they learned what recovery was all about at arm's length from official surveillance. And the margin of freedom was wide enough that the men came to very different views on what it meant to be "in recovery," with interpretations shifting not only from one person to the next but for the same person at different times and places depending on the situation. At Bridge House, recovery was a flexible resource.

* * *

Tim Williams takes a weekend pass from Bridge House. We drive around two hours to Colchester to stay with his family. On this particular night, we are searching for his brother, Dee, who has a custom of giving Tim twenty dollars when he comes to town. The search takes us to a dark bar with a low roof and too-loud music. I shout at Tim that I will have a beer and ask what he wants. He says he wants a beer too, then turns to talk with a friend.

It catches me off guard. Tim is on parole and spends his days promoting abstinence in the Clearview Crossing recovery scene. A failed Breathalyzer could mean return to prison. Now he wants a beer. I fumble crumpled bills from my pocket, confused about what he just said. The bartender interrupts to ask for my order. I buy us both a Budweiser.

Finding a spot behind the speaker where the music is slightly quieter, Tim reassures me: "You know how they say, 'One is too many, and a thousand is never enough'?" he says, rehearsing the twelve step mantra. "With me, it *is* enough."

"How long since you had a beer?" I ask.

"Seven years," he says, nodding. "Sometimes my wife has wine coolers, and I have a sip, but then ah," he says, waving a hand away.

I am anxious about the ethics of the situation. I certainly do not see myself as Tim's minder with a duty to tell him how to behave. But I would have felt better if he bought his own beer. My having a beer and buying his adds an element of encouragement that makes me uncomfortable. I decide that one beer is my limit for Tim. When I return to the bar for a second, he approaches just long enough to say, "Fuck it, man. Matter of fact I'll have another one." I buy only mine.

A man in a color-matched outfit and flat-rim cap buys Tim a beer anyway, paying from a bundle of notes in a money clip. Over the music, I hear him shout a welcome: "You home, man!"

When the bartender calls last drinks, Tim convinces another man who he calls "uncle" to hand over one of two just purchased Coronas. After some back-and-forth jostling, Tim wrestles the bottle from his hand and drinks it quickly.

In the parking lot outside, Tim chugs a beer from a man wearing a do-rag and Roman sandals. He tells a story about getting "popped in the mouth" at the bar. Apparently, he returned later that night with a gun and fired shots in the air. "That's why they all respect me in there," he says.

The elusive Dee finally calls on the phone. He left the city for a weekend in Connecticut. I tell Tim that I can drive us home because I have only had three beers, but he seems unconvinced that I did not have more. He places chewing tobacco under his lip in case we are pulled over by police and both Breathalyzed. We drive through dimly lit back roads to avoid detection.

The next day we drink again. Tim says he was lying that the Budweiser was his first drink in seven years. He always drinks on weekend passes.

* * *

It turned out that Tim was living something of a double life. At Bridge House, he presented as devoted to the twelve steps, leading meetings at a mental health clinic and volunteering daily at an addiction-recovery drop-in center. On weekend passes, he was a casual drinker. Choosing to drink alcohol may seem a small thing—most adults drink. But for Tim, it carried serious legal and social risks. His housing and freedom from prison relied on being sober. Drinking was incompatible with the social identity he claimed as "clean."

For context, you need to understand Tim's hustler's disposition.[3] In our interviews, he replied to simple questions with elusive answers, talking in circles, with details changing from one moment to the next. The narrative was full of subtle and not-so-subtle boasting. It was impossible to pin down timelines or the specifics of events. He was like a politician at a press conference, answering not the questions asked but the questions he wanted to be asked. Just talking about hustling filled him with energy.

In a public park one day, Tim talked for forty minutes about prison hustles without pausing. He jumped from the chair to demonstrate hiding a Wellbutrin pill from the prison nurse so it could later be sold: placing a pinch of chewing tobacco under his tongue where the pill would go, sipping from iced coffee, throwing two hands in the air to show innocence, then waving his tongue back and forth to fake that it had been swallowed—before finally revealing the hidden tobacco. The act was brimming with excitement and laughter.

Then Tim told me he approached recovery as a hustle—not so different from hustling in the street:

"When you hustle, you gotta go out there and advocate: 'Yo, son, I got this good shit. You wanna try it?' But in recovery, you gotta let dudes know, like give 'em the opportunities that you have. That they be like, 'Man, how can I do that?'

"It's hustlin', man. Lettin' 'em know, 'Yo, look, son, I been out here.' Like, I told people I been out here for a year, and I'm doin' more jobs and more outreach than people who been out here fifteen, twenty years. 'Cause they ain't got no hustlin' bone in they body. They can't even sell no mother-fuckin' bread to them seagulls. I can. Nigga, I sell water to a whale.

"You gotta be able to sell a dream to a dream catcher. And that's what I do: I sell—I don't sell dreams, I tell real live, hardcore, uncut stories that happened to me when I was a kid, man.

"You gotta network. And networking's part of hustlin', man. 'Cause if I could call you and get your number and say, 'Yo, Liam, I needa a gram a dope,' then why can't I call somebody and say, 'Yo, I'm about to relapse?'

"Same thing, man. Flip it over, man. Turnin' negative into the positive. And that's what I do. I turn a—if I was out there hustlin' and talkin' to any- and everybody out here, I could go in the [Ray of Hope recovery] center and talk to any- and everybody. Whether ya high or not. Same thing."

I am smiling and chuckling.

"Why you laughing, man?" Tim says with a broad smile.

"It's funny, man, like, ah, recovery is a hustle, right."

"Yeah. It is. 'Cause listen, I'ma put it to you like this: you could look at it how you wanna look at it, but a lot of people don't realize it's *always a hustle.*"

* * *

Tim Williams publicly embraced recovery not to pursue abstinence but as a reintegration strategy. Most immediately, it kept at bay overlapping systems of parole and halfway house regulation and, more generally, opened access to social support for a thirty-five-year-old Black man confronting a set of structural obstacles akin to a racial caste system.[4] Tim came to Clearview Crossing after release from state prison because that is where a place in a program was available, and he arrived broke, with no bank account, entering a deindustrialized neighborhood where racialized criminal stigma amplified already-overwhelming barriers to employment.[5] Recovery was the most visible pathway to gaining a foothold in this hostile social order.

Tim spent most days at an addiction-recovery drop-in center downtown: Ray of Hope. It was run on a peer-to-peer model, with members taking the lead in decision-making, and provided an accepting social space where the people were familiar and a prison history came with legitimacy more than stigma. Tim described his role as "outreach" and connecting others with services. He volunteered at the front desk greeting visitors, ran orientations with new arrivals, went on commitments to talk at other recovery institutions, and led group trips to the city art museum. He was awarded a prize for member of the month and had his story printed in the newsletter. Tim hoped the unpaid work would lead to an internship at the center, a system of recruiting members for positions paying $100 for ten hours of work each week. He talked about training to become a licensed drug and alcohol counselor and named as a model Marcus, an ex-convict who was a long-term employee at the center and went on to run a recovery program in state prison.

Along with employment, Tim pursued through recovery another central pillar of reintegration: housing. By outwardly accepting the dictates of the program, he gained a bed at Bridge House, not only a site of carceral surveillance but a place to stay. The landscape of alternative options was bleak, and the house was far preferable to a crowded shelter or the street.

It all depended on Tim selling an image of himself as dedicated to the twelve steps. The salesmanship made use of existing skills, the product switching from dope to addiction recovery. And the site switched too, from networking in the underground economy to networking in the neighborhood recovery scene. There he presented as a changed man and worked to convince others to transform themselves by abstinence-based recovery. Recovery was a hustle.

I only learned about Tim's double life because we shared a bedroom at Bridge House and became friends. I was part of the recovery hustle, a source of free rides in the car and even takeout food sometimes. To be fair, I had my own ethnographic hustle going. Tim constantly pulled me into interesting situations and provided access to things that were otherwise hidden. We also had a great time and laughed constantly. The around six weeks we were roommates was probably my most enjoyable period of fieldwork. Tim woke me in the morning with freshly brewed coffee, shaking hips and clicking fingers, singing loudly, "Wake up, everybody. No more sleeping in bed!" He invited me to visit with family not only because it saved him train fare but because we were getting along well.

Most of the men did not invite me on weekend passes. My sample of participant-observation was heavily skewed toward their lives inside the house rather than outside. And traveling with Tim was a reminder that the program was a front-stage space, clean and tidy, where the men were pushed to present as reformed to staff and volunteers who cycled through daily. There may have been others who outwardly adopted the language of recovery but secretly broke from program expectations—and Tim's narrative of recovery as a hustle points to the potential rewards of this identification regardless of whether it was matched with a practical commitment to drug abstinence.

The discourses and technologies of addiction recovery have become increasingly central to reentry governance around the United States.[6] Consider the evolution of modern parole. It began primarily as a form of coerced employment, inserting released prisoners into the industrial labor market,[7] but from the 1960s, the political and economic foundations for employment-based parole were stripped away by large-scale social transformations.[8] In the wake of capital flight and deindustrialization, the Black and white middle classes alike fled from crumbling city neighborhoods, and the state systematically withdrew investment in welfare and public services.[9] The war on drugs changed the racial profile of the incarcerated, sweeping up record numbers of African Americans who faced caste-like exclusion from employment after release.[10] No longer able to insert clients into jobs, parole systems turned instead to addiction recovery and drug testing, with the "clean" parolee replacing the industrial "good worker" as the picture of parole success.[11]

There were men at Bridge House who did find paid work despite the difficult conditions in postindustrial Clearview Crossing: around one-third of the twenty-nine residents I lived with during the project were in regular employment. Mostly they pieced together incomes from precarious jobs at poverty wages: like Peter Tennant and Bobby Jones doing day labor at the same temporary work agency, Aidan Meaney hanging sheet rock for a friend's small residential construction company, James Stephens working the front desk at a just-opened cross-fit gym in an old warehouse, and Peter Hanks landscaping for a church volunteer he met at the Bridge House evening meal. A small number were able to gain more stable positions: Jimmy Flag, the delivery driver for Consumer Auto Parts; Michael Peters, the skilled mechanic at an established garage; Mark Richards, the grill cook at Denny's; and Ryan Davies, the heavy-machinery operator for a sand and gravel manufacturer.

At some level, these men were success stories who gained employment in the face of myriad obstacles. But they often struggled at Bridge House as they confronted the difficult task of juggling the work they were paid to perform with the time-consuming routines of "working the program." They spent their days in often physically draining labor, doing long shifts at low wages, leaving little left over to meet the demands of the halfway house and the twelve steps. The evening meal at 6:00 p.m. assumed a regular working day and often clashed with their erratic hours and long travel times to work in insecure labor markets. Their bosses may have overlooked criminal pasts in hiring, but anytime the program impinged on the job, they were forced to discuss potentially embarrassing details about their residence at a halfway house.

At Bridge House, gaining employment created frictions in a reintegration ritual based on addiction recovery.

Work as Recovery

Paul Barry works long hours as a compounder at a sealant factory, combining chemicals in a thousand-gallon mixer to create coatings for driveways and roads and basketball courts. With a combination of a personal loan and hard-earned wages, he had bought a Nissan Xterra work truck and parked it in the Bridge House driveway (he says it cost $11,000). Then Paul met Sarah Kennedy through an online dating website. He moved into her apartment almost on the day his parole-mandated period at the program was complete.

I sit with Paul at the kitchen table of the apartment. He has a shaved head and thick brown eyebrows, beard bushy but well groomed. Paul is fresh from a day's work. He strips off his top to do the interview shirtless in big boots and dirty blue jeans. He pours a mug of Coke and serves our plates of KFC: fried chicken, potato and gravy, coleslaw, and biscuits. With Sarah at work, he looks after the two kids, ages four and six, who watch TV but interrupt repeatedly.

It is a picture of working-class reintegration. Very quickly, Paul gained what many desistance researchers consider the key institutional moorings for men like him—a so-called "steady job and the love of a good woman"[12]—as well as stable and independent housing. He might have been a poster child for Bridge House, publicly celebrated as evidence of an effective program. Yet his experience there was characterized more by conflict. Unlike Tim, who poured his energy into unpaid recovery work, Paul was short on time and constantly struggled to meet official demands.

"I tried really hard to do everything that was asked of me in that house," he said from across the table. "But at the same time, I want better for myself. I don't wanna live in that house for years on end. That house was a stepping-stone. It allowed me to get to the next step. Unfortunately, I fell in with such a good job, and I didn't wanna jeopardize my job because of the house. But I didn't wanna jeopardize the house because of my job. So it was a juggling act.

"Luckily I had a really understanding boss. I cut it close a few times, but I managed to pull it off. I had to find ways to get to and from [work], and I'm not one to ask for help. I had to call on people to get to and from—and people did, like yourself. So yeah, at times the house manager, Kevin, was upset with me, but at the same time, I'm not the one sitting there paying my bills with food stamps. I'm whipping out hundred-dollar bills and paying in cash."

"Can you remember any particular times when there was a conflict or juggling act?"

"Yeah, there were times when there wouldn't be the generous people that come in from outside to bring dinner, and I already stayed out two nights from dinner to work," he says, referencing an agreement he negotiated with Kevin to miss two evening meals a week.

"And my question was, 'If there's no cooks, we're not all gonna sit and break bread together, why do I need to be home? You know I have a legit job. I have legitimate paid work that I can show you where I am.' And yet he made it an issue to say, 'No, you already missed two dinners. Cooks or no cooks, you have to be home,' which jeopardized my job, jeopardized me making money."

I clarify, "Is that what's making it hard for you to work while living there? Having to be home at particular times?"

"Right, yeah. Having to be there at particular times. It's just hard to work around. Because for the person like me that didn't want to get by on food stamps, that wanted to have a job—which is hard to find because of the [criminal] record I have or because it's hard to find a job even if you have a college degree—and I finally come across a job, now I have to tell them, 'Oh, look, I have dinner at six o'clock. I have to be home,' or, 'I have to be back at a certain time,' when the job relies on me being there.

"It was really difficult. I mean, how do ya do it? Because some places wouldn't be as understanding as my boss. He'd be like, you know—they just wouldn't. So how would you do it? And again, I didn't make enough on food stamps to pay rent. And luckily I never got to the point where I got that far behind that I was like, 'Okay, Kevin, what do I do? Are you gonna kick me out? Because I don't have enough food stamps to pay you?' Then what happens? If I get kicked out of that program, because I'm one of the mandated ones that has to be there [as a parole condition], what do I do? Go back to jail? It's a really awkward position."

"Do you go to meetings now?" I ask.

Paul pauses to think, then shakes his head. "No, I don't go to meetings."

"Do you have a sponsor?"

"Technically. Nobody's gonna hear this, are they?" he asks, gesturing to the voice recorder on the table.[13] "No, I don't go to meetings."

"Who would care if you were going to meetings?"

"Kevin, my parole officer. I still have to fill out the card [as a record of attendance]. And my girl, she does it for me. But I don't get out of work until late. Yesterday I worked from 6:00 a.m. to 10:30 at night."

"Let me ask you this: Do you consider yourself an addict?"

"Yes, without a doubt," he says.

"And the house is designed to get people into recovery. Was that helpful for you?"

"I dunno. To me, it's just a weird topic. Like . . ." Paul pauses to think. "Really, when it boiled down to it, it was just a matter of being ready. Like, there were other times where I was going to meetings, and I was lying to everybody including myself, because I was still using. I went to a month-long in-patient rehab that cost my mother $5,000—a very posh place that had tennis courts, volleyball net, hiking up the mountain, natural river that flowed down the mountain, lodge on the side of this brook—a very nice treatment facility. And I was gettin' drugs delivered to me while I was there.

"I wasn't ready. I wouldn't say I was 'in recovery,' 'cause I wasn't done using. But now that I *am* in recovery, I dunno, like everybody has their different ways. The program I was in in Springfield, they taught me a lot. One of the things they said was that an addict will, like—a lot of times, addicts in recovery will take one addiction for another, whether it's going from using drugs to going to the gym, to stay clean, or becoming an absolute health nut or just focusing on work or playing a sport.

"I get that, 'cause that's what I'm doing now. I'm taking one addiction and applying it to this job. And not even the job—I'm applying it to life. Like, I used [drugs] every single day and did everything and anything I could as a means to get more. Well, now that's my job. That's my recovery. Work is my therapy. It keeps my mind occupied. Some pay people to sit in front of them and ramble on. Others punch a punching bag. Other people meditate. Mine is work, man. Why not do something you're gonna get paid for? Going to meetings don't pay the bills. Work keeps my mind focused. It keeps it focused on the right goal. Even if I have a bad day, which could be a traumatic event, I work through it because I know I have to be there tomorrow. I don't feel that I have to get out of work and run and use, because—you know what?—it's part of life. Traumatic events are gonna happen.

"I used to have drug dreams, wanting to use or just feeling I wanted to use. Now after a day of working, I come home, I'm exhausted, I'm beat, I'm tired. I eat dinner and take a shower. I relax, and I'm ready for bed. And when I go to bed, I close my eyes and I'm out. 'Cause 4:30 in the morning comes fast. So I don't have time for the urge. I don't have time to wanna use.

"If I stay busy and focused, then I'm dealing with life on life's terms. I've heard people say that, but I mean it. I'm not letting a traumatic event get in my way. Or I had a bad day, so I'm gonna go use. No. I gotta job I gotta go do."

* * *

Paul followed a traditional path to reintegration, finding factory labor and working relentlessly. This brought him into conflict with a halfway house that prioritized working the program. Getting home for a 6:00 p.m. dinner with the volunteers was difficult with a boss constantly wanting overtime. Paul was able to negotiate with Kevin to miss two dinners each week. Yet there were times when no volunteers were scheduled or did not show up. Paul argued that he should be allowed to work late on these nights, regardless of how many dinners he had already missed. Kevin disagreed and forced him home.

Reintegration systems once disciplined by inserting people into factory work, a way to exhaust time and energy that may otherwise be used making trouble.[14] Yet Paul experienced employment as extra to program requirements, with the halfway house and the factory separate disciplinary systems pulling differently on his time. The institutional tensions materialized as personal tensions with Kevin and his employer, the power brokers on each side. He was grateful for an understanding boss, but resented being forced to talk openly about his criminal status anytime the halfway house impinged on work commitments. He said it was a constant "juggling act" that he was not sure how anyone could properly manage.

The personal conflicts had high stakes. Paul knew that with a long criminal record, his employment prospects were poor and felt lucky to have found a stable job. It was a shot at financial independence and escape from the halfway house. Threats to the job were threats to his freedom. Yet the job made it difficult to meet the demands of the program, where he lived as a parole condition. A major fallout with Kevin or failure to make it work there could mean reimprisonment.

In navigating these institutional arrangements, Paul skewed his time toward the factory. He celebrated paid employment and devalued the unpaid recovery work fostered by Bridge House. Whereas other residents used the language of "working a program" to legitimate time-consuming recovery activities, Paul emphasized instead the lack of financial returns, pointing out that "going to meetings don't pay the bills." He positioned residence at the house as a form of welfare dependence where people get stuck for "years on end." This justified his decision to prioritize factory labor and use the house as a short-term "stepping-stone" to better things.

Paul saw himself as fundamentally different from other residents, symbolized by his wage earning and their receipt of food stamps. For some context, Bridge House charged $75 weekly rent but, when residents could not afford this, allowed them to pay using debit cards provided by the government for people on low incomes to buy food. Kevin used the cards in grocery shopping for the house. Paul stated repeatedly that he used wages to pay rent, linking this to a core difference in character, as a "person like me," who was prepared to work hard and "didn't want to get by on food stamps."

Putting employment ahead of recovery involved institutional deception. At Bridge House, Paul sometimes did not attend the three mandatory twelve-step meetings each week—and falsely signed the card where the signatures of meeting chairs are used as evidence of attendance. By the time we interviewed at the apartment, he had stopped going to meetings altogether and was having Sarah sign the card to show his parole officer. These risky actions emerged from Paul's effort to manage competing demands on his time. Ultimately, he simply refused to participate in the meetings that are perhaps the most time-consuming part of recovery.

Paul continued to identify outwardly as "in recovery" even as he refused the associated practices. He justified this by arguing that it was paid work, not the twelve steps, keeping him clean and sober, with employment a form of "therapy" providing a deep sense of purpose and personal responsibility. Paul did not structure his autobiography as an awakening narrative splitting the past from the present, as twelve-step groups encourage, but told stories that centered on a stable core identity as a hard worker. He was the type of kid who dug "five-foot holes in the sandpit" and got a heavy-machinery license as a teenager. In his narrative, even drug dependency was a form of hard work that he later redirected to factory employment.

At Bridge House, outward acceptance of twelve-step philosophies was consistent with diverse underlying approaches. Notice how Paul adopted the catchphrase "life on life's terms" to narrate his experience but reinterpreted the meaning of the words. Officially, it encapsulates the belief that a person needs to deal with problems that come along without complaint or reverting to substance use. Paul used it instead to express the benefits of dedication to industrial labor.

Paul's creative use of twelve-step language helped in navigating competing institutional demands. Outwardly identifying with recovery kept parole and the halfway house off his back, while treating employment *as* recovery allowed him to use scarce time not in meetings but on the factory floor. For Paul, the path to reintegration lay in the labor market.

* * *

We lean on the hood of my Toyota Camry outside the apartment and smoke a cigarette. Paul is still shirtless on a warm evening. The sound of crickets fills the air and the last of the blue sky shines through trees lining the street. A Chevy Silverado pulls up next door with planks of wood on the roof and country music playing out the window.

The racial symbolism of the country music and tree-lined suburban street is palpable. Paul and I are both white. So are Sarah and her kids and the next-door neighbor. We are only a twenty-minute drive from Bridge House, but it feels like a different world. The program may have had a majority of white residents, but it was still not quite white,[15] marked by the symbolic coding of "criminals" and "former prisoners" as Black[16] and a location in an "urban" neighborhood where people speak Spanish on the sidewalk and bass-heavy Latin music booms from cars driving slowly down the main road.

Paul describes relief at getting away from the program. I hear it as racialized relief about leaving the colored space of an urban halfway house for suburban whiteness. This is amplified as he distances himself from other residents and singles out Tim Williams in the process: "Everybody in that house I kept at arm's length. Because they are all in there for some reason. And as much as I would love to because I want it done to me, to forgive and move on, some of those guys have deeper ulterior motives.

"Some say they wanna preach about what they went through for the rest of their lives. Yet they can't follow it on a day-to-day basis. Tim I have no respect for, none whatsoever. I'm not one to live on Social Security. I felt like an asshole even being on food stamps. That's not me. That's not how I was raised. That's not the work ethic. But other people, that's all they know."

I push back a little: "The thing is, some of these guys have pretty different lives, you know. Your parents owned businesses. Like Tim, he's basically never had a job, he's Black—"

Paul interrupts: "The fuckin' president's Black."

I start laughing. "This is a whole conversation we're gonna have very different views on."

He continues: "Like, women's rights: women have fuckin; more rights than we do now. I could go on about that too, but what it all boils down to—I listen to news talk radio, and it was like people that grow up— these young kids that are having kids that grow up in poverty. They're just creating more poverty and creating a worse life for the future. It's just an ongoing thing. Unless it changes at some point in one of their lives, it's not gonna change. That's all these guys know. Unless they strive to be better, that's the end of it."

"I mean, Tim works. He's out of the house every day. He's all over the place," I say.

Paul interrupts: "But see, again, you wanna help people, and you wanna tell people what *not* to do. I couldn't only go that far in life. If he wants to honestly do that for the rest of his life, he's only gonna get as high as to say, 'Don't do what I did.' That's gonna be his life."

I push back: "What alternatives are there, though? Tim is making a life out of recovery, and to me, it's a smart option for him. Really, what other opportunities are open? He's been in jail pretty much the last fifteen years on and off, he's never really had a job, he finished school in his early teens. You know, again, he's Black—"

Again Paul interrupts: "It's the same thing. He can meet that one person that gets him into an opportunity and gives him a chance. And he needs to run with that chance. And you may only get one. And if you fuck it up, you fuck it up. You may never get another one. Which is why with this opportunity, I'm doing everything I can. Because yeah, I came from means, I came from wealth, and I want that back. They never had that, so they turn to easy money and drugs."

* * *

Paul explained Tim's pursuit of recovery as a form of welfare dependency and failure to strive for anything better. He drew a sharp distinction between their respective work ethics. He evoked racist stereotypes that often pass for common sense about Black marginality in the United States: a culture of poverty in which some people are raised to accept welfare,[17] the election of Barack Obama showing that *they* could make it out if only *they* worked hard enough.[18]

Absent from the account is the pervasive labor-market discrimination facing Black job seekers like Tim.[19] One study famously found that when searching for employment, you have more chance of success having a criminal record than having Black skin—that is, white applicants with records do better than equally qualified Black applicants without them.[20] Further, Black applicants are penalized far more harshly than white applicants when both have convictions. Audit studies suggest that criminal records reduce the number of employer callbacks by around 30 percent for whites but 60 percent for Blacks.[21]

There were racial patterns in employment even over a small sample of Bridge House residents. Of the ten men who gained regular paid work while I lived there, all were white except one. The exception, Bill Morris, patched together an income working at the front desk of an old warehouse that had been converted into a cross-fit gym, his wages tied to commission for recruiting new members. Not that these patterns were talked about openly. Like most Americans, residents were usually color blind in their understandings and reluctant to acknowledge how individual fates are tied to racial advantage and disadvantage.[22]

When Paul explained his success in terms of work ethic—and the failure of others in terms of laziness and low aspirations—this was typical of a prevailing ideology of rugged individualism at the house. No doubt, he showed enviable grit and determination making it work under tough conditions. Nonetheless, his ability to reintegrate through the labor market needs to be understood in the context of advantages gained by whiteness. These include how he and his criminal record were perceived by employers, as well as his background experiences, like a history of skilled trade work beginning in family-owned businesses.

Most residents could not follow in Paul's footsteps even if they wanted to. His social advantages were coupled with physical strengths as a thirty-two-year-old in good health able to work long hours on the factory floor. Many residents experienced various forms of human and bodily frailty that limited their ability to think clearly, without pain, and bring energy to the daily rounds.[23] Their struggles to gain employment went beyond discrimination or criminal records, with physical vulnerability ruling out the manual occupations typically filled by men like them.

In contrast to the industrial labor market, the twelve steps welcomed Black and white, young and old, frail and physically healthy. Anyone could pursue a strategy of reintegration by addiction recovery.

Awakening

I sit on a park bench in downtown Clearview Crossing with Joe Badillo. We smoke home-rolled cigarettes in a shady spot under a tree, deliberately finding a place away from the procession of old friends who usually want to stop and chat in more crowded parts of the city common. Joe has been at Bridge House around fifteen months and pouring his time and energy into addiction recovery, attending a meeting of Narcotics Anonymous almost every day. During the summer, he often comes to this park after meetings to play cards and socialize. It is a great place to talk among the green grass and ambient noise: birds and car motors, sirens and the voices of people mingling together. And this particular day is a chance for Joe to take stock of progress made and articulate goals for the future.

"I no longer fantasize about my life," he declares. "I want the house, I want this and that—the only way for that to be possible was selling drugs. I don't want that no more. What I want is to be happy—normal life, maybe a little apartment for myself, going to the movies with my girlfriend, going out to dinner, going to parks.

"I don't need to buy sneakers, even though I like sneakers. I don't need drugs to achieve my goals today. Yeah, that's the word that I'm looking for: I no longer need the drug life, or that hustle life, to achieve the goals that are in my life today. Whereas before, the goals that I put in front of me were only achievable if I was out there hustling—and being a successful hustler at that, which in the end I wasn't no more.

"When I walk up and down or drive up and down Main Street, I see past that 'look at me, I'm selling drugs.' You might see the glamour, but I see the pain, because I know the pain. He might have nice clothes, nice chain, nice car, but I see their inside and say, 'Man, look at that fuckin' pain he's got to go through to get to where he's at.' He's not sleeping good at night. He's always looking behind his back. He's always worried about the cops coming. He's worried about he's gonna get robbed. I don't want that. So what, he's got a nice car—look at what he's got to go through to have that."

"Let me ask you this: You have a good mind-set, you're positive, you know—where do you think that comes from?"

"Listen, man, I was given another chance at this thing called life. Literally. Who am I to curse the morning, because I got to stretch for an hour to get out of bed, when there was a time when I didn't know if I was gonna get outta bed? That's where my positive attitude comes from. When you're told you never gonna walk again, even if it takes me an hour to walk somewhere, I'm walking. Who am I to curse the morning? Who am I to curse that I'm getting out of bed? How selfish can I be?

"I don't think you've ever seen me in a miserable day, man. I mean, I can't remember the last time I was miserable. My attitude's been the same since I got into Bridge House. It has. I'm very grateful. And I think that comes from the fuckin' experience that I went through and the hurdles I jumped over. Like I said, man, yo, if there's a day where I wake up and I'm mad because I got to stretch for an hour, shame on me, man. Ssshhaaammeee onnn mee, man."

"Did you always have a positive outlook?"

"When I was hustling, no. When I was out using, you don't. You curse the fuckin' morning. You curse waking up. You curse everything around you. That lifestyle is like being in the desert, and you see a mirage, and you get all excited. Then when you walk ten fuckin' miles, you get there, and there's nothing there.

"It's the same as being out there hustling, man. When you're far away from it, and you're looking at it, it looks so glamorous, so exciting. Then when you walk that ten miles, and you're in the hustle, and you look around, there's nothing there. You say, 'What the fuck?' It's all a fuckin' illusion, man, a mirage. Your eyes see something that's not there.

"That's the biggest trick of it all, man. We perceive this lifestyle as being glamorous and fuckin' exciting. 'Oooohh ahhhhhh. Man, I envy him. He's a drug dealer with all this money, all this fast money.' But you know what? When you're there, you've finally walked them ten miles to get into his shoes and you're finally in his shoes and you look around you, you look at your life, you say, 'What the fuck? What a trick that was. Who tricked me?' You got bamboozled. Not what it seems, bro.

"I'm content with my life today. It doesn't take much to make me happy today. A good seafood salad makes me happy today. *America's Got Talent* makes me happy today. Where before I needed all kinds of glamorous stuff, materialistic stuff in my life. Today's the opposite. I don't need much, man. I see this positive attitude following me for the rest of my life, man. As long as I keep it simple and I humble myself, yeah, man,

I'll always remain happy. Liam, there's nothing really—if I stay clean and sober, there's nothing that should make me miserable again. Nothing.

"I lived a lifetime of misery. That should last. All the misery I lived, that's enough for one person's lifetime and some. So there's not enough room in my life today for any misery. Are there gonna be bad days? Of course. Am I gonna be miserable again? I can't see it, man. Being miserable and having a bad day are two totally different things. Being miserable means that you are tired of even living. I don't think that will ever happen again—as long as I stay clean and sober."

"I want to ask you about what helps you do well but just to ask about what makes it hard first. Are there other things that are a struggle?" I ask.

"Well, if I don't get [public] housing. My income is gonna be a burden determining where I live: what kind of neighborhood, what kind of environment. If I don't get housing, I don't know where I'm gonna be. That's just the reality of the fact. Right now I don't worry about it, because I have a place like Bridge House, who tell me, 'Hey, listen. Don't worry. You don't have to leave right now.' But if they tell me to pack my stuff and leave tomorrow, I'm right back on Main Street, man, even with all this [clean] time behind me.

"Would I pick up? I don't know. Are the chances that I start hustling again against me? Absolutely. I don't want to find out if I'm strong enough to live on Gilmore Street [an area with a reputation for drug use]. I don't want to find out if I'm strong enough to live in that environment. Is that saying I'm not? No. I might be. But I don't want to shake the dice on it.

"My income makes it hard. If I don't get housing—a lot rides on housing, man, how my life plays out. Them two things play a big part in how my life turns out. Not saying that if they don't work, then it's gonna fuck up, but it's gonna make life a lot easier if I get these things.

"In the same token, I want to get back into work where I don't have to be dependent on this fixed income. I can't do no physical labor, but shit, there's nothing stopping me from getting my CADAC [certificate of alcohol and drug addiction counseling], going back to school and being a counselor, working in this field that I know, that I had all this experience in. That would make my income much better, where I don't need to worry about living on Gilmore Street. So that's another option I have working for me.

"I can see myself working in the field of recovery. I really want to get into the field of recovery for young adults. I see myself doing a lot of activist work, being more involved in the community. Because if I'm not a voice for people that can recover—and people do change—then they're just gonna have that concept that we're not worth fighting for, that we're always gonna be pieces of shit. We need people in them places. We have a couple, but we need more.

"I'm not gonna be rich working there. I'll probably just be able to pay the bills. But it's more than that. You get a lot more. Even when I go and speak at detoxes, I get a lot out of it. It's rewarding. And come on, let's be honest, man. Am I gonna be a school teacher? [*I laugh*]. Even if I go to school for it. Am I gonna be hired as a school teacher? Chances are nah, man. And who better to be a counselor than a person that went through the mud."

"Do you want to talk a little bit about your volunteer work around the place? What kind of things are you doing?"

"Two weeks ago, I went to state college and spoke with the youth group up there on the dangers of drug use and gangs. I go to DYS facilities, youth lockups, and talk about the dangers of gangs and drug use. I go around to different organizations that donate money to Bridge House talk about the importance of Bridge House. Because the Bridge House is the foundation of my recovery. I owe a lot to Bridge House. Absolutely. I am forever indebted to Bridge House. They gave me that chance and are still playing a big part of me continuing where I am. Because I've been there over year. They could've said, 'Pack your bags and go.' But that's not what their program is about. That's not what that house is about. And thank God for that.

"I go to the Justice Coalition, work on changing some laws, help changing some laws that are affecting convicts and ex-cons. Not every week but some weeks, I go on Main Street and pass out food to the homeless and to addicts.

"And what I'm learning is—the biggest thing I'm doing as far as giving back is remaining clean and sober and out of that lifestyle. Because other people I used to get high with are looking and saying, 'Wow, man, if he can do it, I can do it too.' Just sitting in the common today, people see me and are like, 'Wow, man, you're still clean?' I had a girl come up to me today and say, 'I just wanna give you a hug, man. If you can do it, anybody can.' Yeah, that's helpin' somebody. I think that's really the biggest contribution I can give back is staying positive and remaining clean and sober. It's giving other addicts that 'if he can, maybe I can.'"

* * *

Joe Badillo may have been living at a halfway house, hanging out in the same Clearview Crossing park he had spent countless summer days throughout his life, but he presented a narrative of fundamental change. In the twelve-step meetings that were central to his daily routines, he had learned a vocabulary for articulating this change and practiced weaving his autobiography into a story of reform.[24] As Jill McKorkel puts it, "recovery is a process of re-storying the self."[25] And Joe adopted the temporal structure of the classic twelve-step recovery script by splitting his autobiography into two distinct periods: the past and the present, before and today.[26] He used a series of oppositional metaphors to lump together the diverse events within each period and present them as homogeneous phases with diametric moral charges. Before was a time of materialism and fantasy, negativity and misery. Today was a time of humility and reality, positivity and happiness.

The imagery of getting "clean" linked the transition from past to present decisively to drug abstinence. But it was also much more than a shift in practices of drug consumption: Joe's account described a process of awakening to the truth—another key narrative device of the twelve steps[27]—developed through the metaphor of a mirage evaporating. He said that in the past, he believed he would get rich by hustling, chasing street wealth like a lost traveler chasing a desert illusion. This past was represented by "Main Street," the site of his hustling and the center of the Clearview Crossing drug economy. And Joe said that when he drove that same street today, he could see the false glamour of the men out there with sneakers and jewelry, for now he knew the truth of their pain and suffering. The mirage had evaporated.

Joe described Bridge House as the "foundation" of his recovery. This was not about any formal drug-treatment intervention but the housing provided by the program: Joe was still on the public-housing wait list and raised the possibility that he might never get it, and if he was forced to find a place to stay in the private sector on inadequate Social Security income, was anxious about the kind of drug-addled environments where rent would be affordable. This was the context in which Joe talked about Bridge House—and especially the policy of open time frames—as effectively preventing his homelessness. As Joe put it, "If they tell me to pack my stuff and leave tomorrow, I'm right back on Main Street, man, even with all this [clean] time behind me."

It was a two-way relationship: as Bridge House provided support to Joe, in turn, Joe's story of personal success promoted the success of the Bridge House program. He was increasingly being invited to perform his awakening narrative in public—entering detoxes and youth justice facilities, for example, as a role model for others to emulate. And one specific audience he mentioned was "organizations that donate to Bridge House." An important part of the story he told in these settings was gratitude for the support being provided by Bridge House—as it was that day with me in the park—and this contributed to the program's perpetual work of attracting the funding needed to make it a relatively comfortable place to live.

Unlike Tim Williams and Paul Barry, who presented quite differ- ent narratives of recovery in public and in their conversations with me, Joe very consistently talked about recovery as a process of fundamen- tal change and awakening to the truth. And despite the account of a sharp break from the past obscuring important lines of continuity— including his ongoing carceral control—it was very compelling. He *did* seem to have changed dramatically, and this *did* seem crucially linked to his staunch commitment to drug abstinence. The Joe I got to know in those days was thoughtful and calm—quite different from the ruthless and violent drug dealer he talked about being historically. And when he presented his awakening narrative, the contrast between the present and this "miserable" past of chaotic drug use was backed by his visible physical disability. Walking with a cane and a limp was a marker of au- thenticity supporting his spoken account of the dangers of addiction and, by extension, the promise that recovery could enable triumph over enormous obstacles.[28]

Joe talked about recovery not only as a process of personal change but as a potential field of employment. Large-scale studies of job seeking among people leaving prison suggest that recovery and social services more broadly are a marginal source of paid work—certainly compared to industries like manufacturing and food services.[29] But in the institutions of reentry governance, these mobility pathways become especially visible,[30] as programs run informal apprenticeship systems grooming the next generation of staff by linking the promise of recovery to the potential for paid employment.[31] And Joe could see a clear example right inside Bridge House: Kevin Smith had turned his success as a resident into long-term work as operations manager at the program.

The contrast between Joe's narrative of fundamental change and his continued structural marginality points to important contradictions in recovery as a change project. For one, recovery is a never-ending process. The twelve steps teach that an addict will *always* be an addict, and recovery does not mean becoming normal but learning to live with dysfunction as peacefully as possible.[32] A former prisoner successfully embodies recovery when they admit their deficiencies and submit to being a lifelong work in progress.[33] And even in the relatively rare cases in which people turn a "clean" identity into upward mobility, becoming counselors or program staff, their employment ties them to the circuits of drug dependency that they have personally left behind.[34]

Still, Joe's narrative of recovery at some level worked as he navigated an institution of carceral care—satisfying the punitive edge of Bridge House while securing access to the assistance it provided. And there was good reason that he targeted recovery for employment given his long criminal record. As he put it, "Let's be honest, man. Am I gonna be a school teacher?" But for the time being, Joe remained in a precarious position. It was a harsh environment, even for those who are publicly celebrated as success stories of it, and his progress hung on a knife edge. Simple choices that large numbers of Americans make every day—drinking alcohol or smoking marijuana, for example—would be considered "relapse" and involve a sudden withdrawal of his most basic social supports, beginning with housing. Never mind that medical practitioners treat relapse as a normal part of addiction. In this world of forced abstinence and the binary division of "clean" and "dirty," it would mean losing everything.

6

The Drug Crisis Outside the Door

Ross Whitaker bursts into my bedroom at Bridge House.

"Yo, I need your help, man. My son's mother just called. He got in a fight, and he's all fucked up. She wants me to go down there. Can you give me a ride?"

We speed through dark city streets while Bill Morris, another resident at the house, tries to get details about what to expect. Ross talks in circles about his son being drunk and having a fight with someone who owed him money. We park under the orange glow of a streetlamp, and the car goes quiet. Ross's son, Keith, appears from the darkness partially supported by his mother, Chanelle, one hand on a brick wall topped with barbed wire. They bundle into the backseat, and the smell of booze wafts through the car.

"What you doin', man? Why you even out here?" Ross asks angrily.

"I been out here. I been in the street," Keith responds, slurring.

"What you mean, in the street?"

"Come on—I been out here for like the last year."

The three disappear inside Chanelle's apartment while Bill and I smoke cigarettes on the street, and when Ross returns, he explains the situation. Apparently, Keith had been dealing heroin, and when a fight broke out and brought police to the scene, he swallowed a fistful of small bags to avoid detection. Some had come up with fingers down the throat, but others remained in his stomach; and because Keith was a heroin seller—not a user with established heroin tolerance—any leak could be deadly. They were now frantically trying to remove the bags.

"I just poured like half a bottle of shampoo down his throat," says Ross.

I offer to drive them to the hospital, but Ross worries that it could lead to police involvement and "catching a case." Standing on the sidewalk, Ross and Bill debate the likely consequences of a hospital visit, the argument hinging on their different interpretations of the legal term "intent to distribute." Ross argues that if they pump Keith's stomach and find the individually wrapped bags, the drugs would be used as proof of intent and lead to criminal charges. Bill says that Keith only needs to claim that swallowing the drugs was part of a suicide attempt to avoid prosecution. In the back-and-forth, both men appeal to their personal histories facing similar charges as evidence of their expertise.

"I been arrested for distribution right on this street!" Ross exclaims.

Bill seems relieved to learn that the heroin is double wrapped in balloons—a system designed for safety in case of swallowing—and concedes that maybe they can avoid the hospital. But when Ross heads back inside the apartment, he dismisses the whole makeshift response as "jail shit" and says that if a rich person's kid had heroin in their stomach, they would have already been to the hospital. He shakes his head talking about the madness of selling heroin when media have been reporting a spike in overdose deaths and estimates that Keith, working for someone else, would have only made about thirty dollars selling the bags that are now in his stomach. The next time Ross returns, Chanelle comes out too, and they ask for a ride to CVS to buy a magnesium laxative.

From the backseat of the car, Chanelle calmly announces that she is reaching a limit: "I'm about to have a nervous breakdown," she says. "If this don't work, I'm calling an ambulance. I don't care about no charge. He can hate me later, but I'm not having my son die over this."

It is almost midnight back at Chanelle's apartment. Ross is anxious about the Bridge House curfew despite having talked to Kevin Smith on the phone and getting clearance to leave. I was not told the details of the negotiation but sensed that I was somehow involved, my presence providing some kind of reassurance that he would return without trouble. Ross is eager to get back to the house anyway, worried a broken curfew will bring unwanted attention, with Kevin looking into what happened and talking about it with others. He waits awhile for the laxative to take effect but emerges before learning if the plan has worked, saying goodbyes standing in the doorway:

"Call me, all right. Keep drinking water, man."

We make the short drive back to Bridge House.

* * *

The Bridge House curfew separated Ross Whitaker not only from the "drug crisis" in some abstract sense but from his family in a moment of turmoil when he was desperately needed. Ross might have spent the night with his son, comforting Keith in the morning and providing guidance based on lessons learned from his own experience of similarly chaotic situations. He had moved into Bridge House outside any criminal justice sanction or requirement of community corrections, an attempt to access support for his recovery and self-improvement goals, and perhaps that night would have been an opportunity to model the potential for positive change with Keith. Instead, he left the family and rushed back to the program—leaving Chanelle to deal with the situation on her own.

The family's response to the whole ordeal was saturated with carceral power. Ross's assessment of the situation stemmed from his own history of criminalization: including his evaluation of legal terms and norms and how he imagined the consequences for Keith if the heroin were discovered. He claimed to have been arrested for drug distribution on the very same street. And as Ross and Chanelle made the gut-wrenching decision to avoid the hospital even under life-threatening circumstances, instead improvising with shampoo and laxatives, Ross was also weighing the demands of the halfway house in which he lived. The confinement was subtle, but it was confinement nonetheless. Even after Ross was able to get the curfew temporarily waived, he still feared that staying away too long would stoke suspicions and lead to stigmatizing revelations of his drug-related family problems. The curfew remained a powerful control despite being explicitly relaxed.

Ross lived under a regime of coercive drug abstinence that aimed to create a community based on idealized standards of restraint and personal responsibility that few people meet in the wider society. But the policing of boundaries around this community—through curfews, for example, and evictions for failed drug tests—only partially severed his relationships to the broader communities of which he was also a member. These other communities included his own family and often lacked the kind of stable housing and social support that fostered drug abstinence inside the program. Keith, who I learned later was himself the father of a six-week-old baby, was drawn into the drug economy not by personal use but by what Bill estimated were incredibly meager financial incentives, and by extension, Ross also remained intimately connected to the drug crisis.

It was a deeply liminal social position. Stone-cold sober, Ross watched his son flirt with death over a handful of heroin-filled balloons.

* * *

The intimate connections between Bridge House residents and the drug crisis unfolding in Clearview Crossing were rooted in the broader socio-geography of the American halfway house. Consider the political and economic forces shaping program placements around the country, with affluent white communities blocking the location of halfway houses within their borders[1]—by influencing policy decisions over zoning and state subsidies, for example—while entrepreneurs in postindustrial neighborhoods convert abandoned buildings into burgeoning networks of recovery homes.[2] In the field of prisoner reentry, the organizations tasked with meeting the needs of former prisoners are overwhelmingly concentrated in the same neighborhoods that prisoners come from.[3] These communities are beset by structural problems of economic abandonment and public-sector breakdown—and are ground zero in the drug crisis.[4] The routine siting of halfway houses in close proximity to the most destructive patterns of street-level drug dependency is a central contradiction of the institution.

Program managers confronting these challenges routinely respond by reasserting separation and boundaries and expanding the use of carceral technologies. Indeed, many halfway houses strictly control their borders with security measures like chain-link perimeter fencing, video cameras, electronically operated doors, and uniformed guards at the entrance.[5] Yet there are trade-offs involved: these measures transform the social and built environment in ways that undermine the ability of halfway houses to operate as meaningful alternatives to prison by making the programs themselves more like prison. The very idea of an institution halfway between inside and outside blurs the demarcation between prison and program,[6] and in practice, many US halfway houses already look more like minimum-security prisons than houses.[7] Where do you draw the line between an "open" prison with liberal provisions for work release and furlough and a "closed" halfway house relying on high-security border maintenance? And what specific carceral practices might make a halfway house for all intents and purposes a prison?

Pat Townsend had a vision of Bridge House as a "supportive community" with an approach starkly opposed to the "punitive mind-set" of the criminal justice system more broadly. In part, this involved constructing the physical space to resemble a family home and avoiding some of the more invasive practices common in contemporary reentry programs. There was no secure perimeter or marked institutional entrance, and like most other homes on the residential street on which it was located, there was not even a fence separating the property from the sidewalk outside. And Pat's ability to generate private donations provided a degree of autonomy to resist pressure to introduce more heavy-handed security in exchange for state funding. For example, he said that they refused to bid for a contract with the Massachusetts Probation Service, despite being encouraged to do so, because it would have required staff to search residents entering Bridge House and check that the men were in bed several times a night. For Pat, these practices expressed "a mind-set of jail that doesn't fit" what Bridge House does.

Pat may have spurned the idea of staff monitoring whether residents were in their beds overnight, but the Bridge House curfew still made it mandatory, it was just monitored more informally. The program was small enough that anyone regularly leaving at night would soon be discovered—especially if they did not return before morning—even without a staff member on site doing scheduled checks. At one level, the system was simply a subtler form of spatial confinement that involved residents in the surveillance of each other. But it is not difficult to see why Pat might view the approach as more conducive to the Bridge House philosophy than staff patrolling the hallways would be. And his distinction between bed checks and the curfew emerged from an uneasy combination of critique and use of carceral power.

The punitive edge of Bridge House operations centered on enforcing abstinence through a system of drug testing and eviction—with the power of these practices closely linked to the precarious legal status of residents and potential for further criminal punishment. Pat justified the approach not as opposed to his vision of the program but as a necessary part of it. As he once put it, "If somebody is using drugs and alcohol, it can pollute the whole community. [So] in order to preserve the community, you need to sometimes put your foot down in regards to drugs and alcohol." It was a way of articulating carceral practices that resolved core tensions of halfway house governance: against the backdrop of a drug crisis swirling in the surrounding streets, Pat presented asserting control as a core component of providing care in a supportive community.

As Pat decided where to draw the line in the appropriate intensity of carceral control at Bridge House, he rejected resident searches and bed checks but adopted curfews and drug testing. The ambiguity in these choices points to the practical challenges of constructing a halfway house as a meaningful alternative to mass incarceration and the war on drugs.

* * *

The men gather on the Bridge House porch for the customary after-dinner cigarette. A conversation starts about three people dying of overdoses from the same batch of heroin in an apartment around two miles from the house. Joe Badillo, Ross Whitaker, and Kevin Smith exchange notes and try to figure out the names of the dead. They check their phones for Facebook posts appearing as they talk. As I write up fieldnotes later that night, an online article is posted by the city newspaper—"Suspected Drug Deaths Part of a Surge: 22 Overdoses in Less than a Week." But the news breaks first on the porch.

I wake in the morning to find a newspaper report describing three more overdose deaths—bringing the total to eight in five days. When I get to the kitchen for breakfast, Joe is already talking about the news on the phone. It is the first thing he says to me after hanging up. One of the dead is a friend, Jerome, a regular at Ray of Hope, the addiction-recovery center where he volunteers. Joe shows me photos on his phone. I have seen Jerome around plenty of times.

On day three of the overdose drama, CBS News shows up at Ray of Hope with cameras. Tim Williams also volunteers there and gets interviewed. He is excited by the shot at celebrity, calling friends and family and telling anyone who will listen that he is about to be on television. At the Bridge House dinner, Kevin tells the volunteers that we do not usually have TV, but tonight will be an exception because of Tim's appearance. By six o'clock, we are huddled around the evening news in anticipation. Tim leans forward with elbows on knees, Joe and Ross record on their phones, the volunteers are on chairs with slim television angles by the lounge entrance. The anchorman opens the story announcing two more deaths, bringing the total to ten in six days, and says, "Those who knew the victims of the epidemic are skeptical things will change soon."

Tim is shown at a computer on reception. The room cheers, and he claps with excitement. Ross and his girlfriend, Sarah, also make appearances. But Tim's interview gets cut, and he has no speaking part. Residents turn on him in an instant and, as the gathering spills outside to the porch, berate him relentlessly with mock sympathy.

"I would call them if I was you—tell 'em, 'Unless you use my part, we boycotting. We ain't watching Channel 5 no more.'"

"Damn, Tim, I'm mad about that. I might have to write to them."

"I should call her up and tell her, 'Yo, you took this man's shine away, bro.'"

"We might have to call up Channel 5 and put in complaints, man. What you think? We get enough of us maybe they'll reair it."

"You gotta tell her shit that's relevant, Tim. Were you saying shit that's relevant? Or was you like, 'Yo, we got a fashion show coming up. I'm gonna be security. Then over here we're havin' a basketball tournament.'"

Ross interrupts and takes center stage.

"People droppin', man. That's crazy," he says. "I seen Jayme on Main Street like this. I'm at Mike's Liquor waitin' across the street, and she's like this." He raises both arms straight up in the air and arches back from the hips, top half of the body curved until eyes look out backward, upside down. "I said, 'What the fuck is she on, man?' Dope, man, that dope."

The men laugh loudly. Steve jumps in with his own imitation of the "dope lean," bending at the knees, dropping his head loose at the neck, and waving back and forth.

"How do they not fall over, man?!"

It is classic porch conversation: loud and boisterous, full of humorous insults and laughter at the expense of others. Yet today there is more serious subtext. Even as the men continue to laugh and joke and circle back to hassling Tim several times, they exchange important information about the overdoses.

Everyone wants to know who died. Kevin says that "names got surfaced quick" in the early deaths. But the identities of the two most recent have not been announced. Residents try to put pieces together. They cannot work out specific people and wonder if they are men or women. As Ross puts it, "They [officials] not tryna say no names—but we are."

They talk about the location of the overdoses. One body was found in high-rise apartments behind the Registry of Motor Vehicles, one off Astle Street next to the park, another pulled from an apartment on Castle Street—the same road as Ray of Hope—not long after CBS finished interviewing. There may be others in the wider county. But the men agree that the heroin was almost certainly sold in the city.

The most important information is the nature and potency of the source drugs. The men discuss whether it is more likely to be an especially strong batch of heroin or simply cut with fentanyl, a powerful opiate pain medication. Joe says that they will not know until the autopsy reports come back, and the lab work might take months, but it is probably cut with something. The alternative would be finding the dealer who sold the drugs. Tim says that someone at Ray of Hope claimed to know the identity and was going to tell police.

It would be easy to miss the specialist knowledge being circulated. The facts of the case are buried in busting balls, packaged as humorous anecdotes or squeezed between the insults being hurled around. Information flowed into Bridge House through Facebook posts and phone conversations, traveling through social networks that crisscrossed recovery and the neighborhood street scene. The men are called on by media because they are experts in the social circles where people are dying.

The conversation fades and the porch clears. Tim suggests an evening stroll to stretch legs, maybe to shake off the ribbing he just received. Down the small road from the house and out onto Main Street—almost immediately into drama. Tim calls out to a woman on the other side of the street, who weeps as she walks.

"Don't do that," I say, shaking my head, not wanting to get involved.

"That's Shane's sister Jane," Tim says dismissively.

"You know, Shane that used to live at the house. Their mother's dying. I wanna make sure she's okay."

Jane chokes back tears, mascara running, saying she "relapsed" and is out here "walking the street." I suppress my alarm when she says a doctor gave her a "whole bunch" of Klonopins, a powerful sedative with a notorious reputation for causing blackouts and memory loss.

I sit on a concrete ledge by the footpath and smoke a cigarette.

"You don't have to get high," Tim says. "There's people who wanna help you."

"You don't understand. You have no idea how I feel right now. I just wanna die."

Tim reminds her about kids at home and pushes her to get help. Jane replies with beaten words and no eye contact: "I just wanna die," she says again.

From the concrete ledge, she twice shouts out to men driving past to pull over.

Tim gets increasingly frustrated, waving arms and shouting: "Yo, ten people died since last Sunday!"

"I know I can't believe Jerome died," the woman says softly.

"That should make you not wanna get high!"

Losing the argument, Tim steps to one side and calls the staff member at Ray of Hope to ask for detox phone numbers. As he talks, Jane calls out to a white van driving past: "Hey, Kevin, pull over!"

She heads off into the night.

* * *

Back on the Bridge House porch, darkness is descending. Nick Jones talks out the window of a blue Nissan parked in the driveway. Tone somber and pausing often, he tells Joe about his girlfriend overdosing last night.

"Where's she at now?" asks Joe from the porch.

"I think in the loopy land. I'm not sure."

"What, back out there?"

"I dunno. I didn't call her today. I don't wanna talk to her."

He pauses and goes quiet, then waves a hand over the backseat.

"Right here in the car last night, blue."

Nick believes that the man who sold to his girlfriend is the source of the heroin behind the overdose deaths being publicly reported: "Ricky, Puerto Rican Ricky, mechanic Ricky."

Joe says that the woman is a "lightweight," so it could have been a different batch from the rest.

Nick is back on the porch the next night, and in the meantime, media have reported the arrest of Ricky the mechanic. Joe believes it will be a long sentence, maybe even manslaughter, and says if it were his dope, he would have flushed it down the toilet and left the city the moment deaths were reported. Nick and Joe tell heroin stories: memorable busts and kilo prices, Dominican control of the trade.

Nick leans over the porch handrail to show photos of his girlfriend's overdose, first to Joe and then to me: a picture of her unconscious with eyes closed in the dark backseat of the car, another of her being rushed down a hospital hallway in a stretcher surrounded by white and light-blue coats. The car engine runs quietly in the background while a song by Drake floats out the window just loud enough to hear the words.

Then there is a more theatrical retelling. The very car where the overdose took place is parked behind Nick, providing a prop for a story illustrated with character voices and waving arms. He describes pulling up outside the hospital and swings open the back door, calling out, "Soomebbbooodddy heellp herrrr!" He describes the hospital staff swarming around her unconscious body and stands in the very position where they stood in relation to the car.

Sitting with Joe on the porch—halfway out the halfway house—we watch the dramatic reenactment of the drug crisis.

* * *

My fieldwork at Bridge House took place in the wake of intertwined surges in legal and illegal opiate use,[8] creating what the Center for Disease Control and Prevention has called the "worst drug overdose epidemic in [US] history."[9] In 2016, around sixty thousand Americans died of drug overdoses, substantially more than the number killed by either motor-vehicle accidents or gun violence, and nationwide, drug overdose is the leading cause of death for people under fifty.[10] Steep rises in overdose mortality emerged in three reinforcing waves centered on different kinds of opiates.[11] First came the rapid increase in deaths from prescription opiates like OxyContin from the 1990s, then the escalation in heroin mortality from 2010, and finally from around 2013, a wave of overdoses related to high-potency synthetic opiates like fentanyl—which is widely used as pain relief in palliative care.

This is the context in which Bridge House residents speculated that the wave of overdose deaths was probably caused by a batch of heroin mixed with fentanyl. The assumption was common sense given the close linkages between local drug markets and the corporate mass production of opiate pain medication, which in this case involved dealers potentially using fentanyl as an additive to increase the potency of powdered heroin.[12] Clearview Crossing was awash with opiate pain medications of different kinds: in the six years leading up to the beginning of my fieldwork, four CVS and Walgreens pharmacies within a three-mile radius of the program distributed a combined 16.7 million pills of oxycodone and hydrocodone.[13] And many of the men had personal experience of the overlap between heroin markets and legal and illegal markets in prescription opiates.

Looming in the background were large-scale transformations in US drug policy and production. Consider the recent history of the most popular brand of oxycodone: OxyContin. After the Federal Drug Administration approved the painkiller as "minimally addictive" in 1996, Purdue Pharmaceuticals marketed the drug on the basis of inflated claims that because the oxycodone was released slowly over many hours—the "contin" suffix comes from "continuous"—it did not produce the steep highs and lows that create cravings and lead to addiction.[14] Purdue spent $200 million in a single year marketing OxyContin,[15] and explosive revenue growth continued even after several executives were convicted of criminal misbranding.[16] Annual sales of OxyContin began at $48 million in 1996, increased more than twenty times to $1.1 billion by 2000, and tripled again to $3.1 billion by 2010.[17]

Elaborate synergies emerged between heroin markets and rapidly expanding legal and illegal prescription opiate markets. In the 1990s, an influx of Colombian-produced heroin to the United States and later of heroin from Mexico produced a glut in US supply and a fall in prices.[18] Traffickers aggressively expanded into new US territories in search of customers—some deliberately targeting areas where high rates of prescription opiate use created ready-made demand.[19] Retailers that pioneered the spread of black-tar heroin from the West of the United States to the East avoided traditional markets, like Philadelphia and New York, and fanned out instead to smaller towns and cities to reach customers who were newly dependent on OxyContin.[20] More recent efforts to regulate the illicit trade in pharmaceutical opiates, like the release of an Abuse Deterrent Formulation of OxyContin in 2010, which makes it harder to crush or dissolve pills for injection, have tended to simply increase the number of users switching to heroin.[21]

Popular representations of the drug crisis have focused on the rise of opiate dependency among middle-class whites,[22] and yet the impact has been most severe in pockets of chronic marginalization where opiate producers have made record profits off psychological distress and physical pain rooted in social dislocation.[23] In the area surrounding Bridge House, for example, there were more than thirteen times as many opioid-related hospital discharges in 2015 as in the affluent suburb of the university where I was based during the research—despite these zip codes having similar populations (20,800 and 22,300).[24] And in Clearview Crossing, drug dependency was intertwined with poverty and homelessness and was a very visible feature of neighborhood public space.

Analytically, the drug crisis is best understood as a symptom of deeper dynamics of social marginality and alienation. But at Bridge House, it appeared as a quite concrete feature of the daily rounds, with residents confronting the human consequences anytime they stepped out the door, where emaciated sex workers walked the streets and heroin users nodded sleepily on concrete stoops. Many of the men had friends and family among the dead—or had even come close to death themselves. It was personal when overdoses swept through Clearview Crossing.

* * *

For Joe Badillo, Clearview Crossing was much more than a "criminogenic neighborhood"[25] or "dumping ground,"[26] as these areas are sometimes described in the literature on halfway house placement. It was also home. And Joe's thick social networks in the neighborhood not only fostered ongoing connection to the drug crisis but were an invaluable source of support. He may never have gone to Bridge House in the first place if it were located in an affluent suburb, and he almost certainly would not have stayed: the access to friends and family was among the biggest draws of the program.

Bridge House was most obviously designed to reintegrate residents to the social mainstream, but day in and day out, the time Joe spent cultivating relationships was concentrated in a neighborhood recovery scene inhabited mostly by other people like him. Not only did he live at a halfway house, but the program mandated that he regularly attend twelve-step meetings, gatherings of men and women who also had histories of drug and alcohol dependency. And in the recovery scene, reintegration for Joe often looked less like gaining access to the components of full citizenship—as the process has been defined in the literature[27]—than more literally *re*integrating to the social relationships he already occupied before arriving at Bridge House.

Joe spent many years engaged in street-level drug markets run not through abstract bureaucratic processes but through constant face-to-face interaction. I came to think of him as a bit like a small-town grocer who knows the names and faces of everyone in the neighborhood—the countless microinteractions of market exchange making him a familiar community figure. The men he grew up with tattooed shared images on their bodies and risked their lives together, and at middle age, those who survived called each other "brothers." At Bridge House, the challenge for Joe was how to leverage these relationships for support at a time of desperate need.

The wider Clearview Crossing recovery scene provided the institutional forum. Lots of people Joe knew were looking for a way out—and they came together in twelve-step meetings to plan escape from the drug crisis. In the daily rounds of "getting clean," his social circle did not change a huge amount, and the people around him were not only similar in social profile and demographics but oftentimes the very same individuals from his past. It was a change project less about mobility than redefining a static social position and converting relationships that were once mobilized in the drug economy into networks of mutual support for addiction recovery.

I want to develop the liminality of Joe's residence at Bridge House by locating him in the key sites of his involvement with the neighborhood recovery scene, like Ray of Hope recovery center and the noontime meeting of Narcotics Anonymous. But let us start where it all began.

* * *

Walking down the hill from Bridge House, along the cracked and broken sidewalk and past the triple-decker homes rented by the room, taking a right onto Main Street and heading toward the city, you only need to walk half a mile from the corner to reach where Joe Badillo grew up: Avon Street.

Joe leads a guided tour in my car, showing me the house where he was brought back from the hospital as a baby and then the public housing the family moved to down the road. He talks about the history of the buildings on the street—some that were abandoned or empty lots, others that had been rehabbed or replaced. We take a photo on the corner of Avon and Main.

It is a hot summer day, and Joe wears a white tank top and blue jeans. He poses under the Avon Street sign, bushy grass growing from sidewalk cracks and white paint haphazardly covering graffiti on the wall behind him. Joe tucks his thumb and index finger into his palm, fans out the other three fingers, and presses them against his chest in a gang sign. With his body twisted at an angle, his left bicep is almost front on, showing a jailhouse tattoo of the words "Avon St" scrawled in thick block lettering.

"Basically this thing on my arm is a warning, 'Don't fuck with me,'" Joe says, as we continue the tour back in the car. "It can also go against me, but the chances of someone saying, 'There he goes. Let's fuck him up,' was slimmer than them saying, 'He's Avon. Don't fuck with him.' Even if I was in the wrong neighborhood or approached by a couple of guys, and they looked at my arm and seen that I'm Avon, chances are they'll let me walk on through.

"I think 90 percent of us have the tattoo somewhere. Even if it's Adidas, Adidas sneakers—because that was our thing: we were known for wearing Adidas. When we throw up the three, we are throwing up the three stripes. Either we have a tattoo of Adidas, a hand going like [*Joe demonstrates making the Adidas stripes with three fingers*], AP in it [Avon posse], JKP, which is 'junior Avon posse,' MKP, which is 'miniature Avon posse.'"

Joe stops to point out a passerby: "There goes my cousin Kevin. His brother was murdered," he says nonchalantly.

"Is a lot of reason for Avon Street existing about protection?" I ask.

"Nah, man, we was a bunch of kids that hung out and started trouble, then when we started selling drugs—I mean, this little street from here to the top of Main Street, both sides, would be loaded with cars of people trying to buy drugs, man. I mean, this thing was twenty-four hours a day. Tens and tens and hundreds of thousands of dollars coming through here every fuckin' month, man. Look how big this street is, [and] it's right off Main Street.

"So cops came down, and we caused a lot of trouble for cops. They started calling us the 'Avon Posse,' so we ran with that. We didn't say, 'All right, guys, let's get together. We the Avon Street Posse.' We would have never thought of nothing like that. The cops named us. We would go to a party, and there would be a big fight and somebody got stabbed. Who did it? They would say, 'Them Avon boys.' The next thing you know in the newspaper, 'Avon Posse involved in stabbing,' 'Avon Street involved in shootout,' 'Avon Posse member gets stabbed,' 'Avon Posse member arrested for cocaine.' So when they did that, we made these hats that said, 'AP.' Money-green hats. We just ran with it."

As Joe tells the story, the formation of "Avon Street Posse" appears as a classic case of labeling theory.[28] It was less about coming together and consciously choosing to form a gang than developing relationships organically through shared residence and involvement in the drug trade. It was the police who called them the Avon Street Posse, which became a self-fulfilling prophecy, as they internalized and advertised that marker. They developed a set of symbols to communicate their allegiances and turned their stigmatized location into a badge of pride.

Joe and the men he grew up with used these symbols to communicate their control of a territory.[29] The name of their gang was also the name of the particular street they claimed as their own. And the use of consumerist signs—money-green hats, Adidas stripes—points to the economic basis of these claims. Knowledge of these symbols became a prerequisite to gaining an economic stake in a lucrative drug market. When Joe tattooed "Avon St" on his body, it was not only a statement of belonging in this community but part of a collective effort to protect a financial resource.

Joe says that when the war on drugs came to Clearview Crossing, police cracked down on Avon Street, and they were forced to move operations. The next focal point became a housing project around a mile away. We continue the tour by driving there.

"What up, Kee!" Joe calls out the window to a passerby.

Joe explains that Kee "came up underneath" him. And Joe uses him as an example of how a younger generation of dealers learned from their mistakes, in particular, about the dangers of smoking crack cocaine. He says that while he never injected heroin, because he had seen the damage it did to people older than he, he was part of the first wave of crack users decimated by the drug. Kee watched and learned, Joe says, choosing not to smoke crack and becoming very successful.

As we do a slow loop of the projects and pass Keke again, Joe stops midsentence: "You can get up outta here before—I don't want Keke thinking I'm riding around with a fuckin' . . ."

"The cops," I say, laughing.

"Or he think I probably fuckin' relapsed, and I'm geekin' riding around in a circle. I'll probably get phone calls like, 'Joe, are you all right?'"

We make the short drive back to Bridge House, passing slowly through the webs of social relations and symbolic meanings of a past that Joe is desperate to overcome—but that remain draped over the territories of Clearview Crossing.

* * *

The term "Main Street," a metaphor for middle America in the popular imagination, had more nefarious connotations at Bridge House. If a resident said they were "out on Main Street," it passed as a commonsense reference to engaging in drug use and street crime. The men gave the street names like the "dirty boulevard" and the "combat zone." And these associations had practical consequences: simply being seen on Main Street invited suspicion.

Walking from Avon Street away from Bridge House and into the city, traveling around three-quarters of a mile along Main, you arrived at a central hub of the street-level drug economy in the neighborhood. There was a New York chicken spot, a discount clothing store, a usually empty parking lot—and an open-air drug market often operating on full public display.

Joe Badillo asks if I want to join him in handing out food in this spot. The charity event takes over the whole area: eight white gazebos on one side of the footpath, a big truck with an US Navy sticker on the road out front, a line forming to the table where people collect meals. We sit on folding chairs on the sidewalk at the edge of a parking lot. Joe points to a dirty corner backing onto a concrete wall.

"That's where I used to stand all day," he says, "bangin' sales."

It is a steady stream of Nike sneakers, tattoos on necks and forearms, faces with scars and deep lines. The women's clothes are tight and the men's loose. A man rushes past half a dozen times, bringing people from point A to point B. A woman makes a purchase with two kids in hand. Everyone seems disgruntled. Colleen Milford, a street-level sex worker and old friend of Joe's, stops long enough to say that yesterday she stabbed her "sugar daddy" in a car when he refused to give her any money.

"He pours money into the machines at Foxwoods," she says, "but don't wanna give it up for me? I don't think so."

Colleen asks Joe if he likes recovery.

"I love it," he replies in an instant. "That waking up dope sick is misery. When I compare recovery to being out here, yo, those two things don't even compare."

Joe does not help set up the event or distribute food. Instead, he sits for two hours in a chair on the sidewalk under beating sun, chatting with people like Colleen. He is on first-name basis with the passersby. This is his world. The event is run by a friend of Joe's, Carlos Gonzalez, a reformed convict and evangelical Christian. Carlos delivers a sermon by microphone walking back and forth on the sidewalk. There is symbolism in the location: a charity drive taking over a hub of the street-level drug scene, saving souls and saving lives.

Joe's presence is symbolic too. From a folding chair a few feet from where he stood hustling and selling drugs, he announces to the community that he is now in recovery from addiction. And he invites others to join him.

* * *

Joe Badillo's favorite meeting of Narcotics Anonymous is held in a Lutheran church basement around 150 meters from the Main Street charity event. The men at Bridge House call it "the noontime." Joe goes most days, and the first time I join him, residents Matt Carmine and Peter Tennant are also in attendance. I sit with Matt in a folding chair against the wall. Exposed pipes cross and clutter the low ceiling. The air is thick with heat and sweat forms on my forehead.

The "chair" of the meeting, Keith Richards, addresses the gathering in front of a painting of Jesus on the cross. He opens with a personal introduction that locates him as a fellow participant in the program—"my name's Keith, and I'm an addict"—and recites the "serenity prayer" that opens many twelve-step meetings: "Please, God, grant me the serenity to accept the things I cannot change, the courage to change the things

I can, and the wisdom to know the difference." Matt has the prayer engraved on a silver ring on his finger.

I sit next to a young man named James with a shaved head and a friendship bracelet engraved with the phrase "Fight the Addiction." James sobs quietly through the early part of the meeting, tissue gripped in one hand, and begins to cry as Keith begins to call people forward to collect medallions marking milestones in the accumulation of "clean time." James is the only person to collect a medallion for twenty-four hours "clean." Matt leans over to say how embarrassing it is to reveal such recent drug use. On James's slow walk to the front, another man rises from a chair and hugs him for around thirty seconds. Another five people also stand and hug on him on the walk back.

The ritual awarding of medallions helps construct the boundary between "clean" and "dirty" as common sense in these meetings—despite the categories being deeply ambiguous. Nowhere does Narcotics Anonymous name which drugs a person needs to quit to "get clean," and in a world of ever-proliferating chemical substances, creating such a list would be virtually impossible. The most direct references to abstinence in official literature state that members must avoid "any mood-changing, mind-altering substance."[30] Yet this prohibition is so broad that it seems to include food, and in practice, the drugs nicotine and caffeine are often used openly in the twelve steps—coffee provided free at meetings, cigarettes integral to the debrief afterward. Many members are prescribed drugs that can be powerfully "mood-changing" and "mind-altering," including stimulants like Adderall, antidepressants like Lithium, and anti-anxiety medications like Diazepam. Inside and outside the twelve steps, drug taking is a near universal human phenomenon.[31]

The twelve steps provide a ritual allowing James to transition from "dirty" to "clean" in twenty-four hours, but in the social world of the noontime meeting, the commonsense notion that these categories mark out clearly distinct groups collapses on close inspection. The same person can be "clean" one day and "dirty" the next, then "clean" again. The "clean" and the "dirty" walk Main Street together and chat on the sidewalk—they are friends and family members. They gather at the noontime, where Bridge House residents collect "clean time" medallions and people wander off the street to share stories of morning heroin use.

The peer-to-peer networks of recovery blur together with the peer-to-peer networks of the street-level drug economy.

James is the first to speak when Keith opens the floor for "sharing" personal testimonials. He tells a story about overdosing and waking up in the hospital on life support, not knowing where he was. It sounds like he was kicked out of a program and is now homeless. There is a stream of other painful stories about the misery of life in the street. The whir of a rickety old fan makes it hard to hear. People saunter in and leave the room throughout. Some chat among themselves right through the confessions. It is just another day at the noontime.

* * *

Joe increasingly spent his days at a recovery drop-in center, Ray of Hope, located around a mile from the noontime meeting. And if the Clearview Crossing recovery scene generally blurred together with the neighborhood street scene, this was especially so at the center, because Ray of Hope was built to be the visible storefront and interface of a large drug-treatment organization attracting newcomers right off the street. There were daily recovery meetings and classes of different kinds, but more than any real structured program, the center provided a welcoming space for people to hang out and pass the time. It had air conditioning on hot summer days. There were comfortable couches and tables for playing cards. The kitchen had a microwave and coffee for a dollar. And along with a hospitable physical setting, the center fostered an accessible social environment by adopting a "peer-to-peer model" in which staff and volunteers were not outside experts but people who had much in common with the target clientele.

Joe volunteered to work at the Ray of Hope reception desk greeting visitors and running orientations with new members. And his position as a Clearview Crossing local left him well suited to the role—sitting at reception, he was often greeting familiar faces coming through the door. The founder and director of the center, Thalia Andrews, was once a sex worker in the neighborhood and had a shared history with Joe in the street. And there were other Bridge House residents among the regulars, like Tim Williams and Toa Mackie, as well as some of Joe's oldest friends, like Guy Jordan and Carter Price.

At Ray of Hope, Joe found a philosophy of recovery with important differences to the more hard-line approach to abstinence at Bridge House (and more broadly in the twelve steps). The model promoted by the center was dubbed "all recovery," and within this generally forgiving and all-inclusive framework, it was accepted that some members might choose to use some drugs, particularly as medicine, as a positive part of their recovery. At Ray of Hope recovery meetings, there were no medallions awarded for the accumulation of "clean time"—avoiding the sharp division of "clean" and "dirty" at the core of the twelve steps—and members were encouraged to identify as "in recovery" rather than as "addicts" (and to generally avoid using stigmatizing language).

These philosophical differences had practical stakes informing how drug regulation shaped access to services and support within the Clearview Crossing recovery scene. Consider the contrasting approaches to a drug considered controversial in these circles: Suboxone. Suboxone is widely prescribed by doctors as a medical treatment for opiate addiction, but it is also itself a potentially abusable opiate and is viewed as problematic within recovery models based strictly on the abstinence principle.[32] Suboxone was banned from Bridge House, and residents were unable to use the drug even if it were prescribed; and more broadly, using it disqualified a person from accumulating "clean time" or collecting medallions within the network of twelve-step groups in the neighborhood. At Ray of Hope, in contrast, people using Suboxone were viewed as legitimately pursuing recovery and allowed to participate as full members of the center.

I want to end this chapter with Joe articulating his own evolving perspective on what recovery was all about. These views emerged not only from his reflection on the different ideas to which he was exposed but, more pragmatically, from his efforts to meet the demands of a halfway house that attempted to enforce the strict division between "clean" and "dirty"—using this divide as a core principle of social exclusion—within a wider community setting that was far more liminal than these categories allow.

* * *

Sitting with Joe in the Clearview Crossing common downtown—on a park bench around five hundred meters from the Ray of Hope recovery center—I ask about his views on the contentious substance Suboxone:

"In AA or NA meetings in traditional twelve-step format, if you're on Suboxone or methadone, you can't get a key chain," Joe explains.

"Let's say you are a full-blown heroin addict on Main Street and go get Suboxone. Now you're not even touchin' heroin no more. You got thirty days. You're doin' everything you're doin', you're goin' to every meetin'. When they say, 'Anybody got thirty days clean?' they can't get that coin.

"That's why in the recovery center they have meetings they don't call NA meetings. They call them 'all recovery.' The format of all recovery meetings is that we don't discriminate or promote anybody's pathways to recovery. If you are starting off in the methadone clinic, that's your pathway to recovery. If you're on Suboxone, you're not sellin' your ass on Main Street, you're not sittin' your ass on Main Street, then you're in recovery, you're recovering. Some people need that. I don't see nothing wrong with it as long as you're not abusing it."

"What about that guy Mike who died?" I ask, referencing a mutual acquaintance before continuing. "I'm pretty sure he was on Suboxone, and I'm pretty sure he was going to the NA meeting at the church [the noontime] and saying he had clean time."

Joe takes over: "An individual can consider themselves clean as long as they are not using heroin. But the organization as a whole will not. Which is not right." You're really discouraging people to even fuckin' get clean. I see that a lot. I see a girl that goes to the NA meeting to this day, and she says, 'I'm doin' real good. I haven't touched heroin in six months, but I'm not clean because I got Suboxone.'"

"Are there any meetings it would it be acceptable to take Suboxone and still go up and get a coin?"

"Well the all recovery don't have a coin ceremony. The coin ceremony started in AA, and it's basically just in AA and NA."

"Is it in writing that NA doesn't accept Suboxone?" I ask.

"The NA fuckin' professors, I like to call 'em, will take—now I don't know how old that format is. I'm pretty sure it wasn't written in 1940 whether people were takin' Suboxone or not or whether they even had the concept that was gonna be available one day for somebody in recovery. Same as constitutional rights, like, they were written for that time period. Laws need to be changed with the times, man. And like if this Suboxone's saving somebody's life, who are you to say she ain't clean? See, a lot

of people have that argument without understanding some of this literature was written in '50s and '60s. It doesn't really contain to our times.
Our times are changing, man. Our addiction has progressed so much, so
our recovery should progress. Like, it's Suboxone that helped people stay
clean. You're not shooting dope. You're not selling your ass for crack."

"Are there other things like Suboxone that some people would think
are legitimate but that NA says no?"

Joe pauses to think for a few seconds, then continues: "If you're prescribed Percocets by a doctor because of your back pain. Let's say, I can
get Percocets right now if I want. I can. I have legitimate reason why to
take 'em—because I'm in pain. I won't lose my clean time, as long as I'm
doing them as the doctor prescribed. But you go to the doctor and get
Suboxone, who prescribe this medication that's gonna keep you clean
because of the pain of being sick or being a drug addict, they ain't consider that."

"Why Percocet but not Suboxone, do you think?"

"I don't know why. Them are the NA professor rules. Like, that's 'cause
in the literature it says abstain from any and *all* mind-altering drugs,
all mind-altering drugs. Now, I got a guy I know who got like ten years
clean. But he has a drink once in a while. Not every day, not every weekend. He might go to a wedding and have a glass of wine. He might have
two. Next day, he fine. Now he don't say, 'I lost my . . .' To him, he kept
it [his clean time], but in that community, he'll lose it. Even if the last
thing he was was a alcoholic on the street. Like, this guy just used drugs.
Alcohol wasn't even a problem in his life. That happens to a lot of people.

"Do I see that as wrong? No, if you wanna have a glass of wine, go
ahead, man. If you can have a glass of wine, so be it, man. I know a lady,
just ran into her, that I used to smoke crack with and do heroin with,
and she's been clean five years but smokes marijuana. Whatever! As long
as you not doing what you're doing, man."

Then Joe says sarcastically, "Okay, 'You're not a crack smoker no
more, but you're shootin' dope. Oh, that's cool.' No. But if you're smokin'
a joint here and there, man, or havin' a beer at a family cookout, go
ahead. Who the fuck am I to say you're not clean, man? That's what all
recovery teaches. Hey, you're recoverin', man. Recoverin' means recoverin', man. It doesn't mean lockin' yourself in a room."

I take over to ask another question: "Are there other things some people would think are okay that NA says no to? That says you need to reset your [clean] time?"

"Methadone's a no-no. Suboxone's a no-no. There's a new saying now, and I've seen this on Facebook—it was a post that said, 'You say you have clean time, but you're poppin' Jonnys,'" he says, referencing the street name for the medication gabapentin. "I mean, I'm on Jonnys, and ain't nobody tellin' me I ain't clean. That's why I don't go to NA no more. When you get politics involved, man, and it's interfering with somebody who's tryin' to do the right thing, man. Who cares, man? Really, who cares, man? I mean, if you're on Suboxone—I know a girl who's on Suboxone who got her kids back. The state said, yeah, 'You're good enough to get your kids back from bein' on Suboxones, but you're not good enough to get a thirty-day coin'? Where does that make any sense, man? Like I say, you're really discouraging people from even going to meetings like that. Then what? Then they start using because they don't have the support team. You don't have a support team because you don't recognize the good work he's doin' or she's doin'."

"When you said the NA professors, what do you mean by that?"

"Oh, just a bunch of guys that got clean time, and all they do is read the NA books and just dissect it and read it as verbatim, quote it, find every loophole in it. Yeah, that's NA professors."

"At the all recovery meeting, if you showed up there and said, 'I'm clean, but a couple of times I smoked weed,' and you just said it openly, how would people respond to that?"

"Fine. We would hope it wouldn't become a problem, where it starts interfering with your everyday life. Same with people come in there all the time and say, 'I'm on Suboxones, but I been clean,' sustained from using heroin and crack. I think our main focus should be on alcohol, crack, heroin, oxies [oxycodone], and all that, man. But if somebody's tokin' a marijuana joint once in a while—"

I interrupt: "Who gives a fuck—exactly."

"Who cares, man. I don't think a marijuana joint gonna have you out there suckin' a dick."

"I think what someone in NA would probably say is that those things become gateways. Like that guy you said has a drink occasionally. I mean, I have no problem with that—sure, have a drink—but once you're a little bit drunk, your willpower . . ."

"Exactly, and that's why I don't drink. Some people can, and some people can't. But he don't go into meetings and promote that. He don't even mention that. He don't say, 'Oh, I had a beer last night.' He don't even mention that, man."

"I think that's all over the place," I say. "Like NA has this thing of total abstinence is the only way to recover. But I think a lot of people are doing exactly what that guy's doing. They do what works for them, and then they come to a meeting, and you have to say total abstinence. I'm sure there's lots of people—"

"There's gotta be. There's gotta be, man. And you know what? You're recoverin', you're recoverin', man."

"When you think about what recovering means, what is it?" I ask.

"Recovery to me is starting to learn. Putting down the drugs doesn't mean you're gonna stay clean. You gotta do some inside work. A lot of us addicts have something wrong up here, went through something in our childhood that makes us try and forget those things. We need to let it out. I think professional help as far as going to see a psychiatrist. Recovery to me means that you're no longer doing those habits you were doing: stealing, lying, cheating, robbing. I believe in the NA step work, you know, makin' amends to people you hurt, finding out about yourself, loving yourself first—all that good stuff. I believe in all that. But recovery is finding yourself again, man. And like I said, goin' to a hundred meetings doesn't mean your recovered. That's why a lot of people relapse. 'Cause they do all this stuff in meetings: 'I gotta go here. I got a sponsor.' But you're not really takin' a look deep inside you and finding out what's the cause of you pickin' up them drugs, man."

"I mean, its kinda interesting, because recovery is strictly learning not to use drugs and alcohol, but you're saying there are some people who can still drink or smoke weed occasionally and be in recovery. And there's also people who are totally not using anything who are not really in recovery—"

"At all—and you'll usually see 'em relapse. Recovery is also about giving back, man, doing community work as far as helping out the unfortunate, doing something for your soul, man. Addiction attacks three things: physical, mental, and spiritual. So you have to repair all them three things."

Joe sees Carter Price walking through the common and calls him over to chat.

"What up, player?" says Carter.

"Hey, I dunno if it's true or not, I just wanna give you a heads-up. Somebody said you went to the recovery center [Ray of Hope] and tried to sell 'em some Suboxone."

"Man, I talked to Thalia about that. That's all a bunch of bullshit."

"Yeah, that's what I told her."

"Come on, man, that's bullshit."

"That's what I told her—I said, 'I don't think that's true.' I'll have a talk to her. So what's goin' on, bud?"

"Been down at Bicare," Carter says, referencing a substance-abuse treatment center. "Got about an hour and fifteen in—the first day I'm back, and it feels good to be done, Joe."

"Did you go to the meeting today?"

"Nah, man, went to Bicare, got down here about 12:30, and I just went to the gym. Then I thought I'll just come hang out for a little while before it's time to go home."

"I was telling him [me] about the difference between all recovery and NA-AA, and I didn't know all the answers. And I was explaining like even on methadone, they consider that not clean time."

"Listen, man," says Carter, "if you let other people get to you—this is *your* recovery. Everyone recovers different. If it's gonna stop you from rippin' and runnin' on Main Street, then the more power to you. Who is it for them to tell me if I'm clean or not clean? Do your own program. Don't do my program. If it stops a person like me and Joe from bein' out there rippin' and runnin'—

"Then I'm recoverin'," says Joe.

"Damn right! You can say whatever you want, that doesn't matter to me. I know, God knows. That's all that matters to me. Know what I mean? When I take care of my friggin' house, now I'm able to take care and put food in there and do things for my girl, and you're gonna tell me that I'm not recoverin'? Get the fuck outta here!"

"That's what I told him," Joe says, referring to me.

"A lot of them people in NA are full of shit," Carter continues. "I'm tellin' you, I've been around here all my life. I've been around that meeting for like thirty years almost. I'm forty-six years old. I remember I first went to a meeting when I was seventeen. So I been around that meeting for so long, man, them dudes they really don't wanna help you. These NA dudes full of it, a lot of 'em. Talkin' about how they got twenty-three years clean—but you're buying and selling Percs [Percocet] on the street. Get the fuck outta here. You're selling Percs! To pay your rent."

"Sixteen years clean, and you selling Percocets," Joe agrees.

"If you're buying and selling Percs, you're in the commission of a felony," says Carter. "Your committing a felony. But you're still saying your clean. Go to Bicare, there's a whole bunch of people that are just there 'cause the courts got 'em there. I stay away from them. They outside tryna buy stuff. Half of 'em nodding out in groups."

I chime in: "I mean, even things like, no one's totally clean. I mean, cigarettes, caffeine, those are NA staples."

"Right," says Joe.

"What are you gonna say that a person is not clean?" Carter asks rhetorically. "When they really have a lotta problems from using drugs, where they have to take doctor's meds? They have to! Or they gonna be in so much pain! What you gonna say? They're not clean? Because they take prescribed meds? Come on, man."

"Can either of you remember a time when there was an argument over somebody who said they had clean time and other people said no, they don't?"

"A lot of 'em," says Carter. "Like Suboxone, they'll be the first ones to say, 'Oh, you not clean if you're on Suboxone. Let me tell you something: Suboxones don't do nothing. It might do something the first time, but after that, they don't do anything. They don't get you high."

"Unless you don't do 'em. Like, if I take one, I'll get fucked up," Joe says.

"But if you take one the very next day, it'll be—"

"Nah, nah, nah."

"If you take one today, you'll probably feel nice, but after that, you don't feel nothing. You know a lot of 'em are robbing NA. They put up all these functions, then you say, 'Where did all the money go?' They say, 'Oh, we sent it to area.' Get the fuck out. What you think I am? Johnny knuckle-head?"

Joe agrees: "That's why I don't like going down there—you know what, they get money every day, and they won't serve coffee."

"Exactly. How you not gonna have coffee? Because believe me, that helped me out a lot. When I was at the noontime, when I used to go make the coffee, then I used to clean up after the meeting. That helped me stay clean. It felt like I was giving something back. Just like Joe, how he is now. A lot of people see him, and a lot of the time, you don't even have to say nothing. Just by them seeing him and seeing where he came from, and they're struggling, they might try and go in a detox. Like, I know this guy was just as bad as me out here and look at him now—he's clean going on three years. That's the hope shot right there."

* * *

Joe spent day in and day out in a social world saturated with legal and illegal drugs of different kinds, living in a halfway house with a policy of mandatory abstinence, but intimately connected to the most destructive patterns of street-level drug use. He was part of a web of social relations in which widespread drug dependency was coupled with intense but selective and sometimes unpredictable criminalization of some drugs but not others. Joe's ideas about the boundaries of recovery evolved in the context of his efforts to maintain a socially recognized status as "clean" within this deeply liminal space.

Joe ran into an old friend as we talked about recovery at the city common. Carter had been accused by someone at Ray of Hope of dealing a medication prescribed as treatment for addiction, Suboxone, signaling the importance of brand-name pharmaceuticals to illicit drug markets in the neighborhood. And whether or not the claims were true—Carter forcefully rejected them, and Joe sided with his friend—the fact that they were believable enough to dispute speaks to the proximity of these markets to the daily rounds of the men in recovery.

Joe and Carter constructed a joint critique of the hard-line abstinence stance of Narcotics Anonymous. Carter argued that "everyone recovers different" and that anything that prevents "a person like [him] and Joe" from "rippin' and runnin' on Main Street" should be viewed as legitimate. He said some people *need* to take prescribed medications to deal with serious pain and was indignant about their being excluded because of that choice. Carter argued that there are plenty of people using deception to accumulate "clean time" anyway—or, in his words, "a lot of them people in NA are full of shit"—and having just been accused of dealing himself, he turned the tables on a hypothetical longtime member of the twelve steps dealing Percocet to pay the rent.

Joe nodded along in agreement throughout. Before Carter wandered past, he derided the "NA professors" wedded to an outdated official literature, a situation he compared to those who interpret too strictly the US Constitution. Joe said recovery needs to "progress" with the times, and the authors of official literature would have no idea about contentious contemporary issues like the status of Suboxone. He criticized NA members who insist on using this literature as justification to exclude people on Suboxone from being "clean"—even in situations where it could be "saving somebody's life."

Joe's views on the boundaries of recovery seemed increasingly divorced from the issue of abstinence. He included as "in recovery" specific people who smoked marijuana, drank alcohol, or used Suboxone and, at the same time, excluded others who were more committed to abstinence but not making behavioral changes. Joe presented a narrative of recovery as a broader process of personal development that included "giving back," doing "community work," and "takin' a look deep inside you." It was less about quitting drugs than about quitting a set of behaviors that he associated with using drugs: "stealing, lying, cheating, robbing."

Joe said he was being prescribed "Jonnys," a slang term for the medication gabapentin, for dealing with chronic back pain. And he described a recent Facebook meme posted by a friend making fun of people who claim to have "clean time" while they are also "popping Jonnys." This may seem like an innocuous online exchange about an obscure pharmaceutical drug, but for Joe, the implications were more threatening. The status of the substance gabapentin within recovery shaped his access not only to health care but also to housing and the community of mutual support that he relied on most.

Joe said he could use Percocet, if prescribed by a doctor, and still accumulate "clean time" within Narcotics Anonymous. But this was hypothetical: Joe did not take Percocet. Perhaps he had personal concerns about the potential for physical and emotional dependence on this opiate-based medication. Or maybe he was more concerned about the close scrutiny that using Percocet would probably have attracted from staff and other residents at Bridge House. But somewhere between these two medications that he could legitimately access to manage pain—gabapentin and Percocet—he drew the boundary between acceptable and unacceptable drugs within his own life.

It was one thing for Joe to advocate flexibility around abstinence while sitting in a park on a sunny day chatting to an ethnographer with critical views on the twelve steps and the war on drugs. And I was encouraging the deconstruction: pointing out that "no one is totally clean" and that the drugs nicotine and caffeine are "NA staples," while scoffing at the idea that someone should be excluded from recovery for occasionally smoking marijuana. But Joe was also a resident at a halfway house that is much closer to the twelve-step than the all-recovery philosophy. Smoking marijuana or drinking alcohol, even occasionally, would be grounds for immediate eviction—a devastating loss of social support.

Joe's arguments for taking a more inclusive view of recovery might be viewed as a form of resistance and attempt to carve out a space for acceptable drug use—both recreational (marijuana, alcohol) and medicinal (Percocet, gabapentin)—within a carceral apparatus based on enforced abstinence. But his practical decisions about his own drug use were more cautious. Even as he talked about the acceptability of occasionally drinking alcohol or smoking marijuana among others in recovery, I never knew him to do either. And Joe seemed quite conservative when it came to the plethora of pharmaceutical drugs on offer for dealing with his serious health problems.

The rewards for Joe walking the tightrope required to "get clean" included becoming a public figure and role model in Clearview Crossing. Joe had been drug dependent in these same city streets. But as Carter put it, "Look at him now—he's clean going on three years." Simply by walking the neighborhood and being seen, without needing to say a thing, he gave others a "hope shot."

The routine placement of halfway houses in close proximity to highly visible circuits of street-level drug dependency creates steep challenges for residents in these programs. But when researchers frame the issue narrowly in terms of crime rates and recidivism, they can easily miss important elements of the story. Because when Joe was sentenced to a halfway house in Clearview Crossing, returning to his own community, the same relationships that fostered his intimate connection to the drug crisis were also relationships of mutual aid and reciprocal support. Carter Price publicly celebrated Joe's success with a visceral understanding of the stakes and obstacles—he shared many of the same problems. Joe did the same for Carter. They exchanged ideas about the meaning of recovery while playing cards at Ray of Hope or hanging out on summer days in the city common. The men shared food and cigarettes and generally looked out for each other. Joe had many relationships like this in Clearview Crossing—and they were an invaluable source of support at a time when he desperately needed help.

7

No Narcotics

Joe Badillo chokes backs tears on the phone saying that the infection in his spine is back. Last time, surgery to cut out the abscess became a nightmare that almost left him paralyzed. Now he is in the hospital on opiate pain medications bracing for a similar procedure.

"I guess I'm not clean anymore," he says.

* * *

I visit Joe one week after surgery. White sheets bunch around limp legs on the hospital bed, his gown pulling apart haphazardly in the middle to show his tattooed chest. A large drip punctures the inside of a thick bicep, blood seeping beneath clear plastic where line meets skin. Carter Price and Caitlin Loren are there too, old friends of Joe's from the street, now fellow travelers in recovery. There is a soft toy penguin by the bed and a helium balloon bobbling with the message "Get Well Soon." Joe jokes that he should be charging admission to all the visitors.

We talk about the surgery. Joe says that it started with chest pain diagnosed as a fractured rib, then bronchitis. But the pain grew unbearable, and strength drained from his legs. The problem was identified as a return of the epidural abscess that first appeared around three years and eight months earlier while he was a pretrial detainee at Richmond County Jail (see chapter 2), which again included osteomyelitis, a spread from the bloodstream or tissue into the bone. I clarify the procedure that had been performed to remove the infection in layman's terms:

"My understanding is they just cut your back open and tried to scoop out as much of the infection as they could, is that—"

"Yeah, that's basically what it boiled down to," Joe says. "But they had to remove the bone too, because the infection got inside the bone. So that's what they did: they removed a lot of bone."

"Some of the spine?"

"Yeah, some spine. From the T-1 to T-5 [numbering of vertebrae at the top of the back]. It's crazy because the first surgery I had a thin line where you could see the incision, but you wouldn't even know, like normal. This one is like I got a big fuckin' crater in my back.

"They didn't want to do more surgery. They wanted to fight it with antibiotics. But I was telling them I want the operation. The medication ain't workin'. My surgeon would come in and tell me, 'Joe, this operation is in the same area [as the first time]. We are going to have to take out more bone. We don't think you're going to walk. You're probably going to be paralyzed for the rest of your life.' That scares the shit out of you. I just didn't wanna die at that point, man. That was my biggest thing: I didn't wanna die, man."

Joe pauses, then continues: "So that's the deal, man," he says matter-of-factly. "I gotta start all over. Bad shape, bro. My mental status is in good shape, but my physical status is in bad shape. The only reason why my mental status is in good status is because I already been through it. When they said the infection came back, I prepared myself like there's gonna be a surgery and I'm gonna be paralyzed again. I already knew because I went through it once. I know the outcome."

"Can you move your legs at all [now]?"

"Yeah, but I'm gonna have to strain them, so . . . When everything's said and done and I'm back on my feet, I have to come back because they want to put rods in my spine," he says, pointing upside-down thumbs down either side of his neck. "See that vest over there," Joe points to a large brace sitting on a chair. "I have to wear that. It's like RoboCop, man. I can't move like this [*swiveling shoulders*], because my bones are so infected, that just looking down the wrong way can collapse my spine. Yeah, my skeleton's gone.

"Just imagine, even like twenty years ago, if you had a spinal injury, there really wasn't much they could do for you. 'Oh, you got a spinal injury. You're done.' They just hear that word 'spinal,' 'Oh, you're in a wheelchair.' Nowadays it's not like that, man.

"Shit, I only got half a spine and I'm still moving."

* * *

Trying to prevent infection festering in the body, surgeons decided not to stitch the wound, leaving it open with flesh and tendons exposed. The

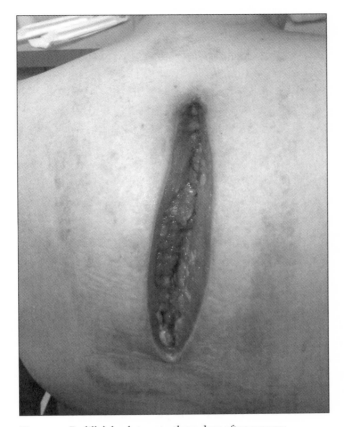

Figure 7.1. Badillo's back twenty-three days after surgery

resulting "crater," as Joe called it, stretched from between his shoulder blades to the curve at the bottom of his back. Nurses cleaned the wound and packed it with gauze several times a day. A little more than three weeks after surgery, he texted me a photo with the message, "looks nasty but to Dr's its healing good" (see figure 7.1).

Joe sent the photo from the in-patient rehabilitation center where he spent around three months after surgery. When I visited, we planned to roll around the block in a wheelchair but stopped just outside the entrance because the footpath sloped downward and he worried about slipping off the front. His legs shook visibly. We smoked a cigarette in the parking lot among gnarled, dead trees, sun melting snow into puddles on the ground. He said it was his first time outside in a month.

Joe's stay at in-patient rehabilitation, like the surgery itself, was covered by health insurance provided by the state—a probably lifesaving institutional opening within a broader context of chronic social marginalization. Many former prisoners around the country lack health insurance,[1] with one large-scale survey finding that 78 percent of men and 66 percent of women were uninsured two to three months after release,[2] and rates of uninsurance for former prisoners remain well above those of the general public even after more recent expansions of coverage under the Affordable Care Act.[3] But Joe was in Massachusetts, where health-care reforms introduced in 2006 had produced among the lowest levels of uninsurance of any state in America (2.7 percent by one estimate).[4] Prison officials built on the reforms by making enrolling in MassHealth—the state version of Medicaid for people on low incomes—into pre-release planning.[5] I never knew a Bridge House resident to be without health insurance.

Still, Joe's health-care access was very liminal: combining institutional inclusion, rooted in geographically specific features of the health system and welfare state, with powerful exclusions visible in micro interactions with doctors and front-line staff. And there was a striking contrast between conditions inside the high-technology medical sector providing his care and the basic social conditions in which he usually lived. Backed by state-funded insurance, Joe entered a US medical establishment boasting assets that no other country can match: cutting-edge technology and equipment, world-leading laboratories and medical schools, a highly educated workforce of doctors, nurses, and technicians.[6] There may have been few better places in the world to undergo complex spinal surgery. But in the aftermath, Joe was left scrambling to find a viable place in the social order as a disabled ex-convict relying on poverty-level Social Security as his primary source of income.

When Joe moved back into Bridge House from in-patient rehabilitation, the program provided crucial stability as he navigated the structural disconnect between a thriving high-technology medical sector and a crumbling welfare state. The program ensured that Joe's fundamental material needs were being met during this tumultuous period—for food and housing, for example, and social connection—which are important determinants of health but nonetheless often neglected by the medical establishment. And yet his residence at a halfway house came with its own structural disconnects. Joe was located in a carceral institution based on a model of coercive drug abstinence while relying on a medical system that was often narrowly focused on drug-based solutions—especially for the kind of serious pain he was experiencing—and he confronted difficult decisions juggling conflicting institutional demands.

I arrived at Bridge House for my last spell of fieldwork not long after Joe moved back into the program. He was out of the wheelchair and using instead a gray plastic walking frame with tennis balls sliced down the middle as stops on the back legs. We spent a lot of time together day in and day out, and as I got involved in shuttling Joe to medical appointments in my old Toyota Camry with a rusty passenger-seat door, the summer unfolded as a slow-burning tour of the health-care sector. It was a chance to see up close the institutional contradictions framing his whole experience of sickness and healing.

*　*　*

Struggling with the pain, Joe spent most of yesterday in bed at Bridge House. He has not had medical support since leaving in-patient rehabilitation around three weeks ago, but we are about to head to physical therapy. He seems relieved at the prospect of help. He wears a color-matched outfit for the trip—black sneakers with red Air Jordan logo, black pants with red Ralph Lauren logo, baggy red T-shirt—and on the short drive from Bridge House to Garden Grove Rehabilitation Clinic, the scenery changes quickly to tree-lined streets of multistory houses with big gardens. The centerpiece of the clinic is a historic Victorian brownstone on a hill surrounded by manicured green grounds. Pulling into the parking lot, Joe says they would not let him stay at Garden Grove after his first spinal surgery because of his criminal record.

Walking with Joe through the entrance, where the air is conditioned and cool, I can *feel* his labored pace of life: the walker pushed slowly forward, followed by a barely raised right foot, then the left, shoe soles scuffing along the ground. Joe says the surgery damaged the spinal nerves that carry automatic messages from brain to legs. Now he has to think the orders to each foot: "Okay, now right foot move, now left foot move." Everything is deliberate.

The receptionist at the front desk wears a Garden Grove polo shirt and name tag around her neck. "Wow, you're so late," she says.

"It's two o'clock," Joe replies quizzically.

"The appointment was one o'clock," she says.

Joe rests a ripped cardboard folder brimming with paperwork on the reception desk. Balancing on the walker, he fumbles through forms, searching for a listing of the appointment time.

"I just had spinal surgery," he says, barely looking up.

The receptionist is stern and unsympathetic. There are no appointments available for almost three weeks, she says, and by then, his doctor's referral will have expired—so he needs to see the doctor before rescheduling. On the slow shuffle back outside, I offer to drive the car around to the entrance.

"Nah, man, I'll walk. I may as well get some exercise while I'm here," he says.

Joe is pragmatic on the drive home. He has never met his doctor, so he calls the hospital and puts it on speaker phone. "Hi, I'm trying to find out who my primary care physician is," he says.

The voice on the other end speaks for only a few seconds, just long enough to say that Joe will be transferred to someone who can help. An automated message says that he will be placed on hold, where he waits for the rest of the drive, eventually giving up without finding out the name of his doctor.

Joe starts talking about getting back to the gym at the YMCA. The thought of him doing self-directed spinal rehabilitation makes me nervous. I decide to have a go phoning Garden Grove to push for an earlier appointment. The call goes to the same receptionist. I tell her that Joe had serious spinal surgery and was told he would never walk again and that he has already gone weeks without help. She stands firm, and I ask to speak with a manager. She says that the paperwork said one o'clock, and he should have got it right. I say it seems like such harsh punishment for a simple human error—that these are issues of "life and death." Still no budging. I ask again to speak with a manager, and she transfers me. It rings once and goes to answer machine. It seems pointless to leave a message, so I do not.

Joe calls me a few minutes later from downstairs. "I think your call to the manager made a difference," he says. "They can fit me in on Monday."

I feel a burst of relief.

"Haha, hell yeah! I didn't even talk to the manager."

"Yeah, well, I still think it made the difference."

"All I did was tell her how serious it was. It seemed like she was just like, 'Fuck that guy. He showed up late and can deal with the consequences.'"

"Well, just remember it's at twelve o'clock—don't let me think it's at eleven."

* * *

When Joe was evaluated for physical therapy at Garden Grove a few days later, he could not feel the bottom of his feet or push his legs against the physio's hands while sitting. He was granted two sessions a week for two months. In this process of rehabilitation, the physical challenges of learning to walk again were compounded by the challenges of navigating a kind of cross-cultural encounter. From the receptionist to the physio, Joe was pulled into interactions with people he would usually not have much to do with. The waiting room was stocked with the most recent issues of *Bloomberg Businessweek* and *Golf Magazine*.

Consider Joe's tense exchange with the receptionist. In the background loomed the challenges he faced accessing care in a disjointed network of health-care bureaucracies—expressed here in confusion over an appointment time and needing a referral for the physio from a doctor whose name he did not know. And he confronted these challenges and their endless paperwork with limited literacy. The receptionist did not know the long backstory or the seriousness of Joe's rolling health problems. She simply saw a man arriving late to an appointment—someone with tattoos and a missing front tooth. Maybe she decided this was a person who needed to be taught that there were consequences to his actions. Whatever the motivations, she responded dismissively.

Joe approached the interaction a little nervously and, when challenged, backed down quickly without arguing. And his ability to argue the case was constrained by the social expectations he faced as a tattooed ex-convict in unfamiliar territory. Even if he had put aside a long history of institutional powerlessness and spoken up, he could easily have come across as hostile and made the situation worse. Perhaps there was also an element of simple pragmatism: if Joe got angry every time things were unfair, he would *always* be angry, and he did not want to live that way.

I was outraged on his behalf. I came to situation with an ingrained sense of entitlement, grounded not only in my social location as a white man from a wealthy private university but more concretely in having successfully exercised power in similar situations in the past. I demanded to speak with a manager more than once and articulated forcefully the seriousness of the surgery—and it worked. None of this is straightforward: Joe was more sociable and outgoing than I during visits to Garden Grove. He exchanged jokes and niceties with staff and other patients and, by the end, even developed friendly rapport with the receptionist from that first day. But it did seem like part of his effort to navigate these relationships involved avoiding confrontation and sacrificing the ability to make demands on the system.

The exclusions were layered and often subtle. When Joe's physio at Garden Grove told him to inform his primary-care doctor that he needed to see a "physiatrist," for example, he could not remember the name of the specialty. He once asked me the title of a "muscle and tone doctor" and, when I did not know, used Google and picked it from a list. Yet asking for a referral was still made difficult by the simple fact that he could not pronounce the word, fumbling over it even on the day he eventually got an appointment.

Joe believed that he was not already seeing the physiatrist because he was on MassHealth. Like many recipients of public health insurance, he felt that it was a stigmatizing marker responsible for hostile treatment from some gatekeepers and at times poor-quality care.[7] I would not say Joe complained about MassHealth—complaining was not really his style—but he did often raise it when things went wrong. Public insurance both opened access to the system and shaped the tone of his experience inside. In general, Joe seemed to treat his health care like it was temporary and could be pulled away any moment, and his philosophical attitude to obstacles was in part because he was not surprised to find them. He got what he could from the medical establishment but was suspicious as well as grateful.

The day after our first visit to Garden Grove, with Joe's access to physical therapy still in doubt, I spent the morning away from Bridge House and returned with him nowhere to be found—but with the walking frame parked in the usual spot by the front door. It turned out that he went to a twelve-step meeting and then to lunch, walking only with the help of a cane, a move that was risky and unsafe but also an impressive physical accomplishment.

I sent him a text: "I see a walker on the porch but no Joe. Look at the man go!"

This was the response: "Yeah just in case they tell me I can't get therapy, I get my own can't hold me back."

* * *

We are smoking cigarettes on the Bridge House porch when Joe takes a phone call. They are canceling his doctor's appointment and rescheduling for July 7—meaning a two-month wait after leaving in-patient rehabilitation. He puts the call on speaker to check his diary.

"I'm sorry for any inconvenience," the woman says.

"Well, you're not the doctor. I know it's not your fault," he replies.

"I wish everyone was like you," she responds.

Joe makes friendly small talk with the woman on the other end of the phone. She says, "Awesome, see you then." He says, "You should use the term 'awesome sauce,'" and she chuckles. When he hangs up, the conversation was so cheerful that I feel the need to clarify that his doctor's appointment was just canceled. I tell him that I think it is bullshit. He agrees, saying that you would think that after spinal surgery, he would be at the top of the list and they would be canceling other people to see him.

But on the phone, he simply accepted gracefully.

* * *

On the day I travel to the doctor's with Joe, I have been thinking a lot about the dynamics of his exclusion and approach the visit as a chance to document both the barriers and his response to them. I am surprised to find a medical facility that seems not only state of the art but welcoming and inclusive. Dignity Health Center is in a freshly renovated building with tiers of shiny glass panels and tall trees out front. A large sign at the entrance announces "welcome" in a host of languages: "bem-vindo" and "bienvence," "miro si vine" and "chao mung." Colorful posters on the wall ask, "Do You Need Health Insurance?" There are wooden booths under a sign reading, "Health Benefits," which like all the hospital signage, is translated into Spanish and Vietnamese. A staff member in one booth speaks Spanish to a patient seated out front.

I ask Joe if the hospital is connected to a university.

"Could be," he says. "This is a clinic. They don't do surgeries, just primary care, prenatal, stuff like that. This is cheap care. It's always so understaffed—there's too many people, man."

"It all looks real new," I say.

"Yeah, well, they just did it all up."

Joe gets called quickly to the appointment. I spend an hour in the waiting room, pondering the disconnect between his account and my own first impressions of the place. There is an enormous flat-screen TV on one wall. A fluorescent blue light marks the place where water is dispensed from a shiny black cooler.

A man in a purple shirt with white pin stripes speaks in broken English to a receptionist with a Spanish accent. Then he takes a seat, leaning forward in the chair, with elbows on knees, and runs a chain of rosary beads through his hand. He is joined by a group speaking Arabic, including a baby in a stroller and an elderly woman in a wheelchair wearing a floral purple dress and matching head scarf. A woman from the group approaches reception on the man's behalf: "He says he needs to see someone *today*," she says, gesturing to the man in the purple shirt.

"But he showed up late—his appointment was at 3:45. The doctor says he needs to reschedule."

There is an exchange in Arabic, and then the woman says, "He's going to have to wait two months? He shows up late and has to reschedule, but when the doctor shows up late . . . ," shrugging her shoulders.

The man in the purple shirt approaches the reception desk and plonks a black case that could have been a laptop bag on the desk. He unzips the top to reveal a bundle of tubes and a face mask and says that the "breathing machine" is broken. Joe reappears with the appointment dispute ongoing. As he shuffles out of reception and down the hospital corridor on the walking frame, I tell him that the man showed up fifteen minutes late and now faces a two-month wait for an appointment. Joe is not much more satisfied with his own experience at Dignity Health: "I sat in the room literally the whole time except for maybe ten minutes," he says, having been gone around an hour. "That's how late she was to see me. I was almost ready to leave."

As we exit for the car, making the short drive back to Bridge House, Joe continues talking about his encounter with the doctor: "I'm telling her I need something for pain, and I don't want it to be a narcotic," he says. "She's like, 'We'll try some different things, but if nothing works, I can get you on Suboxones.' I'm like, 'Suboxones? Ain't that a blocker for heroin and people coming off heroin?' She's like, 'Yeah, but a lot of people don't know, Suboxone's intentioned—what you call it?—design was for pain. But there's no narcotics in it.' I was like, 'Really?' I said, 'Let's try everything but that. I don't wanna be on none of that stuff.'"

"Would you consider Suboxone?" I ask.

"If there's no narcotic in it, man, know mean? I'm in pain, man. I am. I'm in a lot of pain, man. People just don't realize because I don't say nothing. But I'm in a lot of pain. In the morning, oh man. Then you see me trying to stand up, and shit, my legs just start shaking. That shit hurts, man. I mean, it's nonnarcotic. I wouldn't wanna go back on a narcotic, bro, just for the simple fact that—"

"It's a slippery slope?"

"It's a slippery slope, bro."

"People get quite zonked out on Suboxone as well, though ay—"

"But they're taking it because they're mistreating it. Like, if you've got pain, that medication will block the sensors to the pain. But if you're not in no pain, and there's nothin' to block, of course you're gonna get high. If you're taking more than you should be taking . . ."

"That's a difficult spot to be in as a recovering addict whose also constantly in pain."

"Yeah, it is."

"Because, you know, the available treatment's not available to you. If you weren't in the [halfway] house, would you consider narcotics?"

"Not a narcotic, no. Then again—you know what, I was fine when I was on them in the nursing home. I didn't relapse. I would probably give it to my sister to prescribe to me though. I wouldn't wanna have a bottle of fuckin' oxycodone hangin' around my house. But I'm at that point in my recovery where I just don't wanna get high. Not saying that it's not gonna change tomorrow—but today I just don't wanna get high."

"When she said you can try everything else, what is everything else?"

"All nonnarcotics."

"Did she give you something to try now?"

"Yeah, Flexeril."

"What's that?"

"It's a nonnarcotic medication for spasms. So it will also help with the pain and the shaking. We'll see."

"You need someone who's gonna engage with you for more than ten minutes and give you good advice about how you should manage all that, right? I mean, it's complicated questions to know what kind of pain medication would be appropriate, and she's just squeezed it in between a hundred other things she's tryna do today."

"Right."

"And she doesn't even really know who you are."

"She's gonna put me on the Flexeril, and when I go see her in a month, right, she's gonna say, 'How is that working?' If I say, 'It's not working,' she's gonna say, 'All right, try this.' And then we'll try this, and then we'll try this—until there's nothing else to try. Instead of asking me like, 'Where is the pain? When is the pain? What time do you feel most in pain?' No."

* * *

Dignity Health is a federally funded community health center, part of a patchwork of services and institutions known collectively in the United States as the health-care "safety net." Around three-quarters of patients either have no health insurance or receive free or subsidized insurance from the state. When I visited with Joe, the center had recently completed a $7.6 million expansion, including complete renovation of two floors in the main clinical facility.

Yet services at Dignity Health were also being stretched by changes in policy designed to *improve* care among the poor. Reforms to expand insurance coverage created a surge in demand for primary health care, including from people seeking help for previously untreated chronic conditions, intensifying long-standing staff shortages.[8] The changes also redirected stable public funding for community health centers to subsidize individual insurance for people on low incomes, making the centers newly reliant on attracting patients and gaining reimbursements from mainly public insurance plans.[9] These were further strains on a health-care safety net that was already struggling for resources in a system increasingly dominated by market logics and the profit making of large corporate interests.[10]

Joe experienced these system strains as long wait times: the appointment canceled and rescheduled, leaving a two-month gap after leaving in-patient rehabilitation, and an hour milling around before seeing the doctor on the day. When I remarked how nice the center looked physically, he quickly dismissed the appearances, describing it as "cheap care" with "too many people" and not enough staff. Joe was born at Dignity Health, and the recent renovations had not changed his basic impression of the institution.

Joe said that the long-awaited doctor's visit lasted around ten minutes. The doctor's hurried and superficial engagement with Joe's complex medical needs was visible in even a brief scan of the printed visit summary he showed me on the car ride home. There was a spelling mistake at the top of the first page—"meet and *ang* greet"—and a humorously exaggerated documentation of his smoking habits: Joe told the doctor that he smoked four cigarettes a day, and she recorded this as four packs.

One way the doctor managed the constraints of a short visit was to focus narrowly on pharmaceutical treatment. She did not ask broad questions about the context of Joe's pain—the time of day it occurred, for example, or the activities it was most associated with—which may have pulled her into time-consuming engagement with his condition and social circumstances. The doctor came to the encounter as part of a US medical establishment that since World War II has consolidated itself as a high-tech discipline centered on magic-bullet pharmaceutical solutions to a wide range of health problems.[11] She concentrated their short conversation on drugs.

In contrast, Joe approached the interaction as a halfway house resident living under a system of punitive drug prohibition.[12] His experience in the doctor's office was framed by a disconnect between a carceral system of coercive drug abstinence and a medical system that is more reliant on using drugs to treat the sick than ever before. Within Joe's lifeworld, the same chemical substances that health-care professionals presented as cutting-edge medical solutions could be viewed as illicit or even criminalized. Trying to access care in the wake of spinal surgery, he faced the difficult task of making fine-grained distinctions between the plethora of drugs on offer, on the basis of not only their pharmacological properties but how they were perceived socially.

Joe described telling the doctor that he needed help dealing with pain but did not want a "narcotic." The term is ambiguous, often used for opiates but also a more general catchall that labels a drug illicit or illegal—it was a bit like Joe saying that he did not want any drugs that might be considered deviant. He recalled the doctor responding that he could try some different things and, if the other options did not work, turn to Suboxone. Joe was taken aback because Suboxone is most well-known as a treatment for opiate addiction. The doctor reassured him that it was originally designed for pain management and that "there's no narcotics in it," but this designation is open to confusion, because Suboxone is itself an opiate. It is also viewed suspiciously within Narcotics Anonymous, so that people using Suboxone are generally unable to accumulate "clean time" in the twelve steps.[13]

Joe said he responded to the suggestion that he try Suboxone by telling the doctor he "don't wanna be on none of that stuff." But in our conversation on the drive home, after a rare instance of his talking openly about his experience of chronic pain, he softened this stance and suggested that he might be prepared to use Suboxone if "there's no narcotic in it." Joe presented the drug as potentially legitimate by arguing that people only "get high" when taking it inappropriately and that if he used Suboxone medically, it would simply "block the sensors to the pain."

But in practice, Joe did refuse Suboxone, and his residence at the halfway house loomed large in the decision—he said that outside the house, he might choose to use narcotics for pain management. And he pointed to recent successes taking powerful opiates during rehabilitation from surgery at a nursing home—a medical use that neither he nor others in recovery considered "relapse"—without becoming physically dependent. He described being secure enough in recovery that he no longer wanted to get high, opening the possibility of using these medications as treatment with precautions in place, like having his sister administer the drugs.

But this was a hypothetical: Joe did live at Bridge House, and under the constraints of this carceral setting, he told the doctor that he did not want Suboxone or anything else that might be considered narcotic. Ironically, this may have left him *more* likely to be offered opiates.[14] Physicians can be suspicious of overeager patients seeking pain treatment, particularly someone like Joe, who has a long criminal record and health condition associated with heroin dependency. His commitment to abstinence may have communicated to the doctor his ability to use these drugs not for pleasure but for pain management, feeding the counterintuitive dynamic by which "not wanting opiates is often precisely what makes clinicians more willing to prescribe them."[15]

Joe left Dignity Health with a prescription for a drug that he felt comfortable defining unambiguously as a "nonnarcotic medication"—the muscle relaxant Flexiril—hoping it would help with both the back pain and the uncontrolled shaking in his legs. And on the drive back to Bridge House, as we digested his encounter with the doctor, he talked briefly but forcefully about the severe pain he was experiencing day in and day out. Joe almost never complained or drew attention to it, but in this moment, he repeated the word three times in quick succession: "pain."

* * *

This was Joe's second lengthy period of rehabilitation after spinal surgery to drain an epidural abscess. The first time the infection appeared, he was a pretrial detainee at Richmond County Jail, and after a long delay receiving treatment, the surgery almost killed him. When the insurance covering his in-patient rehabilitation lapsed, he left the facility in a wheelchair, moving in with an old friend from the street and sleeping on a couch in the living room. Joe ended up homeless.

I asked him to compare the experience with his most recent surgery.

"The first time around it was eleven months and a couple weeks before they told me, 'Your insurance is no longer paying for your stay [at in-patient rehabilitation].' Well, at that time, I didn't know nobody in recovery. The only persons I know is addicts. So I called an addict—'Hey, can I crash at yours?' That's what I did. I went over his house.

"They gave me all my prescription drugs: I was on fentanyl patches, Percocets. And I went over there. I was, 'Oh, I'm not gonna get high on crack or dope no more.' But I started taking the fentanyl patches, then I started putting double the dose and then triple the dose. Then halfway through the month, I'm dope sick. Then it's off and running.

"This time around I was in recovery. I knew where I went wrong the first time, where I can't be on the meds, man. As good as they feel and as much as they're numbing me and numbing my pain, I gotta get off. I told my doctor, 'I want you to start cutting me down, until when I go home, I don't wanna be dependent on no pain meds.' So that was in our plan.

"Plus they held my room [at Bridge House]. I didn't stress because I knew when I left there I had somewhere to go, a safe place to go. I wasn't being put out on the street. Know what I mean? I was going back home to Bridge House, where there was a big support system, and people around me were gonna help me out and make sure I did the right thing.

"If they didn't hold my room, I don't know where I woulda went. My mom's? But then that would have had to be okay with the landlord, and the rent would have gone up. And you know, I don't think I would have been pushing myself. I probably would have been on pain meds.

"I know if I go to Bridge House, they really don't—they told me I can, but they'll monitor—but in all reality, they really don't want me on pain meds. And I didn't wanna go there on pain meds. If I woulda went to my mom's house, I woulda been on pain meds. 'Ohhhh, I neeed it.' You know, I woulda been using all the excuses. And they would have been sympathetic with me: 'Yeah, he's in pain.' I coulda manipulated with them where they feel sorry for me. Because they don't get the concept of recovery. They don't know that's a danger. Bridge House wouldn't allow—even if I went there on pain meds, they wouldn't allow me to double dose. So I knew I had to get off. That's the main difference."

"So by the time you left the rehab center, you were totally done with the pain meds?"

"I left with one week of pain meds."

"And were there withdrawals?"

"They gave me withdrawal pills. No. No, I didn't feel—I didn't have diarrhea. They gave me these pills—I still got 'em—for withdrawals. I might have took 'em two nights, and not because I was having withdrawals but because I didn't want to have withdrawals more than anything. I don't know if they worked or not, because like I said, I didn't go through the withdrawals. Did the pain come back once I was off? Yeah. Yeah. But is it tolerable? I mean, look at me. I'm on ibuprofen, and that's it."

"Was there ever a time you doubted that decision?"

"No. You know why? Because today I know I'm an addict. I know if I stayed on where I'm gonna be—I just don't wanna live that lifestyle no more, as far as goin; back out there, and I know that's where pain meds is gonna take me, man. Is there's somedays I wish I could pop a

Percocet? Hell yeah. More days than not. But is that the best decision for me today? No. No. Not today. When I get older and the pain—they say when you get older and your bones become more frail and you start feeling pain, maybe down the road, yeah. But today no. No.

"Would the pharmaceutical company like me on them? Hell yeah. Would I have any problem getting them? No. And the doctors they're, 'You sure you wanna go home with no pain meds? You gonna be in some pain.' I'll be all right. It's funny how they, 'Are you sure you wanna go without?' Yeah you want me to be addicted."

I take over to ask a question: "Seeing you go through the surgery and getting better this time, it just reinforces to me how crazy it was you ended up back in the street last time—just like imagining you in the condition you were in, and now it's just, 'I'm out there.' Is that something you've thought about?"

"It is something I thought about. And that's one of the decisions why I decided not to continue on the pain meds. I mean, it's what's motivating me to do the right thing. I was out there on a wheelchair, man. I was out there on a wheelchair for months. And if I wanted to get high or break up—see the chicken spot up that hill? There's a crack house on the fourth floor. They let you break up, smoke there. If I wanted to go up there, I had to walk. So that was my physical therapy, man.

"I used to say this: it's because of getting high that I got out of the wheelchair and started walking. Bullshit. If I wasn't getting high and put in the same effort in physical therapy, it would have been a lot of quicker. But my fucked-up mind: 'Oh, I was walking up and down crack houses. That's why I got stronger.' In all reality, my body would have recovered a lot quicker if I had done all that physical therapy like I am now—"

"Without the crack," I interrupt.

"Yeah, exactly. So my sick mind was giving credit to being a crackhead—'Oh, if it wasn't for me smoking crack, I would still be in the wheelchair.' I had to walk up five flights of stairs to get a hit. That's why I got my physical therapy. In all reality, if I was clean, going to physical therapy, I probably would have been stronger. It took me two years to start walking around with the cane. This time it took me a couple months."

* * *

People in situations like Joe's are often chronically in need of medical services but access them primarily at moments of crisis, becoming frequent-fliers at hospital emergency rooms but staying only long enough to be stabilized before returning to the social conditions that are a key source of their physical distress.[16] Their high-tech emergency medical care can be disconnected from nonemergency social and preventive services. This was the pattern for Joe when the infection first appeared: an expensive state-of-the-art surgical intervention, followed by a return to the same social conditions at the root of the original distress, with Joe homeless during a chaotic period of street-level drug dependency.

The second time around, Bridge House filled the gap in an inadequate social safety net. Joe was still on the public-housing wait list, and while he talked about the possibility of moving in with his mother after surgery (she also lived in Clearview Crossing), he worried that her landlord may not allow him to live there or respond by raising the rent. He would struggle to afford any foreseeable independent alternative in the private housing market—even if a landlord were prepared to overlook his criminal record and history of imprisonment.

Bridge House was the best available housing option. And the long-term outlook of the program was crucial: when Joe went into surgery after the epidural abscess reappeared, he had already been living there almost twenty-one months. He was welcome to stay as long as needed. They even held open his bedroom, with all his clothes and possessions stored as he left them, during the surgery and in-patient rehabilitation afterward. Joe said that this reduced the stress of the whole experience because, unlike the first time, he had "a safe place to go" and "wasn't being put out on the street."

It was more than affordable accommodation that Joe found at the program: he talked about "going back home to Bridge House,"[17] where there was a "big support system." I knew what he meant because I had been watching the support system all summer. Jim Caine washed his clothes, collecting them in a basket, separating whites from colors, and carrying it up and down the stairs to the basement machine. Tim Williams made him coffees to go with the morning cigarette—it was tricky getting to the porch with a cup in the walking frame—and Steve Price cooked breakfast omelets and left boiled eggs in the fridge for him to eat later. During a period of extremely restricted mobility, when Joe might have been isolated and lonely, there was always someone to talk to, and Joe was a central figure in the social life of the house day-to-day.

The price of the care provided at Bridge House was ongoing carceral control. Not that Joe was forced to live there by the criminal justice system—he had long since completed the probation sentence that mandated his residence at the program. He chose to move back after surgery because it provided desperately needed supports that he could not access anywhere else, and in the process, he volunteered to live under a regime including curfews, drug testing, and bans on sex and overnight visitors. His narrative of the program centered not on these penal elements but on the care and support.

Joe's health care in the aftermath of surgery was governed by a medical establishment emphasizing the pharmaceutical management of his chronic pain, but at Bridge House, he lived under a coercive model of abstinence-based recovery. He said that staff would allow him to use "pain meds" with monitoring but that they did not *really* want him to, with this perception of the cultural disapproval of drug use decisive more than any explicit rule. Joe said he probably would use the medication if he were staying with his mother, but when it came to the program, he "didn't wanna go there on pain meds"—even when prescribed by health-care professionals.

As Joe navigated contrasting regimes of drug regulation within these systems—medical and criminal justice—he sided squarely with the abstinence model prevailing at Bridge House. On the one hand, he was critical of doctors and pharmaceutical companies who seemed overeager to prescribe all manner of drugs—even claiming that they wanted him to be addicted. On the other, the strict abstinence stance of the halfway house seemed to align with his own personal goals in recovery. Joe said that Bridge House would help make sure he "did the right thing."

Perhaps endorsement of the abstinence principle was evidence of Joe's internalization of program values after a long period living within an apparatus of coercive recovery. But it was also rooted in quite-rational reflection on his personal experience. After the first surgery, Joe left in-patient rehabilitation using "patches" infused with the powerful synthetic opiate fentanyl. The drug is around forty times stronger than heroin (per milligram) and often used to treat severe pain during palliative care with cancer patients.[18] Joe said that he abused fentanyl and took double and triple the prescribed dose and, as his tolerance rose and prescriptions ran out early, was left "dope sick"—a colloquial term for withdrawals. He said that it was "off and running" after that, positioning his physical dependence on fentanyl as a core reason for his subsequent transition to using heroin and other street drugs.[19]

This time around, Joe told the doctor at the in-patient rehabilitation, "When I go home, I don't wanna be dependent on no pain meds." With the brutal experience of homelessness in a wheelchair still fresh in his mind, he was desperate to avoid a return to the street and believed, "that's where pain meds is gonna take me, man." So he arranged to taper down the medication during the stay and left with pills to help with any withdrawals. And he talked about the process of getting off the drugs as relatively smooth: barely using the withdrawal pills and still not experiencing diarrhea or other symptoms of physical dependence.

Bridge House provided the stability not only for getting off drugs but for sustained engagement with medical services. Joe had a mailing address for receiving letters and a bedroom for storing the ever-accumulating mountain of paperwork documenting the details of his care. He could predict where he would be in the coming weeks and months and even kept a diary, allowing him to plan and keep appointments with long wait times. When people called to arrange visits or provide information, his number was the same, and he was sober and together enough to answer the phone. Joe said that after the first surgery, it took him two years to start walking with the cane, but this time, it was more like a "couple months."

A key difference was the carceral care provided by Bridge House.

* * *

I take Joe to his appointment at the specialist with the title he struggles to say: "physiatrist." It is more of the same frustrations: they recommend Joe for Botox to help with tightness in his legs, but he will not know for at least a month if it will be covered by insurance. The physiatrist says that he should stop going to physical therapy in the meantime, believing it better to wait and use the remaining sessions paid for by insurance once the Botox is available. On the drive home, Joe is annoyed about the lack of support from the primary-care doctor, who he believes "should be like the quarterback calling plays," helping make decisions and weigh options, navigating this complex bricolage of services. Then it is back to waiting to hear from the insurers.

The most striking feature of the visit is the sheer size of the institution: Wakefield University Hospital is part of sprawling complex that also includes a medical school and several research centers and laboratories. On the third floor, where Joe sees the physiatrist, one wall in the corridor is floor-to-roof glass, looking over an expansive green field with a freshly mowed checker pattern. Three towering buildings with sparkling glass windows frame the sides of the field. Everything looks new inside: the polished wooden wall panels, the designer carpet, the comfortable couches in the waiting room. There is valet parking. The complex is the central location of a health-care conglomerate backed by a large state university. The group employs around twenty-two thousand people and estimates its contribution to the regional economy at almost $5 billion annually.

The economic transformation of Greater Boston since World War II has not only been about industrial decline but the shift from manufacturing to services, with industries based on skilled workers and cutting-edge research replacing the mills and factories that ushered in the Industrial Revolution.[20] By the turn of the century, almost one in five of the region's workers were employed in health or education services.[21] And between 2000 and 2012 alone—the period leading up to the beginning of my fieldwork—Massachusetts's health-care and social-assistance sectors added more than 140,000 jobs, while a combined 180,000 were lost across all other industries in the state.[22]

As a way to understand deindustrialization in Clearview Crossing, I walked the old factory district in the neighborhood, writing fieldnotes and taking photos of the abandoned material culture of the Industrial Revolution: red-brick buildings with boarded windows, old railway lines, holes in the ground with bushy grass where factories once stood. Visiting the physiatrist with Joe was similarly a tour of the material culture of the new economic dominance of university research and high-technology medicine. These sites are two sides of the same historical coin: deindustrialization as crumbling factories, the rise of services as a sprawling medical complex.

These sites are also the built environment of Joe Badillo's life. He was raised on the edge of the old factory district. When he was ten years old, what was once among the world's largest manufacturers of textile looms closed a short walk from the family home. And the extreme violence that Joe experienced at a micro-level—inflicted on others as offender, experienced from others as a victim—was inseparable from the macro-level structural violence sweeping away the economic base of his working-class community.[23] The runaway drug dependency that destroyed his life was intertwined with the financial uses of crack and heroin markets in an economic vacuum.[24] Joe's chronic health problems at middle age were rooted in economic neglect and welfare-state breakdown.

It was a strange social world, where Joe was at different moments brutally abandoned and then revived with the most advanced forms of high-technology medicine.

8

Leaving Bridge House

I join Joe Badillo and Tim Williams at an orientation session run by the Massachusetts Department of Rehabilitation. We sit among a group gathered around long folding tables, on brown cushion chairs with barcode stickers still on the back, waiting for the session to start. The room is mostly hushed. As I have come to expect in these spaces, another participant recognizes Joe. The man has neatly trimmed facial hair and a long-sleeved T-shirt decorated with swirling black lines. He tries to make small talk across the table: "You know Ghetto got out?"

A woman who looks like she will make a presentation mills around, wearing thick makeup and green pants resting halfway up her calves, accentuating platform shoes and a gold bracelet around her right ankle. The male presenter arrives right before the session begins, wearing a navy-blue shirt, with a pen in the pocket, tucked into slacks over a pudgy stomach.

"Are you the coordinator?" a participant asks.

He nods.

"Is this about jobs? I don't wanna waste my time if it's not."

"Everything we do here is about jobs," he replies.

"Is it about education?" asks another participant. "I'm trying to go back to school."

"Well, it can be. It depends on the person. If going back to school will help you get a job, then it can be about education."

He opens the orientation with a similar message: "Our mission is to help people with disabilities get to work."

To be eligible for these "vocational rehabilitation services," he says, you need to have a physical, mental, emotional, or learning disability—or a substance-abuse problem. The two presenters take turns narrating PowerPoint slides, decorated with clip art of hands shaking and college caps and gowns, displayed on a TV screen on a rolling cart. The atmosphere is no-frills and direct. A major point of emphasis is the message that there will be three months on a wait list before seeing a counselor—though the male presenter calls it a "processing list"—and then another sixty days while eligibility is assessed. He reassures the group that the wait has been shortened considerably: it used to be indefinite.

Afterward, we huddle in an alcove outside, sheltering from the rain and smoking cigarettes.

Another participant approaches: "So that's it, huh—now we wait three months? You fuckin' kidding me?" he says, walking away before anyone responds.

Tim turns to me and Joe: "What you expect—instant gratification?"

"That is crazy having to wait for three months," I say.

"Like he said, it used to be longer," Joe replies with a shrug. "I need that three months to get stronger anyway."

* * *

Joe attended the orientation still frail from surgery and in a lot of pain day-to-day, only recently out of the walking frame and getting around on a cane. And he had a specific goal in mind: accessing state funding to enroll in a yearlong addiction-counseling program at community college and, ultimately, earning a Certificate in Alcohol and Drug Abuse Counseling—a qualification that the men at Bridge House colloquially called "the CADAC." The Department of Rehabilitation's broad definition of disability, including substance-abuse disorders and learning deficits, made this educational funding potentially available to just about every Bridge House resident. Tim Williams also went to the orientation with the goals of community college and gaining a CADAC.

There were strong incentives for Joe to get the process under way: perhaps most importantly, the income he received from Social Security was not enough to cover basic costs and left him living at a halfway house years after completing his probation sentence. He showed me a letter from the Social Security Administration around this time listing his monthly payment as just $674.50 (after $72.10 was withheld for a previous overpayment). Delivering public aid at effectively unlivable levels has long been a tool of labor regulation intended to promote work effort among the poor[1] and, more recently, has been a key strategy in the neoliberal transformation of the welfare state through which people in need are pushed into precarious low-wage employment.[2] With Joe relying on this system for his sole source of income, he set about up-skilling almost exactly six months after having part of his spine surgically removed.

Joe found the Department of Rehabilitation emphasizing employment and economic independence for people with disabilities. As one presenter put it, "Everything we do here is about jobs." The session was symptomatic of the way contemporary welfare programs promote work both by suppressing the level of public aid and through active labor-market policies that groom and subsidize workers for transitions into employment.[3] Whereas the social safety net once "decommodified" labor by offering people in need a partial reprieve from market pressures, neoliberalism has blurred the boundary between welfare assistance and labor-market participation, with welfare programs designed to press recipients into accepting the worst jobs at the worst wages.[4]

At the same time, Joe's end goal was not the kind of fast-food job often celebrated as a "successful placement" within these welfare bureaucracies, but more meaningful employment as a counselor in the field of addiction recovery. And the department might even fund his education at a community college—a crucial stepping-stone and reminder of the partial openings that remained amid the many structural exclusions he faced. On the drive back to Bridge House after the orientation, Joe said that he had gained a position running a two-hour class each week for the Massachusetts Recovery Coalition (before surgery derailed the opportunity). He said that it only paid $120 a month but was a foot in the door and signal of more to come. And he talked about "building references all over the place," foremost among them the directors of Bridge House and Ray of Hope: Pat Townsend and Thalia Andrews. Joe's growing confidence about his employment prospects came from the potential for education to turn this progress in recovery into a genuine mobility pathway.

"Once I have the CADAC, I'll get a job like this," he said, snapping his fingers.

Joe's optimism belied a long road ahead. The prospect of attending community college, already daunting after decades of educational hiatus, was further complicated by the material realities of his grinding poverty and serious health problems. If Joe successfully completed the six courses and associated "practicum" that were part of the yearlong addiction-counseling program, he would still need to pass an exam for the Massachusetts Board of Substance Abuse Counselor Certification and accrue hours in employment before being granted the CADAC. Then would begin the difficult task of finding a stable job paying a living wage.

The plan relied crucially on the foundational support of Bridge House. Consider the extended wait time to even learn whether he could access funding: the estimates given at the orientation were three months to see a counselor and, after this initial meeting, sixty days to assess eligibility. Yet Joe was able to shrug off the wait—even presenting it as a chance to physically recuperate—in part because the program was meeting basic material needs for food and shelter that his Social Security income was inadequate to cover. Without this support, Joe would have been experiencing desperate urgency to generate additional income by any means necessary. In other words, having the time to navigate the bureaucratic entanglements[5] of accessing education as a welfare recipient was a luxury flowing from his residence at a halfway house that allowed him to stay as long as he needed.

The long-term view of the Bridge House program enabled Joe personally to take a long-term view. He had developed a vision of the future and was taking concrete steps toward it, like attending the orientation in pursuit of a specific qualification and, more generally, developing relationships with working professionals in the recovery scene who might be references in job applications down the road. The plan was based on a rational assessment of the available opportunities: recovery offered forms of employment that were not susceptible to the usual obstacles—working as a counselor would avoid the need for manual labor, for example, and translate his long criminal record from a source of stigma into evidence of experience and expertise. And as Joe mapped out the process, he could be confident of having a stable place to live for as long as it took.

For all this, Joe was only staying at Bridge House because he could not afford housing independently. The program may have been crucial support for his education and employment goals, but it was also a carceral institution, a key reason he was aggressively juggling these goals with complex medical needs and chronic pain. In the wake of spinal surgery, Joe was not only learning to walk again but working hard on an exit strategy from the halfway house.

* * *

Joe and I meet in a city park one block from the family home where he was raised. There is paper and stationery scattered over the gray picnic table where we find shade under a tree. Despite a local university's efforts to renovate the park in recent years, the pond looks more like a swamp, with an old shoe floating in the muddy water. We smoke cigarettes and drink Dunkin Donuts iced coffee from big plastic cups. There are two uniformed police officers at a table nearby.

We both have printed copies of Robert Merton's criminological classic "Social Structure and Anomie."[6] As a first step toward Joe reading the essay on his own, I talk through the basics of academic referencing, describing how each name and year in a bracket links to a published work at the back of the article. We pause to both read the opening paragraph and then talk about what it means—I explain the concept of "social structure," and Joe fumbles over the word "analytically," pronouncing it "antilogicly." I explain as plainly as possible Merton's overarching argument that strain results from a disconnect between a society's culturally defined goals—its "frame of aspirational reference"—and the institutional means for these goals to be achieved legitimately, that when the ideal of the American dream puts pressure on all to accumulate wealth, at the same time as opportunities to do so are closed to many, some people will grab forcefully what they are otherwise denied. Joe engages in a back-and-forth discussion.

We open our essays to Merton's famous typology of adaptations to this socially imposed strain (see table 8.1).[7] I start an explanation with the *conformists*, who accept mainstream cultural goals and pursue them by established institutional means—going to school and building conventional careers. Joe seems to grasp the idea quickly and, before I can get there, interrupts to point a finger at the *innovators*: "This is when you make your own rules up, coming up with your own ideas." It is a fair approximation of Merton's theorizing of responding to strain with deviant entrepreneurialism. Similarly, when I describe *retreatists* giving up on the goals they do not have the institutional means to achieve, Joe suggests as a good example "drug addicts" who "want the other dream."

TABLE 8.1. Merton's Typology of Adaptations

		Culture goals	Institutionalized means
I	Conformity	+	+
II	Innovation	+	−
III	Ritualism	−	+
IV	Retreatism	−	−

The conversation turns toward Joe's own evolving goals: "I was over here," he says, pointing to "retreatism" on the printed copy of the essay.

"Psssh, no goals, I don't care. My goal was to wake up high."

"What's all that husting to get rich?" I ask.

"Yeah, that, but when you realize you can't even hustle, you just wanna get high, you are retreating from the goals. I didn't care about owning a house. I was happy sleeping on Main Street. I wasn't thinking about the goal."

Joe pauses to think, sipping on ice coffee and swirling ice in the cup.

"I'm finding new ways to get it," he says. "I have to go back to school. I have to be content as far as not trying to be in a rush. My goals are still to own my own house, to live comfortably—I want that. Yeah, man, now I understand like, not the American dream, but I *do* want my own home. I think everybody in their right mind would want their own home, or even their own apartment. I'd be happy with my own apartment."

"In a way, you are here, right? 'Conformity.'"

"Today, yeah—because I'm chasing dreams and goals now."

∗ ∗ ∗

When Joe enrolled in community college, I looked for ways to dovetail the research with his return to education and developed a three-month project in which we would read and write together about the American dream. It was a chance to work with Joe as an analyst, rather than simply as a research participant, who might contribute to the representation of his lifeworld being created. Other researchers engaging criminalized people in this kind of collaborative knowledge production tend to rely on artistic outlets like music[8] or photography.[9] But positioning Joe as a writer was a context-specific strategy to advance the research through practices that might be mutually beneficial, a process of data gathering and analysis that also opened space for working with him one-on-one to provide academic mentoring, sharing the cultural capital I was developing through the research.

The ethnographer Mitchell Duneier famously collaborated with the main participant in his ethnography of street vendors in New York, Hakim Hasan, who wrote the afterword to the book *Sidewalk*.[10] But our participants came from very different educational backgrounds. Hakim Hasan had a degree from Rutgers University; had worked a series of jobs as a proofreader in law, accounting, and investment-banking firms; and spent his days selling and talking about books.[11] Joe said he left school at fourteen years-old, and when I asked about other experiences writing as an adult, he thought about it and could name only one: letters to the outside from prison. He said the "deepest he got" with reading was the Greek philosophers like Plato and Socrates (also while incarcerated).

At some level, the project did not really work: we never got to the point of producing publishable writing. But any evaluation depends in part on what you mean by "working." Talking about Robert Merton in the park, for example, was a valuable learning experience on both sides: Joe was gaining knowledge facilitating his broader engagement with education—like how citations work in academic journals—and at the same time, I was developing a more nuanced understanding of both his vision of the future and what return to education looked like in practice. That particular conversation was an important early signal that Joe was adopting fairly conventional goals within what Merton called the wider culture's "frame of aspirational reference"—with a home of his own being a key component.

I was not living at Bridge House during this period and instead traveled to Clearview Crossing weekly to meet with Joe. He did not have a computer, so he wrote using pen and paper, faxed to my department at the university, which I then typed in Microsoft Word and brought printed copies of to our meetings. When he brought a used laptop, I talked him through the basics of Microsoft Word: how to change the font and text size, how to align text on the page, how to "undo" mistakes and "cut and paste" to move text around, how to change the zoom to see better. I showed Joe how to save documents so they could be found later and distinguished from one another—creating and naming folders, labeling files with names and dates—and introduced the thesaurus for finding words. Joe began attaching files to emails and sending the writing electronically instead of using the fax machine.

I may not have been living at Bridge House, but my engagement with Joe was nonetheless facilitated by the program model of cultivating connections between former prisoners and representatives of the social mainstream—especially from universities. Without this ethos, I would probably have never met Joe or been allowed to stay there in the first place. Yes, I was an unusual presence in the program: most volunteers were obviously not ethnographers building long-term collaborations with residents or reading classic works of social theory with them. But the more general way our relationship functioned as a bridge to the mainstream was very consistent with what the program was all about. I even invited Joe to be a guest speaker in a university course I was teaching.

The writing project was also intertwined with the welfare state's active labor-market policies pushing Joe to seek training and employment at a time when he was still reeling from surgery. I sometimes wonder if I should have just left him alone to recuperate during this period. And he got involved not only for the learning but because I paid: the plan was ten dollars an hour, ten hours a week for twelve weeks. I intended this as a tangible way to redistribute the benefits of the research and compensate Joe for the labor he contributed,[12] but in the context of his poverty and halfway house residence, it also introduced an uncomfortable element of coercion. He was in a precarious position and needed the money.

It felt on balance like a meaningful exercise in ethnographic collaboration when the project was going well—like the day we had a good conversation about Merton in the park. But as we transitioned from reading to writing, it was often tumultuous and at times became for Joe a deeply painful experience. For example, writing involved hunching over a keyboard and straining his surgically damaged back, and given that he barely had the money for a secondhand laptop, an ergonomically correct chair and desk setup was a nonstarter. The physical pain was compounded by intense bouts of stress and anxiety. In hindsight, the toll of Joe's return to education should have been obvious. Back then, I found it jarring and unexpected. I had watched him confront enormous challenges over several years while remaining grounded and comfortable in his own skin—and assumed that the philosophical attitude would extend to education. I was wrong.

* * *

Joe starts writing short vignettes about his consumerist dreams as a child and teenager, like the time he brought an Audi he could not drive from a drug customer at fifteen years old. He calls on the phone, bullish and energized, to announce that his writing will be faxed within the hour.

"My arm's about to drop off, and my head's about to explode," he says.

We are scheduled to meet at 3:00 p.m., but Joe waits until the last minute to say that he has a doctor's appointment at 4:00 p.m. It is a long drive, and I am annoyed that we will be cut short. When I pick him up from Ray of Hope, he says that someone stole his phone and that his girlfriend asked him to get a pair of sneakers for her brother who is getting out of jail—but he does not have the money. It is brutally hot at the park. Joe has a vibe of anxiety and insecurity that I am not used to seeing. He loses interest in the meeting and retreats to his phone.

"Stay with me, Joe," I say.

"Yeah, I'm with you."

"You're not with me when you're reading a text."

Joe rests the phone on the table.

"I put down a note to talk about paragraphs. Do you 'get' paragraphs?" I ask, wary that his first round of writing came in one long block of sentences.

"Don't even ask. I won't be able to do that," he says. "I don't know where a paragraph stops or where it begins."

"Nah, you can. You can do that. When you do your CADAC writing, you're going to have to put paragraphs in. The way you have it now is just one long thing, right?

"Yep."

"Just picture it from the reader's point of view. It's hard to read, its intimidating, when you just have word, word, word, word. To break it up a little just makes it that much easier to read."

I hand him the paper copy I typed from his faxed handwritten version.

"So this is yours. I just broke it up into paragraphs."

"Yeah, so *this* is my paragraphs," he says dismissively.

"When you start writing in paragraphs, you'll get a feel about how to use them. A paragraph is just a point or idea, then you go to the next one. In some ways, you can put a paragraph anywhere. Aim for like a hundred words is about what you want. Just start doing it, and don't stress too much about, 'Is my paragraph in the right place.' As you do it a few times, you'll get a feel for it. Just try it."

"All right."

"Yeah?"

"Yeah."

"So I did ask even though you said, 'Don't even ask,'" I say, laughing.

"Nah, I understand," Joe says.

* * *

Joe often arrives hungry to our meetings. Before the first one, I buy lunch at a local diner, and the next week, we go to McDonald's drive-through for iced coffee, Joe mentions being hungry, and I get him a Big Mac. I say that he should eat something before coming. He shrugs his shoulders and says, "Well," which I take to mean that he is broke and does not have a choice.

I have not got much money either. I do not want to create the expectation of lunch every week and start eating in the car on the drive there. I find myself stuffing the scrunched paper wrapper from my sandwich into the center console between the front seats while I wait for him in the car outside Ray of Hope. Another time, I throw my Big Mac box and scrunched brown bags onto the floor of the backseat, but as we drive, I see that my McDonald's cup is still in the holder up front.

I wonder if Joe noticed that I ate on the way.

* * *

Joe sends the following text: "struggling bad . . . mind all over the place."

"whatever you give me will be great Joe, trust me," I respond.

I try to call, but he does not answer the phone.

Then another text: "I am just hit alittle bump in the road in my personal life that renting space in my head."

* * *

Joe moves out of Bridge House four days before starting community college.

The date is August 28, 2015—around three years and three months after he had arrived—and the destination is Father Clarks House on the other side of town. Bridge and Father Clarks are run by the same organization, with movement from the first to the second officially presented as a "graduated reentry process" in which successful residents are selected based on perceived readiness for independent living. I never learn the details of the negotiations through which Joe earns the place or why the decision was not made earlier, but it ultimately depends on the evaluations of Pat Townsend and Kevin Smith. And the close timing of Joe's selection and the start of community college suggests that his return to education may have bolstered his case.

The overlap between these two big life transitions—leaving Bridge House and starting community college—also creates a very stressful situation. Moving to a new house with a disability creates physical challenges, and Joe is experiencing severe foot pain as a complication of determined efforts to walk again after spinal surgery, which will ultimately result in further surgery inserting steel pins into the middle of each toe on one foot. There are bureaucratic entanglements: for example, Joe relies on transport funded through his state health insurance to get around, what he calls his "PT-1," but has time-consuming problems getting the pickup address changed. He loses important materials for his addiction-counseling course during a chaotic move.

Joe is characteristically stoic and almost never draws attention to the many challenges. But writing is different. As I look back, it seems remarkable that he was able to complete any work with me at all during this period, but at the time, I am continuously surprised by how the usually unflappable Joe is so shaken by trying to write. I talk this through with him very directly in one our meetings.

"Your emotional weight around writing still catches me off guard," I tell him. "Because I've seen all the shit you've gone through, and to me, that all seems so much more serious. I never see you complain. Like I've heard you complain more about writing in the last six weeks then I've heard you complain about back pain in fuckin' three and a half years, when they cut half your spine out—"

Joe interrupts: "This is more painful," he says. "It is. I don't know why. It just don't come as—pain you can just deal with it. Writing, you gotta do it. You have to fuckin' do this shit. I'll tell you what: I'm not happy about writing. Your idea of me bein' a writer, that went in one ear, out the other."

"You couldn't imagine a situation where you could come to enjoy it in some way?"

"To what?"

"To enjoy it in some way."

"Pssssh."

"Never?"

"Well, you never say never. But never. I don't think so. Maybe the more time that goes on, the more I'll think about it. But nah, it's too fuckin' stressful, bro. This is stressful shit, bro. Writing is like pssshhh. Like, 'Damn, man, I gotta go write.'"

"Do you wanna just take a second to like—how would you explain to a total stranger what is stressful about writing? And take a minute to think—"

"Nah, I know why it's stressful. It's stressful because you can start a story and get off course. Or you cannot add enough detail, or you can add too much detail. Or for me, I have difficulty putting my thoughts into paper, on paper, I have difficulty—"

I interrupt: "Let me just push back and say, 'Who gives a fuck?' So yeah, you make mistakes—"

"Yeah, yeah, yeah, I know that. That's the thing I have to keep on reminding myself: 'Yo, just writing. This ain't a pass or fail class. I'm not getting credited.'"

"But even if it was. I still haven't heard from you a convincing explanation of—"

"Them are all convincing to me, man."

"Yeah, it's just when I see the other shit that you go through without stressing over, without complaining—like, they seem much harder to me than—"

"They probably are—like dealing with my disability, getting through the day with the pain, you know, just doin' it. I mean, but, in all reality, I have no other choice in that matter. I can't just lay down. I can't. I have to bare through it.

"With writing, it's new. I been through pain and misery and all that. That's something I become accustomed to. I mean, the pain of being out on the street dope sick is far worse than the pain of my back. I rather have another surgery then go back on the street and go through that madness again. That's any given day. My status where I am today, where I have to wake up in the morning and stretch my legs for a half hour, and let them spaz out, and put on sneakers that are, you know, difficulty because my toes hurt, is nowhere the pain that I been in when I was out there in the street."

Again I interrupt to push Joe: "Why can't you say [the same about] this pain and stress of writing? 'When I'm just sitting in a quiet room thinking about my life and trying my best to put my thoughts down is nowhere near the pain of the fuckin' [street] . . .'"

We are both laughing.

"Well, but *because it is*. Because it's new to me, and I wanna do good. It's stressful. It's very stressful. You know writing is stressful. It takes a lot out of you mentally. Like school's fuckin' all new to me again. I haven't been in a real school since I was fourteen. So I'm like pssshh. I think both of them are playin' a part on the stress. I think I got more gray hairs this week than anything else."

"I still don't understand it, man. Basically the only things I'm hearing from you as reasons why writing sucks is because it's new and its stressful. And you don't wanna fuck it up. You wanna do a good job. Those things seem so small. It's like, 'Liam's gonna think I didn't fuckin' write good . . .'"

"Well, maybe me thinkin' like that pushes me. So maybe if I be like, 'Fuck it,' then you wouldn't get the work you get now."

"Yeah, I face the same thing in my writing: to what extent do you be a perfectionist and beat yourself up? Because that helps you to do a good job? But if you're doing that to the point where writing is like torture, and you don't want to write anymore, then you're too far in that direction. You do need to care, but you don't wanna fuckin' torture yourself."

"Exactly what I'm doing, right."

"I can't help but think it's tied up in some unconscious memories of school and just feeling like, 'I can't fuckin' do it.'"

"I think that plays a part. I got ADHD too, so that kicks in. I got PTSD. That's gotta play a part. There's a lot goin' around. It's not somebody who just—you know, it takes a lot."

"Let's say if you were writing a paper for school, like when you write your paper for your class."

"I'm dreading that."

"I guess what I'm tryna get at is how much of it is hard because its forcing you to relive things you would rather not relive, and how much of it is just writing itself?"

"I think both. I guess tryna bring old memories back probably plays a part. But at the same time, I gotta write this paper—basically it boils down to okay, with school I gotta write a five- to eight-page letter, ah paper, and it's gonna be on anything with addiction—let's say single family and addiction. And I gotta do research, and I gotta add where I quote people and then 'Merton said this' or 'This guy said that.' And I'm already stressin' about that, because, one, I don't know where to start; two, I don't know how that's even—I never done that before. I never had to turn in a paper, a research paper, never. Where do you start? Where do you begin your . . ."

Joe stops and pauses, then continues:

"At the same time, it will get done. It might not be a masterpiece, but it will get done to the best of my ability. So that's a plus. I'm not saying 'Psshhh, I'm not doin' that.' I get my moment where I cry, I fuckin' bitch about writing. But I'm not throwing in the towel."

* * *

Joe sends a text: "im having a stressful time with this . . . im going to go over the paper and attempt to edit . . . not happy right now just so you know."

I call Joe, and we talk for around twenty minutes. He says that he had a test at community college last night, and he feels like he has been dumped into the advanced class with a whole lot of lessons skipped in between. There are construction people working on Father Clarks House, and he cannot find a ride to leave for a quieter place to write.

Another text the next morning: "Im sorry I can't do it or do I know where to add stuff . . . i mentally drained . . . all jokes a side I'm having a nervous breakdown . . ."

I try to call twice, and there is no answer.

* * *

I hoped our collaborative writing project would support and complement Joe's transition into community college. And there were ways it did: I typed his handwritten work into printable documents so he could see what a finished product looked like, showed him how to write using paragraphs, and talked him through the essentials of Microsoft Word. This was very direct preparation for the education system. At the same time, our work also fueled the problem by placing further demands on Joe during a period when he was already stretched and vulnerable. Continuing became untenable as classes started, early assignment deadlines loomed, and Joe experienced what he called in a text message a "nervous breakdown." We stopped for over a month.

Joe was pursuing a credential in drug and alcohol counseling as a possible mobility pathway while facing broad social exclusion. Our writing together provided an inside view on what this seemingly conventional plan of turning education into employment demanded from him in practice. Joe described trying to write as more painful than his chronic physical pain. Even as he talked about struggling to put shoes on aching feet and stretching legs that "spaz out" in the mornings, he stood firm on the larger point: writing was more painful. In practice, the psychological pain of writing was not a separate experience to be weighed against the physical pain—Joe experienced both at the same time. And the whole determined effort to up-skill while dealing with serious health problems was rooted in the failures of the social order to recognize his frailty and guarantee a decent standard of living outside labor-market participation.

Joe said he was "dreading" the research paper about addiction that he needed to write. And he articulated the stress in terms of its being a fundamentally new practice: "I never done that before. I never had to turn in a paper." Writing together, I found that the ballooning anxiety associated with education stemmed in part from these unfamiliar skills being learned in a context of social marginality. His often being hungry during meetings was a symptom of inadequate Social Security income and lack of transport making it difficult to access good food, which both sapped the energy he could bring to the work and generally undermined his health and well-being. We usually met at the park because Joe lacked space of his own beyond a small single bedroom at the halfway house.

When Joe moved, Father Clarks House replaced Bridge House as foundational support for his entry to education—meeting most of all the critical need for housing. Father Clarks was physically nicer than Bridge, a single large home divided into four units with some shared living space, and even had a sunroom with one wall mostly a long row of windows to the garden outside. The atmosphere was less restrictive and there was no structured program at all: no weekly meeting or evening meal, no curfew or mandatory involvement in the twelve steps, no formal staff supervision day-to-day. Joe could have me stay at the house overnight without needing to ask anyone's permission.

Despite the material comforts and relative freedom, Father Clarks was still very connected to Bridge, run by the same organization and inhabited by former residents. There was an expectation of abstinence, and Kevin Smith generally kept an eye on the place; so Joe's position was precarious, and he could be removed for a failed Breathalyzer or drug test. After years of carceral supervision, he was out of Bridge House but only just—living in a kind of halfway house from the halfway house. And he was still scrambling for a place of his own.

* * *

Joe and I finished the project across four days working side by side at Father Clarks House, split into two-day blocks in consecutive weeks, during which I stayed the night each time. This engagement marked the end of these years of fieldwork because I was preparing to leave the country and return to New Zealand and, in this context, provided one last chance to examine together Joe's predicament and vision of the future. We blended writing with shared reading and recorded conversation under the broad theme of the American dream. To paint a picture based on fieldnotes: the small wooden table in the sunroom where we worked was small enough that our laptops touched at the back, cords adding to the clutter of empty water bottles, coffee cups, and an Arizona green-tea bottle for cigarette butts. Our respective pads were scrawled with pen-written notes. Joe rested reading glasses on a pile of books and paper. A friend called on the phone and asked what he was doing. "Writing," he said.

In preparation, we both read sections of the recently published *Between the World and Me* by Ta-Nehisi Coates.[13] The book is a partly biographical reflection on the experience of being Black in the United

States, written by Coates as a letter to his son, and has a recurring focus on the American dream as a fantasy that is closed to most people and reserved for privileged whites in comfortable suburban neighborhoods. It provides a powerful account of racialized violence and exclusions—challenging widely held cultural beliefs about meritocracy and the ability of any individual to overcome structural obstacles with determination and hard work. Reading the text with Joe was a springboard for discussing his own prospects for upward mobility in this context of deeply entrenched inequality.

Our conversation about the book cycled again and again around the relationship between structure and agency. And even as Joe drew direct connections between the account of systemic disadvantage in the text and his personal experience—including Coates's descriptions of police violence and being "shackled" by the Baltimore school system—he consistently focused on the opportunities that remained. He talked about his own racial position being different from Coates's, for example, and described the openings presented by having light skin and a flexible racial identity. As he put it, "I don't have to tell nobody that I'm half Puerto Rican. They're not gonna know." Joe even named particular examples of deliberately presenting as white—like ticking "Caucasian" rather than "Hispanic" when filling out forms for parole applications. This narrative of his racial position as a source of opportunity was typical of his generally optimistic view of his individual autonomy.

As we went back and forth talking about the book and reflecting on his experience, Joe articulated a rather orthodox set of goals centered on work and housing: "My dream is just to have a nine-to-five and a home to come home to. I don't know if that's the American dream, but that's my dream." And at one point, he grabbed his printed copy of *Between the World and Me* from the table, flicked through the pages, and read aloud the following passage:

"I have seen that dream all my life. It is perfect houses with nice lawns. It is Memorial Day cookouts, block associations, and driveways. The Dream is treehouses and the Cub Scouts. The Dream smells like peppermint but tastes like strawberry shortcake. And for so long I have wanted to escape into the Dream, to fold my country over my head like a blanket. But this has never been an option because the Dream rests on our backs, the bedding made from our bodies."

Finishing the passage, Joe moved to explain the resonance to his own predicament:

"So basically the dream is only surviving or existing because of people like me. I fund this dream for other people. I'm just a piece of stock. My mistreatment or lack of ability to achieve things is beneficial to them who can truly achieve that dream."

"But there's parallels between that passage—it's the perfect houses, the nice lawns—and how you are talking about what you want."

"Well, I guess I want the American dream."

"What about, he [Coates] follows up with, 'for so long I wanted to escape into the Dream. To pull my country up over my head like a blanket." But "it's never been an option, because that Dream rests on our backs." The whole thing is—"

"Yeah, our sweat and blood." Joe pauses. "I bet you he [Coates] owns his own home by now."

"I bet he does too."

"So I think his view changed. If he don't want to admit it—but he has.

"When you talk about, 'I just want a nine-to-five and a home,' that's very American dreamy right?"

"Of course it is. Absolutely."

"Is there some level of making a deal with the devil?"

"Yeah, you're definitely shaking hands with the devil when you buy into the dream. But I don't know, you can look at it different ways. My biggest fear right now is being homeless. That's my biggest fear. Especially being in recovery, I don't know if I'm going to trip and fall. My plans are not to, but I'm sure everyone's plan was not to trip and fall. I can make one little tiny mistake and go out and have a couple beers and come home, and Kevin sitting at the door waiting with a Breathalyzer. And then what's my next move?

"See when I think of chasing the dream, chasing the dream has never been closing my eyes at night and waking up at six in the morning to go to work. The dream was closing my eyes and waking up with the house. There was no work involved. That was the dream. It's a different dream, I guess, where you close your eyes and you instantly have everything, as opposed to closing your eyes and seeing a plan, how to achieve them things. As far as setting goals, my dream is to have a house and family to come home to. But it involves goals and going back to school and putting in long hours and working."

"There's something all very conventional in it," I say. "Go to school, work hard, the house, you know? The way you talk about it is a classic model. It's a model that society sets. It's like, I'm trying to think of the politics of it all, like this whole fucked-up American system is based around these ideas about 'well, all you gotta go do is go school, then work, you get your house—"

"No, no, that's a lie. It's a lie, we all know that. Even hardworking people been living in the same apartment for thirty years because they can't get into a house, because their jobs don't pay enough. I mean, you figure how many people risk their lives to get into this country, and it's still happening today, but even more so back in the late 1800s and into the 1900s. All these immigrants coming to America for that dream and being so disappointed when they get here and realize there is no dream. Because you're Irish, you can't work at this job or you can't be in this status."

"It sounds like you think it *is* open to *you* though. Like, 'If I go to school and work hard . . .'"

"Well, see, I'm thinking in a different sense, because why wouldn't it be available for me?"

"Because of the fucked-up system with all kinds of poverty—"

Joe interrupts: "But there's proof and evidence in front of me that I *can* achieve that goal. I have friends that put down the drugs and went to school and worked hard and now own their own homes. So why couldn't I?"

"Are you thinking of Trell there?" I ask, referring to a friend of Joe's who got a psychology degree and works as a counselor.

"Yeah, I'm thinking of Trell. I have like five, six friends that own their own homes. All raised smoking crack, selling drugs, gangbanging. But they went back to school. They worked. So I see that as a goal. Will it be achieved? I don't know."

"What about when someone says, 'Well, what the fuck are you guys complaining about with the 'America, everything's wrong'? You're living proof that anyone can do it—'"

Joe interrupts before I can finish: "No, no, no. It's not living proof that anybody can do it. It's just living proof that I'm not giving up on myself.

Doesn't mean I have to give up on my goals. Shit, is the system messed up? Yes. Is there only a certain field that I can get into [alluding to recovery]? Is it difficult? Yes. Is it fair? No. I'm going on five years [clean] and still can't get employed because of my felonies. That doesn't mean in ten years I can't get employed, but is that fair? No. Is there obstacles? Absolutely. I would have to work for the next thirty years before I'm in a house. And I'm already forty-five, so what does that leave me? Like a year in the house? But at the same time, I shouldn't not set goals for myself. That would be injustice for me to think that I can't get the house. If I sat here and said, 'Oh, I can't get that,' then I'd never get it. If I set a goal, there's a possibility I do."

"It's like having some kind of separation between how you think about the way society works and then how you think about your own goals," I suggest.

"The system is not making it easy for me to buy my own home. Definitely not. I mean, it was hard for me to get back to school. The only reason I am going back to school is thank God there's an organization paying for me to go back to school. If not, then . . ."

"Who's paying?"

"The government. The same government that wants me to fail. But the government knows that only a very small percentage of people are gonna be successful through that program. They know that. But they have to put it in place because of politics," he says.

"And they love the idea of people going back to school and trying to—that's their whole model for change," I add.

"It makes them look good," Joe continues. "'What you talking about, we don't care? We got programs for all these people to go back to school. We paying for that.' But they know a small percentage is gonna even be successful at that. They know a very small percentage is gonna graduate. They know a very small few are gonna pursue that career when they get out of school. Like my teacher, on the first day, she said, 'Look around because halfway through the course, half these people won't be here.'"

I laugh. "It's more or less like battling against the odds."

"Battling against the odds."

"But it's also—that's the American dream, baby," I suggest.

"Yeah, that poor immigrant from any country gonna come over here and be successful," Joe agrees, before continuing. "And that's the lie, 'cause out of a million people from different countries, the percentage of being successful are very slim. Do you have 'em? Absolutely. If you have enough people, that dream is gonna—"

I interrupt: "You say it's a lie, but it's also your own goals."

"Yeah, but all right. Look at it like this: America tells you that everybody's dream can come true. And it's a lie because not everybody's dream can come true. But when you put enough people into this equation, somebody is eventually going to achieve that goal. And then they can say, 'Ooh, look see,' and make an example out of them. 'You see this guy came in here with nothing. You see what this country did for him?' That's just playing against the odds, man. It's like going to the casino, playing against the odds. 'We'll let a million people lose, but we'll let a hundred succeed.' That's it."

"It's not stopping *you* grabbing onto that, though, right?"

"Why would it, though? Why would it? Do I want poverty? I *don't* want poverty. I don't. I have to—and I don't know if I'm grabbing onto it, as far as, 'This is my birthright. America owes me this.' But in the sense that I'm holding onto it is because, as bad as this country is, I'm still able to achieve that house. Able doesn't mean that I can. But I have—"

"There's a chance," I say, interrupting, before Joe continues:

"There's a chance. There's a sliver of a chance that I will. Are the odds against me? Stacked. They're stacked against me like me hitting the lottery. But somebody hits the lottery."

9

Alternatives

Joe Badillo's house has an above-ground swimming pool. There is a large television mounted on the wall in the lounge and, underneath, an electronic screen displaying a crackling fire. The floor creaks and slopes unevenly here and there, but the place is tidy and comfortable. The downstairs bath has jet streams, and a well-stocked kitchen looks out over a tree-lined backyard covered with red and orange leaves. There is a dryer and washing machine in the alcove at the front door and, on the wall where no one entering can miss it, a painted wooden sign reading, "Home Sweet Home, Est. 2019" (see figure 9.1).

I stay for two weeks in the spare bedroom, showing Joe a draft of this book and generally taking every chance to talk about the project. But it is hard to find much time: Joe is commuting to Clearview Crossing each day to work as program director at Ray of Hope. He says the annual salary is $52,000. As a drug and alcohol counselor, he is constantly called on to provide advice and support to people embroiled in chaotic cycles of drug-related harm, both at the center he runs and more informally through his own personal networks. He is a board member at a Latino halfway house, mentors young people through a multicultural wellness center on what he calls a "fee-for-service" basis, and has recently taken a sixteen-hour-a-week role as community outreach coordinator at Bridge House. Joe is stretched thin but for the first time has a stable foothold in the formal economy, providing regular income, access to a mortgage and, ultimately, his first home.

Joe's transformation is brimming with contradictions. His employment is a source of not only social mobility but ongoing connection to the social circles of his past. Joe spends his days on the front lines of a street-level drug crisis in the neighborhood where he was born and raised—his many relationships in the scene a key resource he brings to the job—participating now as a service provider rather than drug user and seller. He leverages the stable income to take on debt and purchase

Figure 9.1. Joe Badillo's house

the 2016 Mercedes-Benz SUV he drives from his new home to work each morning (he says the car cost $48,000). It may be a rags-to-riches story of the American dream, but in this particular version, the more things change, the more they seem to stay the same.

The continuities with the past coexist with a host of positive changes. Joe has a long-term girlfriend employed as a social worker in a public school, a completed course at community college behind him, the financial independence to fly to Puerto Rico and reconnect with lost family. He still walks with a cane but his health is greatly improved. In narrower criminal justice terms, he has not seen the inside of a cell or been charged with a crime in over seven years, a remarkable break from the previous two decades cycling in and out of prison and jail. Joe is a well-known success story in the community not only because he drives a nice car but because he has changed for the better in the face of overwhelming obstacles.

Looking back, perhaps the crucial turning point was paradoxically yet another in a long line of criminal justice sanctions—only this time, it was a sentence of probation that diverted Joe from jail and brought him instead to a halfway house.

* * *

In 1976, Michel Foucault gave a talk on alternatives to prison at a conference hosted by the University of Montreal.[1] At a historical moment when many people believed that the future of criminal justice would be led by innovation in community corrections,[2] such as the halfway house,[3] Foucault was skeptical about whether the reforms would be meaningfully more humane than the large, closed institutions they were intended to replace. Drawing on the analysis laid down in *Discipline and Punish*,[4] published the year before, he argued that the "relatively open establishments" being developed were not simply replacing prisons but extending their reach throughout the social order:

> One must not immediately conclude that what is being put in place through these seeming alternatives will be worse than the prison. It is not worse, though one must bear in mind that, in relation to a system of incarceration, there is nothing really alternative in these new methods. It is more a matter of the transmission of the old carceral functions

that the prison implemented in a rather brutal and inefficient way, so that they are now achieved in more flexible, free and also more extensive ways. They are all variations on the same theme of punishment through confinement.[5]

The theoretical vocabulary and style of analysis that Foucault developed during this period provide crucial insights to issues of prisoner reentry and community corrections more than four decades later. The halfway house will always be riddled with the contradictions of an institution designed as an alternative to prison that is itself halfway like a prison. At some level, any transfer of people from prisons to halfway houses is not really decarceration at all, but a movement from one kind of incarceration to another, a shift in styles of social control. More broadly, much of what passes for reentry reform in the United States involves little more than expanding carceral surveillance in ghettoes and barrios that are already subject to violent, militarized policing and historically high rates of imprisonment.

A halfway house placement was helpful for Joe Badillo though. And it was meaningfully different to being imprisoned again—it may have been a variation on the same theme of punishment through confinement, but it was also an environment far more conducive to positive change and healthy development. Joe's successes, with all their idiosyncrasies and personal specificities, are obviously not some kind of vindication of the halfway house as an institution. But they are an opening for thinking through the circumstances under which these programs might provide constructive alternatives even as they are full of messiness and tensions. This is an especially important exercise because the imagery of the carceral risks creating a progressive version of the classic conservative notion that "nothing works,"[6] the idea that all attempts to create community alternatives are inevitably forms of net widening with little impact on the repressive tendencies of the criminal justice system.

Joe's success at Bridge House was based above all else on the unusually long-term view of the program. If he was moved through on a more standard timeline—say the average stay in a federal halfway house of a little under four months[7]—he would likely have ended up homeless again, with social disadvantage compounded by physical disability and a long history of drug dependency, a potentially life-threatening situation.

But he was allowed to stay as long as needed (outside major rule violations). This policy of open time frames partially devolved the decision over when it made sense to leave from the institution to the individual and, in the process, empowered Joe to plan for the future knowing that his basic needs for food and shelter would be met. There were no quick fixes to his complex medical and social problems.

Consider that the Second Chance Act, the signature legislation of the contemporary reentry movement, attempted to extend the length of halfway house stays in the federal system to a maximum of twelve months.[8] The law specifically took aim at a rule restricting placements to six months or 10 percent of a prison sentence,[9] whichever was shorter, but prison managers responded by ignoring the mandate and continuing to impose limits systematically. Bitter legal disputes followed, as prisoners who appeared eligible for release to a halfway house under the Second Chance Act petitioned for relief. The Bureau of Prisons responded by arguing, among other things, that the experience of the agency showed that six months was enough to adequately prepare for reentry.[10]

Six months or twelve months—neither would have been long enough for Joe Badillo. Yet these limits allow correctional managers to cut costs and spread scarce resources more widely at a time when record numbers of people are in dire need of transitional housing. A 2016 review of federally contracted halfway houses, for example, estimated that cutting the length of stay in half (from 180 to 90 days) would also reduce by roughly half the shortage of beds around the country.[11] Missing from this equation is the way choices over timelines shape not only the life chances of participants but the basic atmosphere of programs. Take the decision to hold Joe's room open when his epidural abscess returned and he underwent a second spinal surgery and lengthy period of in-patient rehabilitation. Yes, this left his bed empty for months, unable to be used by anyone else. It also communicated to Joe and the other men at Bridge House a fundamental concern for their well-being—an ethic of care and a promise of stable support at times of need—in the same way that removal in the midst of a health crisis would have communicated neglect and indifference.

The policy of open time frames was especially important at Bridge House because some residents wanted to live there even after completing the placements mandated by parole or probation. One reason was that the program actually resembled a home environment. This may seem like an obvious thing to say, but these kind of small neighborhood halfway houses have been described as a "dying breed."[12] Around three-quarters of the halfway houses contracted by the federal government have capacities of over 40 beds, 41 percent have more than 75, and the largest can hold 317 people.[13] This stretches the definition of what might reasonably be called a halfway "house." And even though the formal terminology has changed over the years—from "pre-release guidance centers" to "community treatment centers," then "community corrections centers" and, most recently, "residential reentry centers"—they are still regularly called halfway houses even in official discourse.[14] But at what scale does a program cease to be a house and become instead an institution or facility or, more ominously, a prison of some kind?

The built environment of Bridge House was consciously constructed to resemble a home rather than a criminal justice setting. The program did not have perimeter fencing or a marked institutional entrance; there were no uniformed staff or guards on the premises, no video cameras or electronically operated doors. These are all common features of contemporary US halfway houses that can make them difficult to distinguish from low-security prisons.[15] Bridge House looked not so different from the other houses on the same residential street. This benign appearance was coupled with more subtle confinements centered on the nightly curfew and other program rules mandating that the men be physically present at particular times. But it was still a much less oppressive space not only than prison or jail but than most halfway houses. Joe described Bridge as "more like a three-quarter house."

The punitive edge of the program centered on a coercive model of abstinence-based recovery, drawing on the twelve steps of Narcotics and Alcoholics Anonymous, which was more in line with the broader field of halfway house governance and prisoner reentry.[16] Drug testing and the associated surveillance practices carceralized Bridge House social relations and, in the context of the precarious legal status of men on parole and probation, aligned the program with more repressive sources of penal power—undermining the extent to which it might be considered a real alternative to the war on drugs and broader system of mass incarceration.

Yet there were important distinctions here too: the Bridge House approach to drug regulation ultimately rested less on coercion than creating a home-like environment within a philosophy of "supportive community" (with all the tensions and contradictions this entailed). There was not even a set program of drug treatment; instead, the men were simply told to attend twelve-step meetings and beyond that largely left to decide for themselves what recovery was all about. What seems most important to Joe's ability to break a long cycle of drug dependency was the way Bridge House guaranteed a set of fundamental human needs over the long term: he had always ignored the threat of punishment for drug use, but a key difference this time was that coercion was coupled with the provision of social support and stable housing. This anchored his engagement with recovery by, for example, reducing the psychological stress of financial insecurity and undercutting incentives to enter the drug economy. Bridge House provided the time and space to address drug dependency as one of multiple interlinked problems. Joe was able to repair his relationship with his daughter, navigate the bureaucratic entanglements of accessing health care for complex medical needs, and take concrete steps toward employment, like volunteering to develop experience and up-skilling through a return to education. This could only be achieved slowly and would have been all but impossible if he were locked in a scramble for survival on unlivable Social Security income.

Let me cycle back once more to Michel Foucault's lecture on alternatives to prison at the University of Montreal. His overarching argument was not only that measures presented as alternatives are often less different from the real thing than they may appear, but also that the very question of alternatives to prison is already limited. It is a loaded question that takes too much for granted and implicitly assumes a narrow choice between different punishments, a bit like, as he put it, "asking a child to choose between being caned or being deprived of dessert."[17] And Foucault's rejection of the question was an invitation to raise more fundamental challenges to penal power and imagine alternatives beyond various forms of confinement.

In Joe's case, the effectiveness of Bridge House rested in large part on the collapse of alternatives outside the field of criminal punishment entirely. Yes, the program providing a home-like environment was crucial to the very positive changes he made during these years. But the broader question is why he was unable to find an actual home outside the carceral apparatus for so long. It is one thing to justify the coercion of a halfway house as part of a sentence handed down by a judge in court, but Joe stayed well beyond because there was nowhere better to live. And the material support provided by the program only became so crucial in the absence of alternative sources of support that did not also impose carceral confinement. As a matter of halfway house policy, granting open time frames expressed an ethic of care, but the more important part of the story is the inability of the social order to meet basic human needs in a less coercive fashion.

Bridge may have been better than prison or jail, but it was still a halfway house.

* * *

The recent history of US criminal justice has been marked by broad-based challenges to mass incarceration. Decades of political organizing from incarcerated people and their allies laid the foundations for sustained public debate over the failures of punitive penal policy and the war on drugs, with unlikely reform coalitions emerging, including conservative critics concerned with the runaway financial costs of prison expansion. Calls for decarceration and prison reform have been coupled with public outrage and movement activism targeting racist police violence against Black Americans, sparked by shocking standalone incidents but raising more fundamental questions about the roots of contemporary criminal justice in slavery and racial caste. As policy makers and ordinary people alike interrogate existing practice and search for alternatives, where might the halfway house fit within the work of reimagining criminal justice? Should the institution be considered a tool for challenging the carceral state and addressing the myriad problems facing the unprecedented numbers of people flowing out of prison and jail each year? Or is the halfway house more an extension of mass incarceration, itself needing to be challenged and dismantled?

Let us begin with one way the halfway house concept might be considered transformative: it targets the systemic relationship between homelessness and imprisonment at the core of mass incarceration. During the years of the prison boom, dramatic increases in correctional budgets were coupled with dramatic declines in spending on public housing.[18] Strong overlaps emerged between prison and homeless populations growing rapidly in tandem—both disproportionately poor and located in racially segregated city neighborhoods.[19] Prisons and jails became a de facto form of public housing, increasingly called on to provide shelter to the poorest Americans.[20] The halfway house presents an institutional mechanism for disrupting the prison-homelessness nexus during a crucial transition—reentry—and places an obligation on carceral systems to recognize social need and guarantee accommodation after release.[21]

The halfway house concept is also subversive to the principle of incapacitation underpinning mass incarceration. The idea that prisons work by "incapacitating" prisoners and preventing crime that they would otherwise commit—rather than, say, by treating or rehabilitating prisoners—has become a kind of guiding philosophy of the system.[22] This can be seen, for example, in the wide adoption of "three strikes" and other mandatory-minimum laws, which force judges to impose long sentences without the chance of parole, and a more general tendency for correctional managers to confine prisoners in high-security settings for the longest period possible, so that increasing numbers are released directly from maximum security to the street. In contrast, the halfway house concept represents a commitment to imposing the minimum intensity of confinement necessary to meet penal ends and provides practical measures for scaling back the overreliance on imprisonment in more severe environments, through both diversion (halfway in) and early release (halfway out).

The disconnect between the halfway house and the prevailing logics of mass incarceration leaves it operating on a tiny scale in many parts of the United States. Consider the situation in Massachusetts. The only halfway house for women leaving prison in the state, McGrath House, was shut down in 2018 because of a lack of funding.[23] This was one among a series of reentry program closures: Span Inc. and Overcoming the Odds were both shut permanently, while the Boston Reentry Initiative was closed and then reopened, with much more limited capacity, after funding lapsed from the Second Chance Act.[24] The president of the nonprofit organization running Brooke House, a sixty-five-bed program also in danger of closing,[25] argued that public funding had so deteriorated that "almost none" of the three thousand people leaving prison in the state each year transitioned through any kind of residential reentry program.[26] It is difficult to know exactly how many because this data is not even reliably collected.

Massachusetts was once a hub of community corrections and rehabilitative prison policy. But despite a decade of resurgent interest in issues of prisoner reentry and a more recent period of bipartisan criminal justice reform,[27] the network of halfway houses in the state is in dire condition. This is symptomatic of a more general breakdown of community alternatives around the country. For decades, runaway spending on criminal justice has been funneled narrowly into prisons, with the web of institutions that once created a post-release bridge not only disregarded but systematically dismantled.[28] No state in America releases any significant portion of its prisoners through public halfway houses, with the institution overwhelmingly outsourced to nonprofits and private corporations, creating a shadow carceral network operating under the conditions of structural neglect and welfare-state retrenchment that stamps the lives of people cycling in and out of prison more broadly.

New Jersey provides a cautionary tale of what halfway house expansion can become once filtered through the racist political economy of mass incarceration.[29] The state has been a national leader in reducing prison populations by shifting prisoners into a largely privatized system of community corrections, with almost 14 percent of all those in Department of Corrections custody now held in halfway houses.[30] A ten-month *New York Times* investigation in 2012 found widespread political corruption:[31] Chris Christie, then governor of the state, used his position to funnel around $70 million a year to Community Education Centers, the company dominating the system, where he had close friends in senior management and had himself worked as a lobbyist. One way corporate managers cut costs and increased profits was to pursue economies of scale and use enormous facilities as "halfway houses." Delaney Hall had a capacity of around twelve hundred, for example, and the Bo Robinson Assessment and Treatment Center had around nine hundred beds.[32] Both were surrounded by high walls and razor wire, and inside, conditions were so poor that some people were requesting returns to prison.[33]

Prison reformers and decarceration advocates who might want to expand halfway houses need to carefully consider the kinds of facilities that would operate under that name. And getting a handle on existing practice is difficult when the institution is highly decentralized, even basic statistics about size and characteristics are not systematically collected, and there is a general lack of empirical research painting a picture of life inside these programs.[34] The available evidence is not especially promising: evaluation studies suggest that halfway house placements generally have little impact on later offending,[35] for example, and those who spend time in halfway houses sometimes have *higher* levels of rearrest and reconviction afterward than similar people who do not spend time in them.[36] But the meaning of these results for the halfway house concept is itself difficult to interpret at a time when many programs are constructed as large, prison-like facilities cycling people through on short stays.

Depending on the way the idea is implemented, the halfway house can be a tool for challenging or extending mass incarceration. It might be a mechanism of decarceration supporting early release from prison, or, people who complete their prison time and would otherwise be released to the street could be subjected to a further period of halfway house supervision, exposing them to both prison and the community "alternative."[37] Similarly, halfway house placements might be attached to probation as a form of diversion from prison, or, used in cases where probation would otherwise be served in the community without any element of penal confinement. In other words, the halfway house can be used either as a substitute for prison or in addition to it.

So much depends on the concrete details of how the halfway house concept is actually practiced. And if the institution were to ever provide a housing-based approach to disrupting the systemic links between prisons and poverty at the core of mass incarceration, the programs would need to resemble houses far more than they currently do. Yet any effort to expand this kind of halfway house would confront sharp problems of scale at a time when more than six hundred thousand people exit prison each year and more than eleven million cycle through jail. What would it look like to develop a network of small neighborhood halfway houses capable of supporting reentry on this magnitude? And even if the political will existed to construct such a system, what would be the social implications of a mass expansion of carceral housing when millions of Americans struggle to access housing of any kind? Might these resources better be used instead to repair a crumbling welfare state and to expand less coercive alternatives, investing in public housing rather than halfway houses?

These questions point to the limits of reentry reform absent a broader process of social transformation. Yet the same conditions of deeply entrenched oppression and exclusion that make large-scale social change so necessary can also make the halfway house a crucial intervention in the meantime—a pragmatic and already-existing alternative. Riddled with tensions and contradictions, yes, but also an opening to provide material support to people in desperate situations and introduce ideals of care into a brutal carceral system.

A halfway house saved Joe Badillo's life.

ACKNOWLEDGMENTS

My first thank-you goes to the man named in this book as Joe Badillo. I was shown so much generosity by the people who shared with me their lives during the fieldwork—and Joe's was the most meaningful of all, the foundation of everything else. So I want to leave a more personal message here: *Yo Joe, remember that time we put chips on Jayme's back while he slept on the beach? What about when Slurpy sent those pictures to the pastor by mistake? You know mermaids don't exist, right? And when are you gonna have a turn wearing the corn suit? We had some good laughs ay brother. But seriously, I learned so much from you over these years, I mean that. I learned even old dudes can change ay? Even when your back's fucked and your legs shake, never too late to change ay? Thanks for letting me stay at your house bro, or more than that, thanks for making me feel at home. I'll never forget your support bro, honestly never.*

I am grateful to so many people for contributions of ideas and support, like the sociology faculty at Boston College, where I did the fieldwork during my doctorate, especially Stephen Pfohl, Lisa Dodson, and Eve Spangler, and now my colleagues at the Institute of Criminology at Victoria University of Wellington, especially Simon MacKenzie, John Pratt, and Elizabeth Stanley. I also want to acknowledge Daniel Botha and Moorea Smithline for excellent research assistance along the way. And I want to say thank you to participants in the Center for the Study of Law and Society speaker series, particularly Jonathan Simon and Tony Platt, along with Elliott Currie, who not only helped me rethink key ideas at a formative stage of the writing but showed great hospitality. My sincerest thank-you also to Ilene Kalish for believing in the project and for incisive comments on drafts and to others with the New York University Press Alternative Criminology series, like Jeff Ferrell, who have worked hard to create space for this kind of book.

Looking back on the longer arc of the book, I especially want to acknowledge William Wood. The first time I applied to do a doctorate in the United States, I was rejected by all schools and gave up on the goal. Then I met Will. He not only convinced me to try again but coached me through it, leaving his door open always and making time for me when he had very little of it. He got me thinking about theory and big ideas and opened a new world of possibilities. I never would have gone to America in the first place without this support. Thank you, Will.

I want to leave a message of deep gratitude here for my mum, Pip Desmond. You taught me to write, mum, these words grew from your words (like cherry tomatoes from the vege garden at Daniel St). You held me close and read aloud, days turning to bedtimes, books and connection. You showed me what it looks like to tell stories and gently, always gently, encouraged me to tell stories too. You read the words I wrote, time and again, year after year—no matter how sore your back, you always made the time. You turned a kid who didn't read much, or even really like books, into an adult who wrote this book. Now we have writing to talk about together, always. *See you on Saturday morning ay mum?*

The last and biggest thank-you of all goes to my love, Aurora Soliz. These words grew from your love Aurora (like Feijoas from the tree at Coburn St). You travelled the whole journey with me, the moving countries, the sleepless nights, the disappearing for months at a time to go live at a halfway house. You came to the house and met the men. And when I got lost in the writing and the academic world, again and again you grounded me in the things that really matter: our precious babies chuckling and hugging, the circle of family and friends, how the people close are doing. You never let me forget there is more to life than a book, even as you filled my life with the love and support it took to write this book.

I couldn't have done it without you.

NOTES

1. CARCERAL CARE

1. The name Joe Badillo and Bridge House are both pseudonyms to protect the anonymity of participants in the research, a convention used throughout the book when naming people, areas, and organizations.
2. For a discussion of the role of criminal records in closing down access to public housing in Massachusetts, see Schneider 2010.
3. Caputo 2004, 171–172.
4. Caputo 2004, 172.
5. Caputo 2004, 174–176.
6. M. Piehl 1982.
7. This average capacity is based on the "total beds" shown for each of the 154 federally contracted residential reentry centers listed in the Bureau of Prisons online directory. See Federal Bureau of Prisons, "About Our Facilities," accessed August 4, 2020, www.bop.gov.
8. Center for Behavioral Health Sciences and Criminal Justice Research 2013, 7.
9. Foucault 1979.
10. Foucault 1979, 298.
11. Foucault 1979, 293–308.
12. Platt 2018, 14–19.
13. Monahan and Torres 2010.
14. Wacquant 2001.
15. Bosworth and Kaufman 2011.
16. Shabazz 2009.
17. McCorkel 2017.
18. Jefferson 2015.
19. Cohen 1979.
20. Miller 2014; Miller and Purifoye 2016.
21. Beckett and Western 2001; Wacquant 2009, 151–164.
22. Stuart 2016.
23. Comfort 2007b, 2013.
24. Miller 2014; Halushka 2017, 2020.
25. Willse 2010, 2015.
26. Wacquant 2005, 3–5.
27. Cohen 1985, 32–36.
28. Kennedy 1964, 3.

29. Garland 2001, 27–53.
30. Cohen 1985, 76.
31. Allen et al. 1978; Keve 1967; Latessa and Allen 1982; Latessa and Smith 2011, 302–304; Seiter et al. 1977; Way 1992.
32. Piven and Cloward 1971, 183.
33. Murakawa 2008, 247–249.
34. An Act to amend section 4082 of title 18, United States Code, to facilitate the rehabilitation of persons convicted of offenses against the United States, Pub. L. No. 89-176, 79 Stat. 674–675 (1965). The act read as follows: "the Attorney General may designate as a place of confinement any available, suitable, and appropriate institution or facility, whether maintained by the Federal Government or otherwise, and whether within or without the judicial district in which the person was convicted, and may at any time transfer a person from one place of confinement to another."
35. Long 1965.
36. Cohen 1985, 40–43.
37. See McMahon 1990.
38. Bullington et al. 1986.
39. B. Martin 1976.
40. LeClair 1978.
41. LeClair and Guarino-Ghezzi 1991.
42. M. Alexander 2010; Weaver 2007.
43. Sasson 2000.
44. Bobo and Thompson 2010.
45. Keough 1999.
46. Romney et al. 2004.
47. Boston Bar Association 2002.
48. Romney et al. 2004.
49. The director of Bridge House, Pat Townsend, described this funding as insecure but providing the program relative independence. He said it was delivered as a contract with the Massachusetts Department of Corrections but, once approved as part of state-level budget processes, was legislatively mandated so not subject to the same controls as typical correctional contracts. And the majority of program funding did not come from the state but was cobbled together through a combination of foundation grants, private donations, fund-raising drives, and the $75 a week paid by each resident.
50. Miller 2014.
51. Mitchell 2011; Ellis and Henderson 2017.
52. Steen, Lacock, and McKinzey 2012.
53. Roman and Travis 2004.
54. Taxman et al. 2010.
55. Center for Behavioral Health Sciences and Criminal Justice Research 2013, 2.
56. Fairbanks 2011.
57. McGowan 2016; Costanza, Kilburn, and Vendetti-Koski 2013; Kilburn et al. 2014.

58. Bluestone and Stevenson 2000; Forrant and Barry 2001; Juravich 2007; Sum et al. 2011.
59. Chomsky 2008.
60. Pager 2003, 2007; Pager, Western, and Sugie 2009.
61. Clear 2007; Roberts 2003; Sampson and Loeffler 2010.
62. Miller 2014, 311–314.
63. Western 2014; Western et al. 2015.
64. Travis 2002, 2005.
65. Pager 2007; Miller and Stuart 2017; Uggen, Manza, and Thompson 2006; Wakefield and Uggen 2010.
66. Demleitner 1999.
67. Mulvaney-Day et al. 2012.
68. Ollove 2015; Pew Charitable Trusts 2015, 2–3.
69. Davis et al. 2011, 87.
70. In a report by the Legal Action Center (2004) examining state-by-state variation in the barriers facing people with criminal records, Massachusetts was ranked the eleventh least restrictive out of fifty states studied. See also Legal Action Center 2009.
71. Turnbull and Hannah-Moffatt 2009.
72. Turner 1967, 1974, 1977.
73. Bell 2009; Grimes 2000; van Gennep 1909.
74. Maruna 2011.
75. Young 1999a.
76. Young 2011.
77. Bourgois 1999, 2158.
78. Bourgois 1999, 2158
79. Ralph 2015a.
80. Smith 1999, 70.
81. Contreras 2013, 17–19.
82. Betts 2014; Rios 2014, 2015.
83. Smith 1999.
84. Blauner and Wellman 1973.
85. Blauner and Wellman 1973.
86. For example, see Brotherton and Barrios 2004.
87. Martin 2018.
88. Diamond 1992, 250; Weston 1991, 9.
89. My approach to editing was informed by Blauner 1987.
90. See also Bourgois 2003, 13.
91. Contreras 2013, 26–28.
92. For examples of ethnographers paying book royalties to participants see Duneier, 1999; Contreras, 2013.

2. A BLESSING IN DISGUISE

1. I also talked with a public defender in Massachusetts who reviewed Joe Badillo's record and assisted in the interpretation. They believed that on each occasion

when multiple sentences had been imposed at the same time, these were most likely to have been served concurrently (based on the shared docket numbers of the cases, for example).

2. Page and Soss 2017; Page, Piehowski, and Soss 2019.

3. Gordon 1987; Pager 2003, 2007; Travis 2002; Miller and Stuart 2017; Murphy et al. 2011.

4. Bobo and Thompson 2010.

5. M. Alexander 2010; Beckett and Sasson 1999; Parenti 2000.

6. Black 2009, 218–221.

7. Brownsberger and Piehl 1997.

8. Given that Joe had a relatively long spell in state prison as a teenager, it might seem unusual that he later spent much less time incarcerated on similar charges and avoided triggering even longer mandatory-minimum sentences under the war on drugs. When I asked Joe about this, he said he took that first case to trial and was found guilty by a jury, but later, the cases brought against him often involved very limited evidence. He believed he could have won many if given the chance at a trial. But with a bad reputation and prior convictions, Joe feared a long mandatory minimum if convicted in court, so he consistently negotiated for short sentences in exchange for pleading guilty. For a discussion of the way mandatory minimums enhanced the power of district attorneys, as the only people able to lower sentences below the fixed limit, and left virtually all defendants in drug cases in Massachusetts plea-bargaining their cases, see Black 2009, 218–221.

9. Kennedy, Piehl, Braga 1996; Braga 2003; Wolfgang, Figlio, and Sellin 1972.

10. Forman 2014.

11. Gilligan 2000; Davis 1998; Contreras 2013, 72–87.

12. Mackenzie et al. 1998, 211.

13. Farmer 1996.

14. In Massachusetts, once a person has served time in state prison, they can be transferred from county jails to state prisons during later sentences through what is known as a "52A." At a time when Richmond County Jail was chronically overcrowded, Joe might seem like a candidate for being moved into the state prison system, but he said this never happened. When I asked him why he thought that was, his explanation was that 52As were only really used at Richmond when people made trouble, but he was generally well liked and well behaved.

15. A. Piehl 2002.

16. C. Haney 2006; Irwin 2005; Simon 2000, 2014.

17. Rea et al. 1992.

18. Mackenzie et al. 1998, 209.

19. Simon 2014.

20. Simon 2016.

21. Comfort 2013.

22. Maruna 2001.
23. Maruna 2001, 97–99.
24. LeBel et al. 2008.

3. HALFWAY HOME

1. Foucault 1979, 302–303.
2. These biographical details come from a recorded interview with Pat about his role at the program.
3. B. Alexander 2001.
4. For example, Alexander, Coambs, and Hadaway 1978.
5. Ross and Richards 2009.
6. See Maté 2018, 140–148.
7. Gowan and Whetstone 2012; McKim 2017; Miller 2014; L. Haney 2010.
8. Sered and Norton-Hawk 2014.
9. Bourgois 2002.
10. Massachusetts Department of Public Health 2016.
11. Massachusetts Department of Public Health 2017.
12. Massachusetts Department of Public Health 2016.
13. Sered and Norton-Hawk 2014, 107–126.
14. Valverde and White-Mair 1999.
15. Gossop 2013.
16. Weinberg 2000.
17. Kauffman, Ferketich, and Wewers 2008; Lankenau 2001.
18. Hochschild 2012.
19. Beckett and Western 2001.
20. Comfort 2013.
21. For example, Sered and Norton-Hawk 2014, 107–126.
22. Travis 2002.
23. Beckett and Murakawa 2012.

4. BRIDGE IS FAMILY

1. Comfort 2007a, 13.
2. Turnbull and Hannah-Moffat 2009.
3. Laub, Nagin, and Sampson 1998; Sampson and Laub 1993.
4. Paylor and Smith 1994.
5. Hyra 2014; Kneebone and Garr 2010; Murphy 2007; Newman and Wyly 2005.
6. Young 1999b.
7. Turnbull and Hannah-Moffat 2009.
8. Wacquant 1996.
9. Desmond and Emirbayer 2010, 152–155.
10. M. Alexander 2010.
11. Valentine 1978.
12. Fishman 1990, 222–261.

13. Fishman 1990, 222.
14. Flores and Hondagneu-Sotelo 2013.

5. THE RECOVERY HUSTLE

1. Denzin 1987, 1988; Valverde 1998.
2. Valverde and White-Mair 1999.
3. Wacquant 1998.
4. M. Alexander 2010.
5. Pager 2003, 2007.
6. See McKim 2017, 6–11.
7. Simon 1997.
8. Miller 2014, 308–309.
9. Wilson 1997.
10. M. Alexander 2010; Pager 2003; Pager, Western, and Sugie 2009.
11. Simon 1997.
12. Maruna 1999.
13. Despite his expression of misgivings about the recording while we talked, Paul gave permission for this interview material to be used in the book with a pseudonym.
14. Simon 1997, 45.
15. Wray 2006.
16. Saperstein and Penner 2010.
17. Bourgois 2001.
18. Bonilla-Silva 2011, 2015.
19. Bertrand and Mullainathan 2003.
20. Pager 2003, 2007.
21. Pager, Western, and Sugie 2009.
22. Bonilla-Silva 2006.
23. Western 2018, 46–63.
24. Denzin 1988.
25. McCorkel 2013, 125.
26. Denzin 1988, 61; Valverde 1998. And for a broader discussion of autobiographical splitting in awakening narratives beyond the twelve steps, see DeGloma 2010, 2014.
27. Keane 2000; Valverde and White-Mair 1999, 400.
28. For an account of former gang members in Chicago turning debilitating physical injuries into sources of authority used in projects of individual and social change, see Ralph 2015b.
29. Harding, Morenoff, and Wyse 2019, 180–181.
30. LeBel 2012; LeBel, Richie, and Maruna 2014.
31. Fairbanks 2009, 92–93.
32. Valverde 1998.
33. Miller 2014.
34. Johnson 1976.

6. THE DRUG CRISIS OUTSIDE THE DOOR

1. Costanza, Kilburn, and Vendetti-Koski 2013.
2. Fairbanks 2009.
3. Miller 2014.
4. Currie 1993; Dasgupta, Beletsky, and Ciccarone 2018.
5. Ross and Richards 2009.
6. Cohen 1985, 40–43.
7. Ross and Richards 2009.
8. A note on terminology: in this book, I use the term "opiate" to describe drugs like heroin, which derive directly from the opium poppy, as well as others that derive indirectly or are synthesized from drugs derived from the poppy, like oxycodone and fentanyl. Sometimes this second group of drugs is distinguished as "opioids." But to avoid jumping back and forth between the terms "opiate" and "opioid," which can get confusing, I have grouped them together as "opiates" (see also Quinones 2016, xiii), which for a long time was the established convention. All originally come from opium and share parallels in effects and chemical properties.
9. Kolodny et al. 2015.
10. Katz 2017.
11. Ciccarone 2017.
12. Ciccarone 2017.
13. Higham, Horwitz, and Rich 2019.
14. Griffin and Miller 2011.
15. Van Zee 2009.
16. Griffin and Miller 2011.
17. Skolnick 2018.
18. Ciccarone, Unick, and Kraus 2009; Rosenblum, Unick, and Ciccarone 2013.
19. Quinones 2016, 164–168.
20. Quinones 2016, 305.
21. Cicero and Ellis 2015.
22. Tiger 2017; Netherland and Hansen 2017.
23. Sered 2018; Dasgupta, Beletsky, and Ciccarone 2018; Monnat 2016; McLean 2016; Quinones 2016, 208–211.
24. Commonwealth of Massachusetts 2018.
25. Kirk 2009.
26. Costanza, Kilburn, and Vendetti-Koski 2013.
27. Western et al. 2015.
28. Becker 1963.
29. Ralph 2015b, 124.
30. Fellowship of Narcotics Anonymous 2008, xxv.
31. Gossop 2013.
32. White 2011.

7. NO NARCOTICS

1. Davis et al. 2011, 87–88; Winkelman et al. 2016.
2. Mallik-Kane and Visher 2008.
3. Farrell and Gottlieb 2020; Winkelman et al. 2016; Winkelman, Choi, and Davis 2017.
4. Berchick, Hood, and Barnett 2018; Mulvaney-Day et al. 2012; Zhu et al. 2010.
5. Ollove 2015; Pew Charitable Trusts 2015, 2–3.
6. Reid 2010, 28.
7. Martinez-Hume et al. 2017.
8. Ku et al. 2009.
9. Mohan et al. 2013.
10. Rylko-Bauer and Farmer 2002.
11. Bourgois and Schonberg 2009, 304–305.
12. Hunt and Arar 2001.
13. White 2011.
14. Crowley-Matoka and True 2012.
15. Crowley-Matoka and True 2012, 704.
16. Bourgois and Schonberg 2009, 225–239.
17. Joe describing Bridge House as "home" in this context was especially significant because he usually used the more impersonal term "the house" (see chapter 3).
18. Ciccarone 2017.
19. Mars et al. 2014.
20. Bluestone and Stevenson 2000.
21. Bluestone and Stevenson 2000, 13.
22. Commonwealth Corporation and Center for Labor Markers and Policy 2016.
23. Farmer 2004.
24. Bourgois 2003.

8. LEAVING BRIDGE HOUSE

1. Piven and Cloward 1971.
2. Soss, Fording, and Schram 2011.
3. Schram, Houser, and Fording 2010.
4. Soss, Fording, and Schram 2011.
5. See Halushka 2020.
6. Merton 1938.
7. Merton 1938, 676.
8. Urie et al. 2019; McNeill 2019.
9. Rumpf 2017; Worrall, Carr, and Robinson 2017.
10. Duneier 1999, 319–332; Duneier 2004.
11. Duneier 1999, 23–25.
12. Blauner and Wellman 1973.
13. Coates 2015.

9. ALTERNATIVES

1. Foucault 2009.
2. Keve 1967; Latessa and Smith 2011, 302–304; Way 1992.
3. Cohen 1985;
4. Foucault 1979.
5. Foucault 2009, 17–18.
6. McMahon 1990.
7. Federal Bureau of Prisons 2018.
8. Mitchell 2011; Ellis and Henderson 2017.
9. Bussert, Goldberger, and Price 2006.
10. Mitchell 2011.
11. Deloitte Consulting 2016, 57.
12. Latessa and Lovins 2019, 326.
13. Deloitte Consulting 2016, 19.
14. Deloitte Consulting 2016, 6.
15. Ross and Richards 2009.
16. Sered and Norton-Hawk 2014; L. Haney 2010; McKim 2017; Miller 2014.
17. Foucault 2009, 13.
18. Wacquant 2009, 159.
19. Herbert, Morenoff, and Harding 2015.
20. Comfort 2007b.
21. Gowan 2002.
22. Simon 2014, 17–47.
23. James 2018.
24. Bentacourt 2019; Jonas 2017; Community Resources for Justice 2018.
25. Community Resources for Justice 2017.
26. Rushing and Larivee 2018.
27. Council of State Governments Justice Center 2017; Jonas 2018, Crowley 2018.
28. Wacquant 2010.
29. Smiley 2014.
30. New Jersey Department of Corrections 2019.
31. Dolnik 2012a.
32. Dolnik 2012c; Dolnik 2012b.
33. Dolnik 2012b.
34. Center for Behavioral Health Sciences and Criminal Justice Research 2013, 7.
35. See Growns et al. 2018. This review of research on supported accommodation for people released from custody concluded that "the majority of studies found no differences between program participants and comparison participants on measures of re-arrest, re-conviction, or re-incarceration" (2187).
36. Center for Behavioral Health Sciences and Criminal Justice Research 2013, 8; Dolnik 2013; New York Times Editorial Board 2013.
37. Greenberg 1975, 12.

REFERENCES

Alexander, Bruce K. 2001. *"The Myth of Drug-Induced Addiction."* Paper delivered to the Canadian Senate. www.parl.gc.ca.

Alexander, Bruce K., Robert B. Coambs, and Patricia F Hadaway. 1978. "The Effect of Housing and Gender on Morphine Self-Administration in Rats." *Psychopharmacology* 58:175–179.

Alexander, Michelle. 2010. *The New Jim Crow: Mass Incarceration in the Age of Colorblindness.* New York: New Press.

Allen, Harry, Eric Carlson, Evalyn Parks, and Richard Seiter. 1978. *Program Model: Halfway Houses.* Washington, DC: US Department of Justice.

Becker, Howard. 1963. *Outsiders: Studies in the Sociology of Deviance.* New York: Free Press.

Beckett, Katherine, and Naomi Murakawa. 2012. "Mapping the Shadow Carceral State: Toward an Institutionally Capacious Approach to Punishment." *Theoretical Criminology* 16:221–244.

Beckett, Katherine, and Theodore Sasson. 1999. *The Politics of Injustice: Crime and Punishment in America.* London: Sage.

Beckett, Katherine, and Bruce Western. 2001. "Governing Social Marginality: Welfare, Incarceration, and the Transformation of State Policy." *Punishment and Society* 3:43–59.

Bell, Catherine. 2009. *Ritual: Perspectives and Dimensions.* New York: Oxford University Press.

Bentacourt, Sarah. 2019. "McGrath Provides Services for Women Leaving Prison." *CommonWealth: Nonprofit Journal of Politics, Ideas and Civic Change,* July 29.

Berchick, Edward R., Emily Hood, and Jessica C. Barnett. 2018. *Health Insurance Coverage in the United States: 2017.* Washington, DC: US Government Printing Office.

Bertrand, Marianne, and Sendhil Mullainathan. 2003. "Are Emily and Greg More Employable than Lakisha and Jamal? A Field Experiment on Labor Market Discrimination." *American Economic Review* 94 (4): 991–1013.

Betts, Dwayne. 2014. "The Stoop Isn't the Jungle." *Slate,* July 10.

Black, Timothy. 2009. *When a Heart Turns Rock Solid: The Lives of Three Puerto Rican Brothers on and off the Streets.* New York: Pantheon Books.

Blauner, Robert. 1987. "Problems of Editing 'First-Person' Sociology." *Qualitative Sociology* 10 (1): 46–64.

Blauner, Robert, and David Wellman. 1973. "Toward the Decolonization of Social Research." In *The Death of White Sociology: Essays on Race and Culture*, edited by Joyce A. Ladner, 310–330. Baltimore: Black Classic.

Bluestone, Barry, and Mary Stevenson. 2000. *The Boston Renaissance: Race, Space, and Economic Change in an American Metropolis*. New York: Russell Sage Foundation.

Bobo, Lawrence, and Victor Thompson. 2010. "Racialized Mass Incarceration: Poverty, Prejudice, and Punishment." In *Doing Race: 21 Essays for the 21st Century*, edited by Hazel R. Markus and Paula Moya, 322–355. New York: Norton.

Bonilla-Silva, Eduardo. 2006. *Racism without Racists: Color-Blind Racism and the Persistence of Racial Inequality in the United States*. 2nd ed. Lanham, MD: Rowman and Littlefield.

———. 2011. "The Sweet Enchantment of Color-Blind Racism in Obamerica." *Annals of the American Academy of Political and Social Science* 634 (1): 190–206.

———. 2015. "The Structure of Racism in Color-Blind, 'Post-Racial' America." *American Behavioral Scientist* 59 (11): 1358–1376.

Boston Bar Association. 2002. *Report of the Boston Bar Association on Parole and Community Re-integration: Parole Practices in Massachusetts and Their Effect on Community Reintegration*. Boston: Boston Bar Association.

Bosworth, Mary, and Emma Kaufman. 2011. "Foreigners in a Carceral Age: Immigration and Imprisonment in the US." *Stanford Law & Policy Review* 22:101–127.

Bourgois, Philippe. 1999. "Theory, Method, and Power in Drug and HIV-Prevention Research: A Participant-Observer's Critique." *Substance Use & Misuse* 34 (14): 2155–2172.

———. 2001. "Poverty, Culture of." In *International Encyclopedia of the Social and Behavioral Sciences*, edited by Neil J. Smelser and Paul B. Baltes, 11904–11907. Amsterdam: Elsevier.

———. 2002. "Disciplining Addictions: The Bio-Politics of Methadone and Heroin in the United States." *Culture, Medicine and Psychiatry* 24:165–195.

———. 2003. *In Search of Respect: Selling Crack in El Barrio*. 2nd ed. Cambridge: Cambridge University Press.

Bourgois, Philippe, and Jeff Schonberg. 2009. *Righteous Dopefiend*. Berkeley: University of California Press.

Braga, Anthony. 2003. "Serious Youth Gun Offenders and the Epidemic of Youth Violence in Boston." *Journal of Quantitative Criminology* 19:33–54.

Brotherton, David, and Luis Barrios. 2004. *The Almighty Latin King and Queen Nation: Street Politics and the Transformation of a New York City Gang*. New York: Columbia University Press.

Brownsberger, William, and Anne Piehl. 1997. "Profile of Anti-drug Law Enforcement in Urban Poverty Areas in Massachusetts." Unpublished report, November. www.prisonpolicy.org.

Bullington, Bruce, James Sprowls, Daniel Katkin, and Harvey Lowell. 1986. "The Politics of Policy: Deinstitutionalization in Massachusetts 1970–1985." *Law & Policy* 8 (4): 507–524.

Bussert, Todd, Peter Goldberger, and Mary Price. 2006. "New Time Limits on Federal Halfway Houses." *Criminal Justice* 21:20–26.

Caputo, Gail A. 2004. *Intermediate Sanctions in Corrections*. Denton: University of North Texas Press.

Center for Behavioral Health Sciences and Criminal Justice Research. 2013. *Halfway from Prison to the Community: From Current Practice to Best Practice*. New Brunswick, NJ: Rutgers University.

Chomsky, Aviva. 2008. *Linked Labor Histories: New England, Colombia, and the Making of a Global Working Class*. Durham, NC: Duke University Press.

Ciccarone, Daniel H. 2017. "Fentanyl in the US Heroin Supply: A Rapidly Changing Risk Environment." *International Journal of Drug Policy* 46:107–111.

Ciccarone, Daniel H., George J. Unick, and Allison Kraus. 2009. "Impact of South American Heroin on the US Heroin Market 1993–2004." *International Journal on Drug Policy* 20 (5): 392–401.

Cicero, Theodore, and Matthew Ellis. 2015. "Abuse-Deterrent Formulations and the Prescription Opioid Abuse Epidemic in the United States: Lessons Learned from OxyContin." *JAMA Psychiatry* 72 (5): 424–430.

Clear, Todd. 2007. *Imprisoning Communities: How Mass Incarceration Makes Disadvantaged Neighborhoods Worse*. Oxford: Oxford University Press.

Coates, Ta-Nehisi. 2015. *Between the World and Me*. New York: Spiegel and Grau.

Cohen, Stanley. 1979. "The Punitive City: Notes on the Dispersal of Social Control." *Contemporary Crises* 3:339–363.

———. 1985. *Visions of Social Control: Crime, Punishment, and Classification*. Cambridge, UK: Polity.

Comfort, Megan. 2007a. *Doing Time Together: Love and Family in the Shadow of the Prison*. Chicago: University of Chicago Press.

———. 2007b. "Punishment beyond the Legal Offender." *Annual Review of Law and Social Science* 3:271–296.

———. 2013. "When Prison Is a Refuge, America's Messed Up." *Chronicle of Higher Education*, December 2.

Commonwealth Corporation and Center for Labor Markets and Policy. 2016. *Health Care Employment, Structure and Trends in Massachusetts: Chapter 224 Workforce Impact Study*. Boston: Commonwealth of Massachusetts, Office of the State Auditor.

Commonwealth of Massachusetts. 2018. "HPC DataPoints, Issue 4: Opioid Epidemic: The Growing Opioid Epidemic in Massachusetts Hospitals." www.mass.gov.

Community Resources for Justice. 2017. "CRJ Asks Supporters to Stand with Brooke House." Boston: Community Resources for Justice.

———. 2018. "Community-Based Residential Reentry: Essential for Recidivism Reduction." Boston: Community Resources for Justice.

Contreras, Randol. 2013. *The Stickup Kids: Race, Drugs, Violence, and the American Dream*. Berkeley: University of California Press.

Costanza, Stephen, John Kilburn, and Susan Vendetti-Koski. 2013. "Are Minority Areas Disproportionately Targeted for Halfway House Placement?" *Journal of Ethnicity in Criminal Justice* 11: 256–276.

Council of State Governments Justice Center. 2017. "Justice Reinvestment in Massachusetts: Policy Framework." New York: Council of State Governments Justice Center.

Crowley, Michael. 2018. "Massachusetts Sets an Example for Bipartisan Criminal Justice Reform." Brennan Center for Justice, May 1. www.brennancenter.org.

Crowley-Matoka, Megan, and Gala True. 2012. "No One Wants to Be the Candy Man: Ambivalent Medicalization and Clinician Subjectivity in Pain Management." *Cultural Anthropology* 27 (4): 689–712.

Currie, Elliott. 1993. *Reckoning: Drugs, the Cities, and the American Future.* New York: Hill and Wang.

Dasgupta, Nabarun, Leo Beletsky, and Daniel Ciccarone. 2018. "Opioid Crisis: No Easy Fix to Its Social and Economic Determinants." *American Journal of Public Health* 108 (2): 182–186.

Davis, Angela. 1998. "Public Imprisonment and Private Violence: Reflections on the Hidden Punishment of Women." *New England Journal of Criminal and Civil Confinement* 24:339–352.

Davis, Lois M., Malcolm V. Williams, Kathryn Pitkin Derose, Paul Steinberg, Nancy Nicosia, Adrian Overton, Lisa Miyashiro, Susan Turner, Terry Fain, and Eugene Williams III. 2011. *Understanding the Public Health Implications of Prisoner Reentry in California: State-of-the-State Report.* Santa Monica, CA: RAND Corporation.

DeGloma, Thomas. 2010. "Awakenings: Autobiography, Memory, and the Social Logic of Personal Discovery." *Sociological Forum* 25 (3): 519–540.

———. 2014. *Seeing the Light: The Social Logic of Personal Discovery.* Chicago: University of Chicago Press.

Deloitte Consulting. 2016. *US Department of Justice Bureau of Prisons Residential Reentry Centers Assessment Recommendations Report.* New York: Deloitte Consulting.

Demleitner, Nora V. 1999. "Preventing Internal Exile: The Need for Restrictions on Collateral Sentencing Consequences." *Stanford Law and Policy Review* 11 (1): 153–171.

Denzin, Norman. 1987. *The Alcoholic Society: Addiction and Recovery of the Self.* New York: Routledge.

———. 1988. "The Alcoholic Self: Communication, Ritual, and Identity Transformation." In *Communication and Social Structure*, edited by David R. Maines and Carl J. Couch, 59–74. Springfield, IL: Charles C. Thomas.

Desmond, Matthew, and Mustafa Emirbayer. 2010. *Racial Domination, Racial Progress: The Sociology of Race in America.* New York: McGraw-Hill.

Diamond, Timothy. 1992. *Making Gray Gold: Narratives of Nursing Home Care.* Chicago: University of Chicago Press.

Dolnik, Sam. 2012a. "As Escapees Stream Out, a Penal Business Thrives." *New York Times*, June 17.

———. 2012b. "At a Halfway House, Bedlam Reigns." *New York Times*, June 17.

———. 2012c. "A Volatile Mix Fuels a Murder." *New York Times*, June 17.

———. 2013. "Pennsylvania Study Finds Halfway Houses Don't Reduce Recidivism." *New York Times*, March 24.

Duneier, Mitchell. 1999. *Sidewalk*. New York: Farrar, Straus and Giroux.

———. 2004. "Three Rules I Go By in My Ethnographic Research on Race and Racism." In *Researching Race and Racism*, edited by Martin Bulmer and John Solomos, 92–104. New York: Routledge.

Ellis, Alan, and Michael Henderson. 2017. "The US Bureau of Prisons' Pre-release Program: Getting Out Early." *Criminal Justice* 31:20–22.

Fairbanks, Robert P., II. 2009. *How It Works: Recovering Citizens in Post-Welfare Philadelphia*. Chicago: University of Chicago Press.

———. 2011. "The Illinois Reentry Imperative: Sheridan Correctional Center as National Model." *Carceral Notebooks* 6:175–200.

Farmer, Paul. 1996. "On Suffering and Structural Violence: A View from Below." *Daedalus* 125:261–283.

———. 2004. "An Anthropology of Structural Violence." *Current Anthropology* 45 (3): 305–325.

Farrell, Caitlin M., and Aaron Gottlieb. 2020. "The Effect of Health Insurance on Health Care Utilization in the Justice-Involved Population: United States, 2014–2016." *American Journal of Public Health* 110:S78–S84.

Federal Bureau of Prisons. 2018. *Program Fact Sheet*. Washington, DC: Federal Bureau of Prisons.

Fellowship of Narcotics Anonymous. 2008. *Narcotics Anonymous*. 6th ed. Van Nuys, CA: Narcotics Anonymous World Services.

Fishman, Laura. 1990. *Women at the Wall: A Study of Prisoners' Wives Doing Time on the Outside*. Albany: State University of New York Press.

Flores, Edward Orozco, and Pierrette Hondagneu-Sotelo. 2013. "Chicano Gang Members in Recovery: The Public Talk of Negotiating Chicano Masculinities." *Social Problems* 60 (4): 476–490.

Forman, James. 2014. "The Society of Fugitives." *Atlantic*, October.

Forrant, Robert, and Shawn Barry. 2001. "Winners and Losers: High-Tech Employment Deals an Uneven Hand." *Massachusetts Benchmarks* 4:12–16.

Foucault, Michel. 1979. *Discipline and Punish: The Birth of the Prison*. New York: Pantheon Books.

———. 2009. "Alternatives to the Prison: Dissemination or Decline of Social Control?" *Theory, Culture and Society* 26:12–24.

Garland, David. 2001. *The Culture of Control: Crime and Social Order in Contemporary Society*. Oxford: Oxford University Press.

Gilligan, James. 2000. "Punishment and Violence: Is the Criminal Law Based on One Huge Mistake?" *Social Research* 67:745–772.

Goffman, Erving. 1961. *Asylums: Essays on the Social Situation of Mental Patients and Other Inmates*. Garden City, NY: Anchor Books.

Gordon, Diana. 1987. "The Electronic Panopticon: A Case Study of the Development of the National Criminal Records System." *Politics & Society* 15 (4): 483–511.

Gossop, Michael. 2013. *Living with Drugs*. 6th ed. Aldershot, UK: Ashgate.

Gowan, Teresa. 2002. "The Nexus: Homelessness and Incarceration in Two American Cities." *Ethnography* 3:500–534.

Gowan, Teresa, and Sarah Whetstone. 2012. "Making the Criminal Addict: Subjectivity and Social Control in a Strong-Arm Rehab." *Punishment and Society* 14 (1): 69–93.

Greenberg, David. 1975. "Problems in Community Corrections." *Issues in Criminology* 10:1–33.

Griffin, O. Hayden, and Bryan Lee Miller. 2011. "OxyContin and a Regulation Deficiency of the Pharmaceutical Industry: Rethinking State-Corporate Crime." *Critical Criminology* 19 (3): 213–226.

Grimes, Ronald L. 2000. *Deeply into the Bone: Re-inventing Rites of Passage*. Berkeley: University of California Press.

Growns, Bethany, Stuart Kinner, Elizabeth Conroy, Eileen Baldry, and Sarah Larney. 2018. "A Systematic Review of Supported Accommodation Programs for People Released from Custody." *International Journal of Offender Therapy and Comparative Criminology* 62:2174–2194.

Halushka, John. 2017. "The Runaround: Punishment, Welfare, and Poverty Survival after Prison." PhD diss., New York University.

———. 2020. "The Runaround: Punishment, Welfare, and Poverty Survival after Prison." *Social Problems* 67:233–250.

Haney, Craig. 2006. "The Wages of Prison Overcrowding: Harmful Psychological Consequences and Dysfunctional Correctional Reactions." *Washington University Journal of Law & Policy* 22:265–294.

Haney, Lynne A. 2010. *Offending Women: Power, Punishment, and the Regulation of Desire*. Berkeley: University of California Press.

Harding, David, Jeffrey Morenoff, and Jessica Wyse. 2019. *On the Outside: Prisoner Reentry and Reintegration*. Chicago: University of Chicago Press.

Herbert, Claire, Jeffrey Morenoff, and David Harding. 2015. "Homelessness and Housing Insecurity among Former Prisoners." *Russell Sage Foundation Journal of Social Science* 1:44–79.

Higham, Scott, Sari Horwitz, and Steven Rich. 2019. "76 Billion Opioid Pills: Newly Released Federal Data Unmasks the Epidemic." *Washington Post*, July 17.

Hochschild, Arlie. 2012. *The Second Shift: Working Families and the Revolution at Home*. New York: Penguin.

Hunt, Linda M., and Nedal H. Arar. 2001. "An Analytical Framework for Contrasting Patient and Provider Views of the Process of Chronic Disease Management." *Medical Anthropology Quarterly* 15 (3): 347–367.

Hyra, Derek. 2014. "The Back-to-the-City Movement: Neighbourhood Redevelopment and Processes of Political and Cultural Displacement." *Urban Studies* 52 (10): 1753–1773.

Irwin, John. 2005. *The Warehouse Prison: Disposal of the New Dangerous Class*. New York: Oxford University Press.

Jaffe, Jerome H., and Charles O'Keeffe. 2003. "From Morphine Clinics to Buprenorphine: Regulating Opioid Agonist Treatment of Addiction in the United States." *Drug and Alcohol Dependence* 70 (2): S3–S11.

James, Claire. 2018. "Massachusetts' Only Halfway House Solely for Women Becomes Latest Victim of Wave of Reentry Program Closures." *Sampan*, April 2.

Jefferson, Brian Jordan. 2015. "From Prisons to Hyperpolicing: Neoliberalism, Carcerality, and Regulative Geographies." In *Historical Geographies of Prisons: Unlocking the Usable Carceral Past*, edited by Karen M. Morin and Dominique Moran, 185–205. London: Routledge.

Johnson, Gregory. 1976. "Conversion as a Cure: The Therapeutic Community and the Professional Ex-Addict." *Contemporary Drug Problems: An Interdisciplinary Quarterly* 5 (2): 187–205.

Jonas, Michael. 2017. "Boston Reentry Initiative Hits the Skids." *CommonWealth: Nonprofit Journal of Politics, Ideas and Civic Change*, May 14.

———. 2018. "Criminal Justice Bill Reaches Finish Line." *CommonWealth: Nonprofit Journal of Politics, Ideas and Civic Change*, April 13.

Juravich, Thomas. 2007. *The Future of Work in Massachusetts*. Amherst: University of Massachusetts Press.

Katz, Josh. 2017. "Drug Deaths in America Are Rising Faster than Ever." *New York Times*, June 5.

Kauffman, Ross M., Amy K. Ferketich, and Mary Ellen Wewers. 2008. "Tobacco Policy in American Prisons, 2007." *Tobacco Control* 17 (5): 357–360.

Keane, Helen. 2000. "Setting Yourself Free: Techniques of Recovery." *Health* 4 (3): 324–346.

Kennedy, David, Anne Piehl, and Anthony Braga. 1996. "Youth Violence in Boston: Gun Markets, Serious Youth Offenders, and a Use-Reduction Strategy." *Law and Contemporary Problems* 59:147–196.

Kennedy, Robert. 1964. "Halfway Houses Pay Off." *Crime and Delinquency* 10 (1): 1–7.

Keough, Robert. 1999. *Prisons and Sentencing in Massachusetts: Waging a More Effective Fight against Crime*. Boston: Massachusetts Institute for a New Commonwealth.

Keve, Paul. 1967. *Imaginative Programming in Probation and Parole*. Minneapolis: University of Minnesota Press.

Kilburn, John, Stephen Costanza, Kelly Frailing, and Stephanie Diaz. 2014. "A Paper Tiger on Chestnut Lane: The Significance of NIMBY Battles in Decaying Communities." *Urbanities* 4:3–20.

Kirk, David S. 2009. "A Natural Experiment on Residential Change and Recidivism: Lessons from Hurricane Katrina." *American Sociological Review* 74:484–505.

Kneebone, Elizabeth, and Emily Garr. 2010. *The Suburbanization of Poverty*. Washington, DC: Brookings Institution.

Kolodny, Andrew, David T. Courtwright, Catherine S. Hwang, Peter Kreiner, John L. Eadie, Thomas W. Clark, and G. Caleb Alexander. 2015. "The Prescription Opioid and Heroin Crisis: A Public Health Approach to an Epidemic of Addiction." *Annual Review of Public Health* 36 (1): 559–574.

Ku, Leighton, Emily Jones, Brad Finnegan, Peter Shin, and Sara Rosenbaum. 2009. *How Is the Primary Care Safety Net Faring in Massachusetts? Community Health Centers in the Midst of Health Reform*. Washington DC: Kaiser Commission on Medicaid and the Uninsured.

Lankenau, Stephen E. 2001. "Smoke 'Em If You Got 'Em: Cigarette Black Markets in U.S. Prisons and Jails." *Prison Journal* 81 (2): 142–161.

Lara-Millán, Armando, and Nicole Gonzalez Van Cleve. 2017. "Interorganizational Utility of Welfare Stigma in the Criminal Justice System." *Criminology* 55 (1): 59–84.

Latessa, Edward J., and Harry E. Allen. 1982. "Halfway Houses and Parole: A National Assessment." *Journal of Criminal Justice* 10 (2): 153–163.

Latessa, Edward J., and Lori Brusman Lovins. 2019. "Privatization of Community Corrections." *Criminology and Public Policy* 18:323–341.

Latessa, Edward J., and Paula Smith. 2011. *Corrections in the Community*. 5th ed. Burlington, MA: Anderson.

Laub, John H., Daniel S. Nagin, and Robert J. Sampson. 1998. "Trajectories of Change in Criminal Offending: Good Marriages and the Desistance Process." *American Sociological Review* 63 (2): 225–238.

LeBel, Thomas P. 2012. "An Examination of the Impact of Formerly Incarcerated Persons Helping Others." *Journal of Offender Rehabilitation* 46 (1–2): 1–24.

LeBel, Thomas P., Ros Burnett, Shadd Maruna, and Shawn Bushway. 2008. "The 'Chicken and Egg' of Subjective and Social Factors in Desistance from Crime." *European Journal of Criminology* 5:131–159.

LeBel, Thomas P., Matt Richie, and Shadd Maruna. 2014. "Helping Others as a Response to Reconcile a Criminal Past: The Role of the Wounded Healer in Prisoner Reentry Programs." *Criminal Justice and Behavior* 42 (1): 108–120.

LeClair, Daniel P. 1978. "Societal Reintegration and Recidivism Rates." Paper presented at the American Society of Criminology Meetings, Dallas.

LeClair, Daniel P., and Susan Guarino-Ghezzi. 1991. "Does Incapacitation Guarantee Public Safety? Lessons from the Massachusetts Furlough and Prerelease Programs." *Justice Quarterly* 8 (1): 9–36.

Legal Action Center. 2004. *After Prison: Roadblocks to Reentry, a Report on State Legal Barriers Facing People with Criminal Records*. New York: Legal Action Center.

———. 2009. *After Prison: Roadblocks to Reentry, a Report on State Legal Barriers Facing People with Criminal Records—2009 Update*. New York: Legal Action Center.

Long, Edward V. 1965. "The Prisoner Rehabilitation Act of 1965." *Federal Probation* 29 (4): 3–7.

Mackenzie, A. R., R. B. S. Laing, C. C. Smith, G. F. Kaar, and F. W. Smith. 1998. "Spinal Epidural Abscess: The Importance of Early Diagnosis and Treatment." *Journal of Neurology, Neurosurgery & Psychiatry* 65 (2): 209–212.

Mallik-Kane, Kamala, and Christy Visher. 2008. *Health and Prisoner Reentry: How Physical, Mental, and Substance Abuse Conditions Shape the Process of Reintegration*. Washington, DC: Urban Institute Justice Policy Center.

Mars, Sarah G., Philippe Bourgois, George Karandinos, Fernando Montero, and Daniel Ciccarone. 2014. "'Every "Never" I Ever Said Came True': Transitions from Opioid Pills to Heroin Injecting." *International Journal of Drug Policy* 25:257–266.

Martin, Bob. 1976. "The Massachusetts Correctional System: Treatment as an Ideology for Control." *Crime and Social Justice* 6:49–57.

Martin, Liam. 2018. "'Free but Still Walking the Yard': Prisonization and the Problems of Reentry." *Journal of Contemporary Ethnography* 47 (5): 671–694.

Martinez-Hume, Anna C., Allison M. Bakers, Hanah S. Bell, Isabel Montemayor, Kristan Elwell, and Linda M. Hunt. 2017. "'They Treat You a Different Way': Public Insurance, Stigma, and the Challenge to Quality Health Care." *Culture, Medicine, and Psychiatry* 41 (1): 161–180.

Maruna, Shadd. 1999. "Desistance and Development: The Psychosocial Process of Going Straight." *British Criminology Conference: Selected Proceedings* 2:1–25.

———. 2001. *Making Good: How Ex-Convicts Reform and Rebuild Their Lives.* Washington, DC: American Psychological Association.

———. 2011. "Reentry as a Rite of Passage." *Punishment and Society* 13 (1): 3–28.

Massachusetts Department of Public Health. 2016. "Unintentional Opioid-Related Overdose Deaths vs. Motor Vehicle-Related Injury Deaths Massachusetts 2000–2013." July. www.mass.gov.

———. 2017. "Data Brief: Opioid-Related Overdose Deaths among Massachusetts Residents." August 31. www.mass.gov.

Maté, Gabor. 2018. *In the Realm of Hungry Ghosts: Close Encounters with Addiction.* London: Vermillion.

McCorkel, Jill A. 2013. *Breaking Women: Gender, Race, and the New Politics of Imprisonment.* New York: New York University Press.

———. 2017. "The Second Coming: Gender, Race, and the Privatization of Carceral Drug Treatment." *Contemporary Drug Problems* 44 (4): 286–300.

McGowan, Matthew J. 2016. "Location, Location, Mis-Location: How Local Land Use Restrictions are Dulling Halfway Housing's Criminal Rehabilitation Potential." *Urban Lawyer* 48 (2): 329–364.

McKim, Alison. 2017. *Addicted to Rehab: Race, Gender, and Drugs in the Era of Mass Incarceration.* New Brunswick, NJ: Rutgers University Press.

McLean, Katherine. 2016. "'There's Nothing Here': Deindustrialization as Risk Environment for Overdose." *International Journal of Drug Policy* 29:19–26.

McMahon, Maeve. 1990. "'Net-Widening': Vagaries in the Use of a Concept." *British Journal of Criminology* 30 (2): 121–149.

McNeill, Fergus. 2019. "Mass Supervision, Misrecognition and the 'Malopticon.'" *Punishment & Society* 21 (2): 207–230.

Merton, Robert K. 1938. "Social Structure and Anomie." *American Sociological Association* 3 (5): 672–682.

Miller, Reuben Jonathan. 2014. "Devolving the Carceral State: Race, Prisoner Reentry, and the Micro-Politics of Urban Poverty Management." *Punishment and Society* 16 (3): 305–335.

Miller, Reuben Jonathan, and Gwendolyn Purifoye. 2016. "Carceral Devolution and the Transformation of Urban America." In *The Voluntary Sector in Prisons: Encouraging Personal and Institutional Change*, edited by Laura S. Abrams, Emma Hughes, Michelle Inderbitzin, and Rosie Meek, 195–213. New York: Palgrave Macmillan.

Miller, Reuben Jonathan, and Forest Stuart. 2017. "Carceral Citizenship: Race, Rights and Responsibility in the Age of Mass Supervision." *Theoretical Criminology* 21:532–548.

Mitchell, S. David. 2011. "Impeding Reentry: Agency and Judicial Obstacles to Longer Halfway House Placements." *Michigan Journal of Race and the Law* 235.

Mohan, Arun, Jennifer Grant, Maren Batalden, and Danny McCormick. 2013. "The Health and Safety Net Hospitals Following Massachusetts Health Care Reform: Changes in Volume, Revenue, Costs, and Operating Margins from 2006 to 2009." *International Journal of Health Services* 43 (2): 321–335.

Monahan, Torin, and Rodolfo D. Torres. 2010. *Schools under Surveillance: Cultures of Control In Public Education*. New Brunswick, NJ: Rutgers University Press.

Monnat, Shannon. 2016. *Deaths of Despair and Support for Trump in the 2016 Presidential Election*. University Park: Pennsylvania State University, Department of Agricultural Economics.

Mulvaney-Day, Norah, Margarita Alegría, Anna Nillni, and Sabrina Gonzalez. 2012. "Implementation of Massachusetts Health Insurance Reform with Vulnerable Populations in a Safety-Net Setting." *Journal of Health Care for the Poor and Underserved* 23 (12): 884–902.

Murakawa, Naomi. 2008. "The Origins of the Carceral Crisis: Racial Order as 'Law and Order' in Postwar American Politics." In *Race and American Political Development*, edited by Joseph E. Lowndes, Julie Novkov, and Dorain T. Warren, 234–255. New York: Routledge.

Murphy, Alexandra. 2007. "The Suburban Ghetto: The Legacy of Herbert Gans in Understanding the Experience of Poverty in Recently Impoverished American Suburbs." *City and Community* 6:21–37.

Murphy, Daniel, Brian Fuleihan, Stephen Richards, and Richard Jones. 2011. "The Electronic 'Scarlet Letter': Criminal Backgrounding and a Perpetual Spoiled Identity." *Journal of Offender Rehabilitation* 50 (3): 101–118.

Netherland, Julie, and Helena Hansen. 2017. "White Opioids: Pharmaceutical Race and the War on Drugs That Wasn't." *BioSocieties* 12 (2): 217–238.

New Jersey Department of Corrections. 2019. "Offender Characteristics Report." Office of Policy and Planning. www.state.nj.us.

Newman, Kathe, and Elvin Wyly. 2006. "The Right to Stay Put, Revisited: Gentrification and Resistance to Displacement in New York City." *Urban Studies* 43 (1): 23–57.

New York Times Editorial Board. 2013. "Building Better Halfway Houses." *New York Times*, April 12.

Ollove, Michael. 2015. "Linking Released Inmates to Health Care." Pew Charitable Trusts, June 11. www.pewtrusts.org.

Page, Joshua, Victoria Piehowski, and Joe Soss. 2019. "A Debt of Care: Commercial Bail and the Gendered Logic of Criminal Justice Predation." *Russell Sage Foundation Journal of the Social Sciences* 5 (1): 150–172.

Page, Joshua, and Joe Soss. 2017. "Criminal Justice Predation and Neoliberal Governance." In *Rethinking Neoliberalism: Resisting the Disciplinary Regime*, edited by Sanford Schram and Marianna Pavlovskaya, 141–161. New York: Routledge.

Pager, Devah. 2003. "The Mark of a Criminal Record." *American Journal of Sociology* 108 (5): 937–975.

———. 2007. *Marked: Race, Crime, and Finding Work in an Era of Mass Incarceration*. Chicago: University of Chicago Press.

Pager, Devah, Bruce Western, and Naomi Sugie. 2009. "Sequencing Disadvantage: Barriers to Employment Facing Young Black and White Men with Criminal Records." *Annals of the American Academy of Political and Social Sciences* 623 (1): 195–213.

Parenti, Christian. 2000. *Lockdown America: Police and Prisons in the Age of Crisis*. New York: Verso.

Paylor, Ian, and David Smith. 1994. "Who Are the Prisoners' Families?" *Journal of Social Welfare and Family Law* 16 (2): 131–144.

Pew Charitable Trusts. 2015. "How Medicaid Enrollment of Inmates Facilitates Health Coverage after Release." December. www.pewtrusts.org.

Piehl, Anne. 2002. *From Cell to Street: A Plan to Supervise Inmates after Release*. Boston: Massachusetts Institute for a New Commonwealth.

Piehl, Mel. 1982. *Breaking Bread: The Catholic Worker and the Origin of Catholic Radicalism in America*. Philadelphia: Temple University Press.

Piven, Frances Fox, and Richard Cloward. 1971. *Regulating the Poor: The Functions of Public Welfare*. New York: Pantheon Books.

Platt, Tony. 2018. *Beyond These Walls: Rethinking Crime and Punishment in the United States*. New York: St Martin's.

Quinones, Sam. 2016. *Dreamland: The True Tale of America's Opiate Epidemic*. London: Bloomsbury.

Ralph, Laurence. 2015a. "The Limitations of a 'Dirty' World." *Du Bois Review: Social Science Research on Race* 12:441–451.

———. 2015b. *Renegade Dreams: Living through Injury in Gangland Chicago*. Chicago: University of Chicago Press.

Rea, Gary, John McGregor, Carole Miller, and Michael Miner. 1992. "Surgical Treatment of the Spontaneous Spinal Epidural Abscess." *Surgical Neurology* 37 (4): 274–279.

Reid, T. R. 2010. *The Healing of America: A Global Quest for Better, Cheaper, and Fairer Health Care*. New York: Penguin Books.

Rios, Victor. 2014. "Decolonizing the White Space in Urban Ethnography." *City and Community* 14 (3): 258–261.

———. 2015. "Reviewed Work: *On the Run: Fugitive Life in an American City* by Goffman." *American Journal of Sociology* 121 (1): 306–308.

Roberts, Dorothy. 2003. "The Social and Moral Cost of Mass Incarceration in African American Communities." *Stanford Law Review* 56:1271–1305.

Roman, Caterina, and Jeremy Travis. 2004. *Taking Stock: Housing, Homelessness, and Prisoner Reentry*. New York: Urban Institute.

Romney, Mitt, Kerry Healey, Edward A. Flynn, and Scott Harshbarger. 2004. *Strengthening Public Safety, Increasing Accountability, and Instituting Fiscal Responsibility in the Department of Correction*. Boston: Commonwealth of Massachusetts Governor's Commission on Corrections Reform.

Rosenblum, Daniel, Jay Unick, and Daniel Ciccarone. 2013. "The Entry of Colombian-Sourced Heroin into the US Market: The Relationship between Competition, Price, and Purity." *International Journal of Drug Policy* 25 (1): 88–95.

Ross, Jeffrey, and Stephen Richards. 2009. *Beyond Bars: Rejoining Society After Prison*. New York: Alpha Books.

Rumpf, Cesraéa. 2017. "Decentering Power in Research with Criminalized Women: A Case for Photo-Elicitation Interviewing." *Sociological Focus* 50 (1): 18–35.

Rushing, Byron, and John Larivee. 2018. "The Missing Piece of Massachusetts Criminal Justice Reform." *Boston Globe*, April 12.

Rylko-Bauer, Barbara, and Paul Farmer. 2002. "Managed Care or Managed Inequality? A Call for Critiques of Market-Based Medicine." *Medical Anthropology Quarterly* 16 (4): 476–502.

Sampson, Robert J., and John H. Laub. 1993. *Crime in the Making: Pathways and Turning Points through Life*. Cambridge, MA: Harvard University Press.

Sampson, Robert J., and Charles Loeffler. 2010. "Punishment's Place: The Local Concentration of Mass Incarceration." *Daedalus* 139 (3): 20–31.

Saperstein, Aliya, and Andrew M. Penner. 2010. "The Race of a Criminal Record: How Incarceration Colors Racial Perceptions." *Social Problems* 57 (1): 92–113.

Sasson, Theodore. 2000. "William Horton's Long Shadow: 'Punitiveness' and 'Managerialism' in the Penal Politics of Massachusetts, 1988–99." In *Crime, Risk and Insecurity: Law and Order in Everyday Life and Discourse*, edited by Timothy J. Hope and Richard J. Sparks, 238–251. London: Routledge.

Schneider, M. L. 2010. "From Criminal Confinement to Social Confinement: Helping Ex-Offenders Obtain Public Housing with Certificate or Rehabilitation." *New England Journal on Criminal and Civil Confinement* 36 (2): 335–358.

Schram, Sanford, Joe Soss, Lina Houser, and Richard Fording. "The Third Level of US Welfare Reform: Governmentality under Neoliberal Paternalism." *Citizenship Studies* 10 (6): 739–754.

Seiter, Richard, Eric Carlson, Helen Bowman, James Grandfield, and Nancy Beran. 1977. *Halfway Houses: National Evaluation Program Phase I Summary Report*. Washington, DC: US Department of Justice.

Sered, Susan. 2018. "Gender, Race, Class and the Root Causes of the Opioid Crisis." Susan Sered's blog, April 24. http://susan.sered.name.

Sered, Susan Star, and Maureen Norton-Hawk. 2014. *Can't Catch a Break: Gender, Jail, Drugs, and the Limits of Personal Responsibility*. Oakland: University of California Press.

Shabazz, Rashad. 2009. "'So High You Can't Get over It, So Low You Can't Get under It': Carceral Spatiality and Black Masculinities in the United States and South Africa." *Souls: A Critical Journal of Black Politics, Culture, and Society* 11:276–294.

Simon, Jonathan. 1997. *Poor Discipline: Parole and the Social Control of the Underclass, 1890–1990*. Chicago: University of Chicago Press.

———. 2000. "The 'Society of Captives' in the Era of Hyper-Incarceration." *Theoretical Criminology* 4 (3): 285–308.

———. 2014. *Mass Incarceration on Trial: A Remarkable Court Decision and the Future of Prisons in America*. New York: New Press.

———. 2016. "California's New Carceral Logic: Health Care, Confinement, and the Future of Imprisonment." *Boom* 6 (2): 22–31.

Skolnick, Phil. 2018. "The Opioid Epidemic: Crisis and Solutions." *Annual Review of Pharmacology and Toxicology* 58 (1): 143–159.

Smiley, Calvin. 2014. "Existing but Not Living: Neo-Civil Death and the Carceral State." PhD diss., City University of New York.

Smith, Linda Tuhiwai. 1999. *Decolonizing Methodologies: Research and Indigenous Peoples*. New York: Zed Books.

Soss, Joe, Richard Fording, and Sanford Schram. 2011. *Disciplining the Poor: Neoliberal Paternalism and the Persistent Power of Race*. Chicago: University of Chicago Press.

Steen, Sara, Traci Lacock, and Shelby McKinzey. 2012. "Unsettling the Discourse of Punishment? Competing Narratives of Reentry and the Possibilities for Change." *Punishment & Society* 14 (1): 29–50.

Stuart, Forrest. 2016. *Down, Out, and Under Arrest: Policing and Everyday Life in Skid Row*. Chicago: University of Chicago Press.

Sum, Andrew, Misha Trubskyy, Joseph McLaughlin, and Sheila Palma. 2011. "The Depression in Blue Collar Labor Markets in Massachusetts and the U.S.: The Implications of Growing Labor Surpluses for Future Economic Stimulus and Workforce Development Policies." *MassBenchmarks* 13 (1): 13–19.

Taxman, Faye S., Jessica Rexroat, Mary Shilton, Amy Mericle, and Jennifer Lerch. 2010. *What Works in Residential Reentry Centers: Executive Overview*. Fairfax, VA: George Mason University.

Tiger, Rebecca. 2017. "Race, Class, and the Framing of Drug Epidemics." *Contexts* 16 (4): 46–51.

Travis, Jeremy. 2002. "Invisible Punishment: An Instrument of Social Exclusion." In *Invisible Punishment: The Collateral Consequences of Mass Imprisonment*, edited by Marc Mauer and Meda Chesney-Lind, 15–36. New York: New Press.

———. 2005. *But They All Come Back: Facing the Challenges of Prisoner Reentry*. Washington, DC: Urban Institute Press.

Turnbull, Sarah, and Kelly Hannah-Moffat. 2009. "Under These Conditions: Gender, Parole and the Governance of Reintegration." *British Journal of Criminology* 49:532–551.

Turner, Victor. 1967. "Betwixt and Between: The Liminal Period in Rites de Passage." In *The Forest of Symbols: Aspects of Ndembu Rituals*, edited by Victor Turner, 93–111. Ithaca, NY: Cornell University Press.

———. 1974. "Liminal to Liminoid, in Play, Flow, and Ritual: An Essay in Comparative Symbology." *Rice Institute Pamphlet—Rice University Studies* 60 (3): 53–92.

———. 1977. "Variations on a Theme of Liminality." In *Secular Ritual*, edited by Sally F. Moore and Barbara G. Myerhoff, 36–52. Amsterdam: Van Gorcum.

Uggen, Christopher, Jeff Manza, and Melissa Thompson. 2006. "Citizenship, Democracy, and the Civic Reintegration of Criminal Offenders." *Annals of the American Academy of Political and Social Science* 605:281–310.

Urie, Alison, Fergus McNeill, Lucy Frödén, Jo Scott, Phil Thomas, Oliver Escobar, Sandy Macleod, and Graeme McKerracher. 2019. "Reintegration, Hospitality and Hostility: Song-Writing and Song-Sharing in Criminal Justice." *Journal of Extreme Anthropology* 3 (1): 77–101.

Valentine, Bettylou. 1978. *Hustling and Other Hard Work: Life Styles in the Ghetto*. New York: Free Press.

Valverde, Mariana. 1998. *Diseases of the Will: Alcohol and the Dilemmas of Freedom*. Cambridge: Cambridge University Press.

Valverde, Mariana, and Kimberly White-Mair. 1999. "'One Day at a Time' and Other Slogans for Everyday Life: The Ethical Practices of Alcoholics Anonymous." *Sociology* 33 (2): 393–410.

van Gennep, Arnold. 1909. *Les rites de passage* [The Rites of Passage]. Paris: Émile Nourry.

van Zee, Art. 2009. "The Promotion and Marketing of OxyContin: Commercial Triumph, Public Health Tragedy." *American Journal of Public Health* 99 (2): 221–227.

Wacquant, Loïc. 1996. "The Rise of Advanced Marginality: Notes on Its Nature and Implications." *Acta Sociologica* 39 (2): 121–139.

———. 1998. "Inside the Zone: The Social Art of the Hustler in the Black American Ghetto." *Theory, Culture and Society* 15:1–36.

———. 2001. "Deadly Symbiosis: When Ghetto and Prison Meet and Mesh." *Punishment and Society* 3:95–133.

———. 2005. "The Great Penal Leap Backward: Incarceration in America from Nixon to Clinton." In *The New Punitiveness: Trends, Theories, Perspectives*, edited by John Pratt, David Brown, Mark Brown, Simon Hallsworth, and Wayne Morrison, 3–26. London: Willan.

———. 2009. *Punishing the Poor: The Neoliberal Government of Social Insecurity*. Durham, NC: Duke University Press.

———. 2010. "Prisoner Reentry as Myth and Ceremony." *Dialectical Anthropology* 34 (4): 605–620.

Wakefield, Sara, and Christopher Uggen. 2010. "Incarceration and Stratification." *Annual Review of Sociology* 36:387–406.

Way, Cory T. 1992. "Innovative Incarceration: Community Corrections in the Federal Bureau of Prisons." *Federal Prisons Journal* 2 (4): 20–28.

Weaver, Vesla M. 2007. "Frontlash: Race and the Development of Punitive Crime Policy." *Studies in American Political Development* 21:230–265.

Weinberg, Darin. 2000. "'Out There': The Ecology of Addiction in Drug Abuse Treatment Discourse." *Social Problems* 47 (4): 606–621.

Western, Bruce. 2014. *Leaving Prison as a Poverty Transition: Preliminary Results from the Boston Reentry Study.* New York: Vera Institute.

———. 2018. *Homeward: Life in the Year after Prison.* New York: Russell Sage Foundation.

Western, Bruce, Anthony A. Braga, Jaclyn Davis, and Catherine Sirois. 2015. "Stress and Hardship after Prison." *American Journal of Sociology* 120 (5): 1512–1547.

Weston, Kath. 1991. *Families We Choose: Lesbians, Gays, Kinship.* New York: Columbia University Press.

White, William L. 2011. *Narcotics Anonymous and the Pharmacotherapeutic Treatment of Opioid Addiction in the United States.* Chicago: Philadelphia Department of Behavioral Health and Intellectual Disability Services and Great Lakes Addiction Technology Transfer Center.

Willse, Craig. 2010. "Neo-liberal Biopolitics and The Invention of Chronic Homelessness." *Economy and Society* 39 (2): 155–184.

———. 2015. *The Value of Homelessness: Managing Surplus Life in the United States.* Minneapolis: University of Minnesota Press.

Wilson, William J. 1997. *When Work Disappears: The World of the New Urban Poor.* New York: Vintage Books.

Winkelman, Tyler, Hwa Jung Choi, and Matthew Davis. 2017. "The Affordable Care Act, Insurance Coverage, and Health Care Utilization of Previously Incarcerated Young Men: 2008–2015." *American Journal of Public Health* 107:807–811.

Winkelman, Tyler, Edith Kieffer, Susan Goold, Jeffrey Morenoff, Kristen Cross, and John Ayanian. 2016. "Health Insurance Trends and Access to Behavioral Healthcare among Justice-Involved Individuals—United States, 2008–2014." *Journal of General Internal Medicine* 31 (12): 1523–1529.

Wolfgang, Marvin, Robert Figlio, and Thorsten Sellin. 1972. *Delinquency in a Birth Cohort.* Chicago: University of Chicago Press.

Worrall, Anne, Nicola Carr, and Gwen Robinson. 2017. "Opening a Window on Probation Cultures." In *Routledge International Handbook of Visual Criminology*, edited by Michelle Brown and Eamonn Carrabine, 268–279. London: Routledge.

Wray, Matt. 2006. *Not Quite White: White Trash and the Boundaries of Whiteness.* Durham, NC: Duke University Press.

Young, Jock. 1999a. "Cannibalism and Bulimia: Patterns of Social Control in Late Modernity." *Theoretical Criminology* 3 (4): 387–407.

———. 1999b. *The Exclusive Society: Social Exclusion, Crime and Difference in Late Modernity.* London: Sage.

———. 2011. *Criminological Imagination.* Hoboken, NJ: Wiley.

Zhu, Jane, Phyllis Brawarsky, Stuart Lipsitz, Haiden Huskamp, and Jennifer S. Haas. 2010. "Massachusetts Health Reform and Disparities in Coverage, Access and Health Status." *Journal of General Internal Medicine* 25 (12): 1356–1362.

INDEX

AA. *See* Alcoholics Anonymous

abstinence, 49, 50, 58, 192; of Badillo, 53, 151–52; Badillo commitment to, 168–69; change from, 123; coercive, 127, 159, 167; drug testing, eviction and, 129–30; ethics and, 103–5; of NA, 151–52; recovery and, 151–52, 173; as reintegration strategy, 106–7; Smith on, 192; in twelve steps, 144; war on drugs and, 153

ACA. *See* Affordable Care Act

Adderall, 142

addiction, 12, 29–30, 40, 69, 121–22, 137; counselor for, recovery, 179; family influenced by, 96–97; language of, recovery, 48–49; to opiates, 144; of OxyContin, 135; recovery, 103, 111, 141, 147–49, 165, 169–70; recovery and labor, 109; reentry and, 108; research on, 42–47, 190, 191; as social failure symptom, 45; Townsend on, 45–46; work *vs.*, 112

addiction-counseling program, 179–80, 187; public funding for, 178

ADHD. *See* Attention Deficit Hyperactivity Disorder

Affordable Care Act (ACA), 158

alcohol, 124; within community, 129–30; counselor, 198; eviction and, 153; prohibition on, 15; Williams drinking, 103–5

Alcoholics Anonymous (AA), 15, 46, 145

American dream, 181–82, 192–97, 200

Anomie, 181–82

Attention Deficit Hyperactivity Disorder (ADHD), 188–89

Avon Street, 137–41

Badillo, Joe (pseudonym), 1–3, 16, 18, 23, 69–70, 71, 130–31, 150; abstinence of, 53, 151–52; alternatives for, 198–209; awakening of, 118–24; at Bridge House, 28, 38, 41, 42; change for, 200; childhood home of, 137–41; child of, 94; at Clearview Crossing, 136, 153–54; commitment to abstinence, 168–69; community college for, 187–91; criminal record of, 24–25; daughter of, 95–98; on detoxing, 29–30; drug testing of, 52–53; epidural abscess of, 28–30, 39–41, 155–76, 172–73; ethnographic representation of, 21–22; family separation of, 98–99; goals of, 194–97; healing of, 159; homelessness of, 36, 40, 72–73; house of, 198, 199; hypercriminalization of, 26–27; incarceration cycle of, 25–27; income of, 198, 200; in infirmary, 29–33; at in-patient rehabilitation center, 157–58; insurance of, 33–35; mistreatment of, 39; mother of, 172; moving out of halfway house, 187; in NA meetings, 118, 141–42; paralysis of, 17–18, 29–30, 31–33, 38–39; physical therapy of, 161, 162–63; prison and jail sentences of, 25; probation of, 53, 72, 173; at Ray of Hope recovery center, 186; record of, 215n1, 216n8; recovery of, 136–37, 153; reentry of, 25–26; rehabilitation of, 155–76, 160–61, 177–80; relationship with, 17–20; reputation of, 36–37; social connection in halfway house for, 100–102; success of, 201;

239

ABOUT THE AUTHOR

LIAM MARTIN is Lecturer in Criminology at Victoria University of Wellington.